Lenore Zann

A Rogue's Tale

A MEMOIR

POTTERSFIELD PRESS

Lawrencetown Beach, Nova Scotia, Canada

Library and Archives Canada Cataloguing in Publication
Title: A rogue's tale : a memoir / Lenore Zann.
Names: Zann, Lenore, 1959- author.
Identifiers: Canadiana (print) 20240359593 | Canadiana (ebook) 20240359631 | ISBN 9781990770630 (softcover) | ISBN 9781990770647 (EPUB)
Subjects: LCSH: Zann, Lenore, 1959- | LCSH: Voice actors and actresses—Canada—Biography. | LCSH: Television actors and actresses—Canada—Biography. | LCSH: Motion picture actors and actresses—Canada—Biography. | LCSH: Politicians—Canada—Biography. | LCSH: Recovering addicts—Canada—Biography. | LCGFT: Autobiographies.
Classification: LCC PN2308.Z36 A3 2024 | DDC 791.4502/8092—dc23

Front cover photo: Katheryn Gordon (www.gordonphotographic.com)
Back cover author photo: Lindsay Rosenberg (www.lnzyrosephoto.com)
All other photos from Lenore Zann's personal collection

Cover design: Gail LeBlanc

Pottersfield Press gratefully acknowledges the financial support of the Government of Canada for our publishing activities through the Canada Book Fund. We also acknowledge the support of the Canada Council for the Arts and the Province of Nova Scotia which has assisted us to develop and promote our creative industries for the benefit of all Nova Scotians.

Pottersfield Press
248 Leslie Road
East Lawrencetown, Nova Scotia, Canada, B2Z 1T4
Website: www.pottersfieldpress.com
To order, phone 1-800-NIMBUS9 (1-800-646-2879) www.nimbus.ca

Printed in Canada on recycled paper.

CONTENTS

Prologue   7

Chapter 1: In the Beginning … My Origin Story   10

Chapter 2: Neptune's Daughter   23

Chapter 3: An Actor Prepares   36

Chapter 4: Waiting in the Wings   41

Chapter 5: Hey Marilyn!: The Good, the Bad, and the Ugly   48

Chapter 6: A Star is Born   62

Chapter 7: "You Gotta Get a Gimmick!"   71

Chapter 8: Hollywood: Craig Russell and the Gay '80s   77

Chapter 9: "Ready for my Close-up"   86

Chapter 10: Shadow Dancing with Andy Gibb, Spielberg,
            Alexa, and the Moral Majority   94

Chapter 11: A Cuban Romeo and Juliet   101

Chapter 12: Back in the U.S.S.R.   107

Chapter 13: Keanu, Nellie, and An Officer and a Gentleman   113

Chapter 14: An Actor's Guide to the Universe (Part 1)   130

Chapter 15: An Actor's Guide to the Universe (Part 2)   139

Chapter 16: An Actor's Guide to the Universe (Part 3)   148

Chapter 17: An Actor's Guide to the Universe (Part 4)   154

Chapter 18: California Dreamin': The Raven and the Gopher   162

Chapter 19: The Way of the Shaman, Shape-shifting,
            and the Good Red Road   167

Chapter 20: Rita MacNeil, Priscilla Presley,
            and a Rock 'n' Roll Wedding   174

Chapter 21: Unidentified Human Remains and the
            True Nature of Love   180

Chapter 22: On with the Show:
            The Power of Radical Forgiveness   187

Chapter 23: The Uncanny X-Men   196

Chapter 24: Losing the Plot and Going Rogue   201

Chapter 25: The Cure   207

Chapter 26: Waiting for Takeoff: Pablo the Intrepid   215

Chapter 27: Rogue Goes to Parliament and
            X-Men Take Hollywood by Storm   222

Epilogue: To Me, My X-Men!   231

Acknowledgements   235

About the Author   236

4

In loving memory of "Pablo the Intrepid" –
dearest Dad – who taught me anything is possible,
and never stopped believing …

"The path is narrow,
grasses and bushes are high.
Evening dew moistens my clothes;
But so what if my clothes are wet?
I choose not to avoid anything that comes."

– Táo Yuanmíng (365 – 427)

"The soul walks not upon
a line, neither does it
grow like a reed. The soul
unfolds itself like a lotus of countless petals."

– Khalil Gibran (1883 –1931)

"Heaven is not a place but a state of mind.
Look underfoot. You are always nearer the divine
and the true sources of your power than you think.
Leap, and the net will appear."

– John Burroughs (1837 – 1921)

PROLOGUE

Choosing the hero's path means that we commit to doing something that takes us out of our comfort zone. It means making a conscious decision to take a special action – to go on a journey – and not necessarily a physical one. The journey will be fraught with danger and there is a very real possibility that we may not even survive. But the hero's path can also be a journey we take within our own minds – our deep subconscious.

Mythology expert Joseph Campbell has said that many people hear the "Call of the Wild" to go on a spiritual quest or journey, but they don't heed it. Those who do usually have a driving desire to delve deep below the consciousness of daily living to discover the mystery that is life – no matter how frightening it may be. Campbell explained that this journey can seem like entering a dark and dangerous forest without a path or the familiarities of "home." But it is necessary to find our own path through this forest and follow it no matter what, in order to be brought to a divine state of grace whereupon we are finally able to discover the treasure we've been searching for and comprehend its universal truth. This is what I've discovered in my own quest for truth and meaning in life in this crazy, tenuous, and often confusing world.

And that's where the X-Men come in. The X-Men too are often heading off on quests – both individually and as a team – and they lead us along with them, helping us face not only the bigger questions of existence, but our own personal fears and misconceptions. And in every hero's journey there are times when we are challenged to face our worst fears, when we doubt ourselves, and even the purpose of our existence.

It can sometimes be so intense that it feels like being sucked into a long, dark tunnel with no light at the end. Sometimes called the "dark night of the soul," this is a time when all of our strength is really put to the test.

However, in order to conquer our fears, it is absolutely necessary to face them. And to do that we must be willing to sit still long enough to discern a different kind of strength that exists within each and every one of us – like a sleeping giant, or superhero, just waiting to be awakened. Take it from me, it is there, ready to be called upon when needed.

Like my alter ego, Rogue of the X-Men, I myself have had to travel the hero's journey and survived fear, self-hatred, loss, and grief in order to finally find self-acceptance. Looking back at some of my earlier escapades as a young woman who constantly threw caution to the wind, seemingly thriving on danger, this memoir is a recounting of how I chose to journey through the dark forest to find the truth I was seeking. And, like the Phoenix itself, to burn with the ashes and rise again. Like the heroes of old in those ancient stories, facing danger and not succumbing is often necessary to discover who we are, where we want to go, and what we are truly able to accomplish in our lives. And when we come through it, we are stronger than ever.

As a female politician I've faced misogyny, death threats, and betrayals. But I have never let that stop me from doing the right thing and constantly fighting for social and environmental justice in order to create a better world for future generations.

As an actor I've been honoured to perform in hundreds of productions around the world in film, TV, theatre, radio, and animation, receiving professional recognition and awards. But nothing has given me as much fulfillment as playing Rogue in *X-Men: The Animated Series.*

Over the years it has become one of the top animated series of all time, with millions of fans worldwide. And I've been moved by the stories of fans of all ages when I meet you on the street, at schools, Comic Cons, and speaking engagements. Because one thing X-Men fans have told me is that, as kids in the '90s, our show was a "safe place." You would race home from school to watch us, or get up early on Saturday mornings in PJs with your cereal. And you've told me that, like Rogue, you too felt different. Perhaps you were bullied in school or abused at home and could therefore relate to Rogue because she was forced to leave home as a teenager by a parent who did not understand her, and hated and despised for being a "mutant." And with recent attacks on the rights of women, diverse and LGBTQ2SIA+ communities, I'd say the X-Men are needed now more than ever. Do not despair.

I'm here to tell you, you are not alone. We are *all* mutants – one way or another. Even though my character, Rogue, is considered the "strongest woman in the Universe" she too has her vulnerabilities. Unable to enjoy an intimate, loving relationship, she must learn to accept herself as she is and find her true purpose and a sense of belonging. It's a yearning we all have in common.

Sometimes it takes a crisis to slow us down long enough to do the emotional work of healing past traumas, dealing with chronic anxiety or depression, or simply accepting ourselves in this busy, busy world. So don't be afraid to slow down and go at your own pace, in your own time. And if you hit a wall and are suddenly forced to come to a screeching halt, please remember these words: You are enough – just as you are. So be gentle with yourself and give yourself some empathy, as you would a beloved child. You are worth it.

We are all here for a reason. And deep inside we each have our own, unique superpower. So when you are ready, just relax, close your eyes, and dig down deep within your subconscious. Awaken that sleeping superhero within you and come up smiling, calm, poised, and ready for action. And meanwhile enjoy reading about my own Rogue's Tale, my quest for meaning in this crazy world. There is no silver bullet that will "cure" us. Our journey is about progress, not perfection. It is a daily discipline. And truth be told, it's hard work. But then again, nobody said being a superhero would be easy.

CHAPTER 1

IN THE BEGINNING ...
MY ORIGIN STORY

On November 22, 1959, a baby girl was born to teachers Janice Rose Marshall and Vincent Paul Zann sometime between 4 and 5 a.m. at the Royal North Shore Hospital in Sydney, Australia. As the tale goes, she was born with what looked to be a mutation of some kind, which manifested as a pair of bright blue legs. Upon first sight, this shocked her father so deeply that he was said to disappear for a while to compose himself. And it took great reassurance from the presiding doctor that this was not an abiding malady, that indeed his daughter was not some kind of mutant (God forbid!), and that her blue legs would soon morph into a healthy pink glow.

Also, as her mother tells the tale, the instant the newborn, exercising her newfound lungs and vocal cords with gusto, was placed in her mum's arms, the child stopped screaming only long enough to open up two huge brown eyes that penetrated her own and seemed to hold the wisdom of the ancients. Her mother's immediate thought was that this tiny force of nature, this wizened creature, was thinking, "My God! I got stuck with you for a mother?" This initial introduction of two fierce Scorpios likely set the stage for the intense dynamics to come.

They named the child Lenore (meaning "Light") for the poetry of Edgar Allan Poe, and Elizabeth (meaning "Beloved of God") for her maternal grandmother, who was soon to become her best friend and chief comforter until her death at ninety-seven. When a friend of her grand-mother first saw the baby sleeping in her crib, she intoned (much like the evil fairy in the *Sleeping Beauty* tale), "Little girl, you have no idea what the world has in store for you."

But, in the beginning, no one had any idea that little Lenore from Sydney, Australia, was destined to travel across the planet to settle on the East Coast of North America in the small town of Truro, Nova Scotia, where, against all odds, she would become, first, an award-winning actor, then a multiply-elected politician, and finally a "superhero."

Really. You can't make this stuff up.

So, as we say in the biz, "Slam cut to ..."

Curtain Up (The Early Years)
"There was a little girl,
  Who had a little curl,
Right in the middle of her forehead.
  When she was good,
  She was very good indeed,
But when she was bad, she was horrid."

Many of us as kids were scolded with this old nursery rhyme by our elders, and my grandmother was no different. Whenever I lost my temper as a young child this is the verse she would recite. My response was always the same: "I don't care!" to which my grandmother would reply with another old chestnut, this time recited in a songsong voice like a child in a playground: "Don't care was made to care. Don't care was hung. Don't care was put to bed – with a good smacked bum!"

But once again my stubborn streak would make me dig in my heels even harder and my response was louder and even more cranky: "I don't care!"

When faced with absolute non-capitulation, my grandmother would resort to the very worst threat of all: "If you're not good, I'll call up the witches, and they'll come here on their broomsticks and whisk you off to Popocatépetl!" I had no idea where that was but I knew I didn't want to be taken there by witch's broom. I quickly learned to smarten up and beg forgiveness. Years later I discovered it's a real place, an active volcano and the second highest peak in Mexico.

I'm laughing today as I recall these memories. What exactly I was cranky about or what I was fussing over I do not recall. But I loved my grandmother dearly, so I would eventually calm down and come around with nary a smacked bum.

I called my grandmother Mummy Marshall because as a child going back and forth between my mother's home and my grandmother's I thought I had two mothers: Mummy and Mummy Marshall. I also thought I had two fathers: Daddy and Daddy Pop, since my mother called her father "Pop."

Mummy Marshall was fond of quoting snatches of poetry for all sorts of situations: good, bad, or indifferent. Rumi, Khalil Gibran, and Omar Khyam were her favourites. Walt Whitman was another. They soon became my favourites as well. You could say my childhood in Australia was idyllic as I would often go between my parents' home in the city of Sydney and Mummy Marshall's house in Newcastle as well as her cottage in the bush that was located in Karuah, a small community north up the coast from Sydney. I loved playing all kinds of imaginary games with imaginary friends and spending time with Mummy Marshall, begging her to tell me more stories of fairies and witches and the unique Australian bush creatures that lived all around us. When my parents bought a small block of land in West Ryde, a suburb of Sydney, to begin building their first house, I got to spend even more time with my grandparents, which was wonderful.

The property Mum and Dad built only cost $5,000 at the time. It was a very modern design for the time, and unique, as the house itself was built high above the ground, on stilts, with a long stairway leading from the ground to the main floor. Most homes in Australia did not have air conditioning in those days, so the Aussies found this a great design to stay cool.

Nowadays stilt-homes built in the 1960s go for millions because they're considered "heritage" classics. My mother often wishes they had never sold ours. We lived there happily at 6 Fir Tree Avenue near my elementary school, Ermington Public, until I turned eight, while Mum taught biology at Marsden High School nearby. We could both walk to school of a morning and I was always very proud to wait at the end of our little cul-de-sac for my mum to come walking home. I loved asking the "big girls" walking by if she was on her way home yet as I was very proud of my beautiful, always well-dressed, very intelligent mother, who seemed to know so many facts about everything.

One day I remember I was really mad at Mum for something and after a heated exchange, I flung myself into my Dad's lap crying and claimed, "You're smarter than Mum!" To which he responded, "Oh no, pet! Never think that! Your mother is one hundred times smarter than I am!" I believe this was one of my earliest lessons in feminism since my dad behaved not only as an "ally" but a defender of women simply by saying that my mother was even more accomplished than he. Over the years, my dad was the one person who constantly told me that girls were just as capable as boys and that we could accomplish anything we set our minds upon. This was another early lesson which became ingrained in my psyche and would come in very handy in my later years, especially once I decided to enter the dangerous battlefield of politics, traditionally a sacrosanct area reserved for men.

The times spent at my grandmother's were incredible. We spent many an afternoon walking in the bush looking at all the incredible Australian wildlife: koalas, kangaroos, wallabies, wombats, platypuses, even snakes (of which my grandmother showed no fear), and brilliantly coloured birds. I clearly remember the sound of the kookaburra laughing, his riotous call ringing throughout the bush as if he were taunting you to dare to find him.

And I spent many sun-drenched hours trying to catch little golden finches that flitted from bush to bush – they were so splendidly arrayed in rainbow colours from head to tail. I dreamed of someday "taming" one like Antoine de Saint-Exupéry's Little Prince, who finally tames his fox. No luck for me, however. Those little birds were too fast and could easily outwit a small child. Probably just as well. After all, why should we need to "tame" any wild creature? They're better off in their natural habitat. And this way they remain a living memory of fleeting and ever-changing colour.

Mummy Marshall had a good friend who lived down the lane from our house. Mrs. Ping was an older First Nations lady who had a large family of adopted children. They were, in fact, children of Indigenous women of the community who had been impregnated by truck drivers or others passing through town. Instead of giving them up to an adoption agency or orphanage, Mrs. Ping chose to bring up these children herself, with love and kindness, teaching them much about their history and culture.

My grandmother and Mrs. Ping would frequently get together at either one or the other's home, often sitting out on the terrace for afternoon tea. When they did this, we knew it was story time as they'd gather us children together to regale us with stories about the bush, the animals, flowers and fauna, as well as ancient myths and fairy tales. Their stories were often also teachings, especially about the connection between humans, all creatures, the land, and the magic. Mrs. Ping taught us that her ancestors were known to follow "song lines" as they travelled from place to place, and that as they travelled to new terrain, the magic of their song created the formations they encountered.

I once asked Mrs. Ping and Mummy Marshall if magic was real. They looked at each other, then rocked for a bit in their chairs, then another look passed between them. Finally, as if deciding to share a great secret, they both looked at us and nodded. Mrs. Ping said softly, "Of course." And Mummy Marshall continued, "Magic is nothing more than a change in consciousness. Mind over matter." Then the two turned to each other and poured afternoon tea, signalling that today's lesson was over.

After a story we'd all go running out into the bush, none of us wearing many clothes because it was so hot and, besides, who was there to bother us? We were young and our grandmothers both believed in us going "au naturel" out in the country. My mates would often show me special berries that could be eaten along the way. Along with Vegemite sandwiches to fortify us, we were never hungry.

One day we came across a bush that was full of witchity grubs. Witchity grubs are white maggoty grubs or worms that live on certain trees or bushes in the Australian outback and the kids were so excited to come across them because these grubs were apparently like the sweetest candy, or the best chocolates money could buy. I will always remember with a smile the look of pure joy on their faces as they stuffed their mouths with those fat wriggling white grubs, juice dripping down their chins, as they excitedly offered me one to try. Although I was adventurous, I did draw the line at this and my young mates had a great time making fun of my timidity, pointing at me and bending over laughing, their eyes sparkling with glee.

On another occasion I asked my grandmother why a bunch of trash had been thrown in Mrs. Ping's yard. Mummy Marshall told me that there were people in the world who were very cruel and who did not understand the unique ways and cultures of our friends, who were the original inhabitants of these lands and who had lived in Australia for 60,000 years before the white man came.

She explained that the white man had come to Australia and made Mrs. Ping's people live on "Reserves" despite the fact that they were used to being travellers, moving to different areas at different times of the year, and that they would never destroy a whole tree to make something out of wood; they'd use a part of a tree and then move on to another, only taking what they needed and never more. They never killed a tree or destroyed an area just for their own pleasure. She told me that these first inhabitants were treated very badly by our ancestors and were still not being given the respect they deserved. She taught me that some had even been put in prison simply for "burning off" certain areas at certain times of the year to prevent bushfires, which the white man did not understand until two hundred years later. They were the original Caretakers of the Earth, so we should respect them and help them continue that tradition.

Mummy Marshall was very angry about the attitude of people who she called "reptile brains" because she said they were still living in the past as if they still had small reptilian brains that could not comprehend the largeness of the universe and the beauty of all the different types of people that make up this incredible world we live in. She told me these unthinking people were "racists" because they believed whites were superior to Black people and that they dumped trash in their yard because they felt Mrs. Ping and her kids were just trash too. I could see very clearly that this was not a correct perception of sweet, kind Mrs. Ping and my friends. My first lesson about hating racism and wanting to stand up for my friends was embedded in my brain, heart, and soul before the age of eight. I count myself lucky to have had two great teachers such as Mummy Marshall and Mrs. Ping.

I believe it was these lessons from so many years ago that helped to shape me into the human being I am today, always championing diverse cultures and Indigenous peoples around the world with a desire to share these teachings with others. Mummy Marshall and Mrs. Ping were allies and taught us children to accept each other for who we are no matter how different our customs may be or what colour our skin is, what language we speak, what religion we follow, or what gender we may be. They taught us we could be whoever we dreamed we could be, just as the Spirit beings in the Dreamtime stories could shape-shift at will.

Mummy Marshall was a true feminist and social justice warrior and as the saying goes, "the apple doesn't fall far from the tree." My mother was the same and between my grandmother and mother, I was taught to respect the importance of reconciliation with First Nations peoples long before the word was bandied about by politicians. As a matter of fact, I can't remember a time when politics and the issues of the day were not discussed in either of our homes by both sets of "parents." Their early introduction taught me much about the governance structures, and injustices often faced by everyday people, as well as a healthy curiosity to travel to far countries and a deep desire to create a better world for all.

Religion was not discussed in either household. The family had all been born Catholic, but after my mother was treated with extreme cruelty by the nuns at her Catholic Girls School, when she turned fourteen, she and her mother made a pact. They made arrangements to switch her to the local public school and they chose a day to go in together to tell the nuns. Their pact was that no matter what the nuns said, they were determined she was to leave.

My grandmother told me this story herself and explained that when they told the nuns Mum was leaving, a group of nuns separated them into two corners of the room and told them both that if they went through with it, they would both be excommunicated and would go to Hell. Despite this threat, they stuck to their pact and after some time, Mummy Marshall pushed the nuns out of the way and took my mother by the hand, saying, "Come on, Janice, we're leaving." She told me that her parting words that day were, "As for you lot, you should be ashamed of yourselves.

If anybody is going to Hell, it should be you – for terrifying innocent little girls!"

Did I mention I have a stubborn streak? I now realize just how much strength it took for two "good Catholic women" to do what they did that day in spite of their fears. Stubbornness can also be called determination, and the women in this family sure have it in spades. My mother and grandmother left that school in Newcastle and left the Catholic Church the same day. They never looked back. Years later when asked what religion she followed my grandmother would proudly say, "I'm a pantheist. Mother Nature is my God." I'm sure that's something she and Mrs. Ping had in common.

Since Mummy Marshall welcomed all creatures as important to the ecological canvas of the bush, she also had a great reverence for snakes and spiders. There was a carpet snake (a type of python) that lived under her house in Karuah. Although they are not of the poisonous variety (of which there are many in Australia), when I first expressed trepidation about the fact there was a huge snake living under the house, she would say, "Don't worry, darling. She won't hurt you. She has an important place in the animal kingdom as she eats mice and any other rodents that might try to get into our house and make a mess." There was also a big spider's web by the front door, and she'd say, "Oh, that's just Mrs. Spider. She won't harm you. She keeps the flies and mozzies [mosquitoes] out of the house."

At this point I do have to say that I developed a very healthy respect for snakes, becuase on our car trips to Karuah we would often come across big snakes stretched across the country road so long that they disappeared into the bush on either end. Now that's a snake!

Back in Sydney, once my parents' new home was completed, I started attending elementary school at Ermington Public. And it was here that I had an encounter with one of Australia's infamous spiders which I will never forget. I must have been six or seven, and like many Australian schools at the time our school did not have indoor bathrooms. We simply had outhouses beside the playground. I remember that on one recess I visited the outhouse. I was wearing my little grey school uniform with its blue and gold tie, and my hair had been done very carefully by Mum that morning with a beautiful big bow on top. When I walked out of the outhouse, I remember clearly hearing a gasp, and when I looked towards the sound, I saw that the playground teacher had gone white, as if all the blood had drained out of her face.

It was like time stood still. All the kids stopped what they were doing and turned towards me. I don't remember any sounds, except for "Lenore! Stand still! Right there! Don't move!"

I froze. Without taking her eyes off me, the teacher slowly picked up a big stick from the ground.

Thwack!

She swung the stick like a cricket bat right at my head. Yet I didn't move. I could tell she meant what she said from the blind terror in her eyes.

Thump.

Suddenly I could hear sound again and things around me started moving. I heard an almost unanimous scream from the kids around me. There in the dust lay a humungous, black, hairy spider – a deadly funnel web, so-called for the funnel-shaped webs they weave, often in the ground or in the eaves of buildings.

I guess you could say that was my first brush with death, although it's funny that after all that time roaming around freely in the Australian bush it took coming back to the city to have this life-threatening experience. This experience could be one of the reasons why my parents decided to move to Canada not long afterwards, a country where their child was not likely to succumb to death by venomous spider or snake.

Ballet classes on the weekend with my best friend Vivian Burns were my favourite activity, especially since my mother had been an excellent dancer herself, winning all kinds of dance competitions. I loved poring over the photos of Mum as a young girl dressed up in gorgeous costumes, and began to dream of someday becoming a famous ballerina myself, with one small difference.

When asked the perennial question adults always seem to ask of small children, "What do you want to be when you grow up?" my response was always the same: "When I grow up, I want to be a ballerina at the circus," for I imagined myself standing on a magnificent white horse doing pirouettes and arabesques as we galloped around the ring – to great applause, of course. (Glad I didn't follow through on that, although some might say that becoming a politician years later was a somewhat similar balancing act.)

After a while my parents decided to drop me off on a weekend afternoon to watch the matinee of a professional ballet. This was where I first developed my love of the theatre: the sights, sounds, and smells, the costumes, the music, the lights and the dark, the excitement and rapture of the audience, and the exquisite beauty of the performers and their amazing craft. Once I remember I even got to see the crème de la crème, the best of the best – Rudolph Nureyev and Margot Fontaine, performing in *Swan Lake*.

One intermission, I got lost, which was terrifying. Surrounded by huge adults bustling about I was too shy to ask for help. I made my way to the front of house and then outside into the street where the ticket booth was located. I was so small that the lady behind the glass couldn't see me. I did something I'd seen in the movies; I pretended to cough. Loudly. So loudly that after she had looked around for a time to see where Camille was dying of consumption, she finally peered over the rim of her booth and saw me. As soon as she did, she cried, "Why, it's a little girl!" She immediately came around to me and knelt down, asking where my parents were. That's when I burst into tears and said they'd left me at the theatre to watch the show. Alone. With a cluck-clucking sound of disapproval, she gave me a big hug and wiped my tears and asked if I wanted to go back inside to watch the second half of the show. Of course, I did. Soon my fears and tears were forgotten as I was once more swallowed up into the dark bosom of the theatre where I felt safe again.

I can see now that this first real taste of the theatre, with all its drama and the excitement it created, sowed the seeds that made me want to be a professional performer. As an only child now living in the city, I often tended to play imaginary games with imaginary friends, including my stuffed animals and dolls.

However, there was one game I made up that I loved to play with Mummy Marshall whenever she would come to visit; I realize now that it was likely the first sign of my interest in acting. At one time we had an old grandfather clock. The rules of the game were that Mummy Marshall would sit on the couch as my audience of one and I would hide behind the clock. Then, whenever I came out from behind the clock, Mummy

Marshall had to guess who I was. And each time I came out I was a different person. It could be a movie star or a TV personality or a family member. I don't remember whether my impersonations were good. I just remember the game. But it's obvious that this was my first attempt at "acting."

My dad was a great influence on my imagination as well, for he was a born storyteller and I loved him reading me stories before bed because he changed his voice to become each character. Dad would make me laugh and often his antics were used to make me eat food I didn't like too. I just didn't want to eat eggs until Dad came up with a game of his own called "The Seven Dwarfs." To play the game I had to swallow several spoonfuls of egg which each time would land on the head of one of the Dwarfs who he said were (somehow) in my tummy. So naturally Sleepy, Grumpy, Sneezy, and the rest reacted quite differently to the egg being dumped on their heads. Needless to say, this was very entertaining.

Dad was travelling to Papua New Guinea at this time to teach elementary school kids. Each time he returned he would bring home carvings, gifts, stories, and music, including tapes of the children singing songs in their native tongue as well as English in beautiful harmony. I remember one song in particular which I loved, "If There Were Witchcraft." These stories of Dad's trips abroad also whet my appetite for travel and, again, I was inspired by my family's interest in Indigenous peoples and their unique cultures, languages, and customs.

Mum was an only child, but her mother and uncles (Uncle Ambie and Uncle Snowie) as well as Daddy Pop are also etched in my memory and I loved spending time with them too. One of their favourite pastimes was attending weekend horse races. We all dressed to the nines, wearing hats and gloves, and trotted off to the races to watch the thoroughbreds. These were big events in Australia, with huge crowds and everyone all dressed up as well. At the intermission there would be a fashion show. My family would let me place small bets on whatever horses I liked. My method was very strategic. I always picked purple. That was it. Sometimes I'd even win.

Mummy Marshall and her two brothers Ambrose (Ambie) and Leonard (Snowie) had long been going to the races as their mother once owned racehorses herself. Bridie Frances Walshe had been a very successful businesswoman in the late 1800s, back when most women were darning socks and baking and having babies. Not Bridie. An orphan from Dublin, she was sent to Australia as a toddler with a governess to live with relatives who were successful in the hotel business in Brisbane. And she grew up in the trade herself. Bridie married Ambrose Rose, whose family was also in the hotel and bar business, and they had just three children when so many other women were having dozens. My grandmother Elizabeth was the eldest of the three. Unfortunately, Bridie's beloved husband died young, at age forty-one. Bridie, now widowed with many businesses to tend, decided to send her three children to Catholic boarding school.

That's when my grandmother first experienced the cruelty of nuns herself and therefore, years later, was able to empathize with my mother about the cruelty she was experiencing, which ended in their pact for her to leave the Catholic school. As my grandmother said, "Not all of them are bad, but the ones who are can scar you for life."

Once I asked Mummy Marshall, "Why doesn't Mum like hugging me? She always pulls away when I try to hug her as if she doesn't like me." Mummy Marshall thought for a moment, then sighed and said, "Oh, that's probably my fault. My mother never hugged me as a child so I don't think I hugged your mum either. When Mother sent us off to boarding school, nobody hugged or kissed us as kids, and when you'd have a bath, you weren't even allowed to look at your own body – they'd say it was a 'sin.' They'd drape a sheet over the bathtub so you couldn't look at yourself. That's what it was like back then. Not like nowadays."

Mummy Marshall also used to tell me about her father and how much she loved him and how he'd take her to look at the tall ships in the harbour in Newcastle near one of the hotels they owned where sailors would come and stay when they were in port. One day, Mummy Marshall said, at about sunset her father took her onboard a huge wooden four-masted schooner that a friend of his owned. She said, "I was a little older than you." She remembered asking her dad if she could climb up the mainsail. He told her she could but not to tell her mother. She said she remembered climbing up that mast "quick-smart" wearing her high button boots and stockings under her dress and when she got to the top she looked around and saw the gas lights all lighting up along the harbour.

These were the stories I lived for. I could see every detail. They made me want to "time travel" and to see the world and have adventures.

My grandmother was truly my best friend for many years until her death at ninety-seven. I could tell her anything. She would never be shocked and she showed me true, unconditional love. For many years as an adult coming home from my own adventures, I looked forward to sharing them with her – Elizabeth, my namesake. I'd say "Am I all right, Mummy Marshall? "And she'd say, "Turn around and let me look at you." I'd dutifully turn around for her.

And each time she would say, "Yes. You look fine to me. You're more than all right. You're right as rain!"

My childhood in Australia truly molded me as a human being and to this day, I'm grateful for not only the time spent with my mum's family but also the many wonderful celebrations with our larger Zann family since Dad was the eldest of five. His dad, Vincent Zann, for whom he was named, had sadly passed away when Dad was just fourteen, leaving his mother Eileen widowed with five children. Dad became the one she leaned on, and instead of studying law as he had wished to do, with a lack of funds and mouths to feed, Dad went instead to teachers college and his first classes were taught at a school in Ryde, Sydney, right beside their Pope Street home. After her husband died, Grandma Zann had to get a job and she worked at Grace Brothers department store for years. She was very sweet and kind. My many cousins and I loved going to her home and playing together in the backyard, and eating toast and Vegemite with the crusts cut off, with hot tea. I am the eldest of our generation and when, twelve years later, my sister Tamara was born in Canada, she became the youngest, therefore making us the "bookends" of this big, loud, brash, fun-loving Aussie family. As a kid in those early years, I loved being part of a big family with so many cousins, grandparents, loving aunts and uncles and great-uncles. It made me feel like I belonged to something bigger than myself. Family. A "tribe." Community.

But this was all soon to change.

CHAPTER 2

NEPTUNE'S DAUGHTER

The summer of '68 was a pivotal point for the Zann family. Although 1967's "Summer of Love" had a lasting effect on the world, since Australia was an island stuck in the South Pacific – long before the internet – social change and trends occurred later than they did in North America.

The Summer of Love was a social phenomenon that occurred during the summer of 1967 when hundreds of thousands of young people wearing "hippie" fashions streamed to California from all over the United States in a search for love, community, music, drugs, and the freedom to be themselves without the conventions they felt yoked their parents to the wheel of staid jobs and capitalism. Coined "flower children," these youth descended upon San Francisco's famed Golden Gate Park and Haight-Ashbury neighbourhood to create a new scene, with anti-war and civil rights themes and hallucinogenic drugs in a "free love" environment.

The excitement engendered by this movement continued to expand internationally, inspiring other young people to break free from conventional societal bonds to embrace "flower power," the "brotherhood of man," and the Women's Liberation Movement, and to get "uptight and outasight," as the Stevie Wonder hit bade them. As free and progressive thinkers, Jan and Paul Zann were no exception. In early 1968, when both Dr. Martin Luther King, Jr. and Robert F. Kennedy were assassinated, the ripples were felt around the world, and Paul and Jan decided to embark on a journey that would change their lives and that of their only daughter, now eight years old, forever.

I can still remember the day Bobby Kennedy was murdered – June 6, 1968 – as it was an emotional one in our home with my mother crying, and I too felt deeply moved by a sharp sense of loss and desperation, my first real sense of death. I remember throwing myself on my bed crying, "I love you, Bobby, Bobby, Bobby!" over and over. Perhaps I was simply affected by my mother's grief, but even at that young age I thought him attractive and felt like I knew him personally. I had no idea that eleven years later I would be starring in a rock musical in which both Kennedy brothers were key characters.

The morning of June 25, 1968, dawned sunny and crisp in Sydney, June being the first month of winter in the "Land Down Under." Mum, Dad, and I were on board the SS *Canberra*, a huge ocean liner, docked in Circular Quay in Sydney Harbour.

Although I didn't realize it at the time, this was the same harbour many of our ancestors had arrived in over the years, also by ship – some voluntarily in search of a new life and prosperity and some involuntarily, as convicts being brought to the British penal colony of New South Wales. A hundred and eighty years before, in 1788, Captain Arthur Phillip had brought a fleet of eleven British ships carrying the first convicts to Botany Bay, and three days later to the deeper waters of Sydney Cove, so named for Lord Sydney, the British Home Secretary. The colony itself was called Port Jackson and the British considered this the "founding" of Australia (although the original Indigenous inhabitants had been there for the previous 60,000 years).

On this sunny June day in 1968, from the deck of the SS *Canberra* we waved goodbye to our family, our home, and our country. We were immigrating to Canada with two thousand other Aussie and New Zealand teachers onboard. Canadian Prime Minister Pierre Trudeau had put out a call to them, inviting them to come to Canada to teach. My parents heeded that call as they had been watching in admiration as this handsome, vibrant prime minister – who was fluent in French and English, wore a rose in his lapel, and who had done a pirouette behind the Queen – was the kind of modern, progressive leader they desired.

As our ship pulled away from the quay, our family all held tight to long crepe paper streamers which had been thrown to the shore from the ship and from families onshore to their loved ones on deck. I can still see our whole family there, and the same lump comes into my throat and tears spring to my eyes as if it were yesterday. There, bravely smiling and waving, were Mummy Marshall and Daddy Pop, Uncle Ambie and Uncle Snowie, and our entire Zann Clan: Uncle Brian, Noel, Aunt Cecily and Moira, along with Grandma Zann (who cried inconsolably as she watched her eldest son leave Australia's shores, as though she already knew we were leaving for good). Mum's best friend Paula Bloch was there as well, whom I counted as another auntie.

The whole image is still there in my mind, but in muted colours and sounds like an old video ... the crepe streamers stretching out straighter and straighter as the ship pulls away, until they're so taut they break one by one and drift behind us, no longer gay but now sodden and sagging in the ship's wake, as seagulls circle and cry above us as if to say, "Come, fly with us on the back of the wind – we're off on an adventure! So dry your tears and turn your face forward and say *yes* to life!"

We visited a number of remarkable countries on our trip to North America and were able to disembark for a day or so at each stop before continuing our trip. In this way, we visited the Tongan islands, New Zealand, Hawaii, and Vancouver, Canada.

During our sea journey there were some terrifying storms. When emergency horns started blaring, no matter the time of day or night, passengers would have to grab life jackets from the cabins and line the hallways of the ship while trying to stand upright as everything was rolling about – and being seasick to boot. Our children's playroom had one long fifteen- to twenty-foot floor-to-ceiling window and I remember seeing humongous waves pounding the top of that window with such force I was sure it would break. It was a lot for a child to take in.

After we had been at sea for a time it was announced we would be crossing the Equator, the imaginary line around the middle of the Earth that is halfway between the North and South Poles, at 0 degrees latitude, thus dividing the Earth into the Northern and Southern Hemispheres. Owing to the tilt of the Earth's rotation relative to the Sun and the ecliptic plane, summer in the Southern Hemisphere is from December to March and winter is from June to August. Interestingly (for some), when you flush a toilet in Australia, the water flows in the opposite direction than it does in North America. And hurricanes, tornadoes, and tropical cyclones also spin in the opposite direction from how they spin north of the Equator. This due to what is called the Coriolis effect, which makes things swirl clockwise instead of counterclockwise south of the Equator. In any case it's a kind of fun fact and when you've been at sea for some time, crossing the Equator is a great excuse for throwing a big party.

The SS *Canberra* was no different. And when they announced there would be a costume contest and parade, I was excited because one of my favourite things to do was to play dress-up (likely another early sign of the actor-waiting-in-the-wings). Mum was great at sewing and figuring out costumes. Her dad had bought her a Singer sewing machine when she was a teenager because his mother had been a seamstress and he thought that a great job for a woman. Little did he know that he'd birthed a feminist firebrand. She would have dearly loved to become a professional dancer, but Daddy Pop thought that was just nonsense. He didn't even want his wife working as he thought it made him look like he couldn't look after his family. I'm told a number of men thought that way back then.

Since I was well-versed in mythology (thanks to Mummy Marshall's tutelage) and since we were at sea, Mum and I decided I should portray Neptune's Daughter. Neptune was the Roman god of the seas and revered as the father of all living things on Earth through the fertilizing power of rainwater. Given a name that means "wet" in Latin, he was first mentioned in Roman mythology around 399 BCE. Neptune is always depicted with a three-pronged fisherman's spear called a trident. The cross at the bottom of the trident represents the root of things, the essence of nature. The three points can be interpreted to have various meanings, including birth, life, and death, or mind, body, and spirit. And Neptune is usually assisted by a retinue of sea nymphs and goddesses.

So we made a trident, a crown, and a gown with many layers of pearl, shell, and bead necklaces that we had acquired in the Tongan islands, and with my hair flowing to my waist I was entered in the costume contest.

And … I won.

That was the first thing I had ever won and I have to say it felt good. As we paraded around the ship in our finery, I felt like Neptune's Daughter riding the waves. And as I experienced applause for the first time I could not help but think of Mummy Marshall, who had told me stories of her younger days as a performer. She had been a great singer and accomplished pianist and had performed professionally as a chorus girl in many J.C. Williamson musicals in Sydney in the 1920s. She'd also sung on the radio and at movie theatres. In those early days of film, the projectionist had to change the reel of film halfway through the movie. To keep the audience entertained during this pause in the show, they'd hire a pianist and singer to perform until the projectionist was ready.

Mummy Marshall told me she used to perform with her former boyfriend, whose stage name was Andre Navarre – and they'd been set to marry. He had a beautiful voice, she said, and they would sing duets in harmony. In 1928 Andre was invited to perform at La Scala Opera in Italy and they planned for her to follow him there. But when the Great Depression hit in 1929, her mother lost a lot of her properties when tenants were suddenly jobless and unable to pay their rents. Mummy Marshall said that her mother Bridie had a soft heart and couldn't simply throw people out of their homes, so eventually the banks took the properties. And Bridie needed her daughter to help her keep the hotel business going. So that's what she did.

Mummy Marshall told me that Andre sent her many postcards and letters begging her to come to meet him in Italy and asking pitifully why she wasn't responding. But she said she couldn't bring herself to write back as she knew she couldn't leave her mother. Eventually she met my grandfather, Thomas Marshall, an engineer. The only problem was he was a Protestant and she was a Catholic. But she told me she decided to marry him "because he was always well-dressed, polite, funny, and he had a motor car."

When they got married in Newcastle her mother refused to attend the wedding because her daughter was marrying a Protestant. But Mummy Marshall said eventually Bridie herself lost faith in her religion because while she had lots of money and properties the local priest came for dinner on many a weekend. And, of course, Bridie was generous with her donations. However, once the family lost its wealth the priest stopped coming. Bridie took note of that as did her daughter and sons. They were not impressed.

Mummy Marshall told me she had chosen "family duty" over love and her career. "But," she added, "don't make the same mistake! You have a special talent. So go out and set the world on fire!" All of this flashed through my mind as we crossed the Equator while I took my first bows high above the waves.

When the SS *Canberra* finally came to North America, we docked in Vancouver, Canada, where we disembarked for three days and took in the sights and sounds of our new chosen country. But instead of simply travelling by land to our final destination, we reembarked on the *Canberra* and continued sailing down the West Coast to San Fransisco.

It was here we experienced meeting "flower children" and "hippies" in the flesh. How intriguing for three little Australians! How exciting! They were wearing brightly coloured dashikis and headbands, turbans and large combs, with beads and flowers, short and long skirts, and it was as if "everything goes" and nothing was out of fashion – except suits. When I saw that most of the young men were sporting long hair and afros, I remember saying incredulously, "Look, Mummy! All the boys look like girls – they've got long hair!" I'll never forget my mother's reply: "Yes! Isn't it beautiful!"

I believe those four words, uttered with such heartfelt approval and admiration, caused my consciousness to open to another level of acceptance. As a schoolgirl in Australia under the British system of education, I had only ever known a life of school uniforms and tidy, bound, or plaited hair for girls, and close-cropped hair for boys. Imagine the freedom this concept introduced in my young mind.

After San Fransisco, we reembarked on the SS *Canberra* for our last leg of the sea voyage. We arrived in Los Angeles on July 14, 1968. And I am so grateful to my parents for this incredible trip because it enabled us to visit Disneyland, which had been a dream of mine for as long as I could remember.

At the end of every week, like most families of the day, we would have dinner, then sit together on the couch in front of our small black and white TV set to watch *The Wonderful World of Disney*, our favourite show. The word "Disney" for me was the equivalent of the word "magic." And at the end of each show when we saw Cinderella's castle with fireworks exploding above, I wanted to go so badly, but it seemed as far off as Never-Never Land. Especially when one looked at a globe and saw that we lived on the opposite end of the planet.

However, my parents worked out a way to get me there, and I have to say that for an eight-year-old kid from Australia it was the most fun I'd ever had in my life. Between the Dumbo, Magic Cup-and-Saucer, and Matterhorn Mountain rides I was giddy with delight. And Cinderella's castle with fireworks right after sunset just capped off the whole experience. It was a dream come true.

And once again, if someone had told us that one day I would be working for Disney myself on a TV series watched by millions I don't think we would have believed it. But for the time being, little Lenore and her folks were simply relieved and happy they'd made it all the way across the globe to visit "The Happiest Place on Earth."

Dad rented a car and after a few days in Los Angeles we headed north towards Canada, where my parents had teaching jobs in Regina, Saskatchewan, in the Prairies. It was here that my dad had accepted a job as a professor at the University of Regina, and Mum as teacher at a local junior high school.

Regina is 1,719 miles from Los Angeles, which could take a little over twenty-five hours to drive, but we took our time in order to see as much of the country as we could. We drove in all kinds of weather through Arizona and the Badlands in South Dakota, through communities with interesting pueblo homes and Indigenous communities. When we got to the Grand Canyon I was deeply immersed in a book, lying across the entire back seat of the car and gazing up at my book since any other way I sat was making me car sick. Dad parked the car and my parents got out.

"Come on, Lenore," said Mum. "Come see the Grand Canyon."

"No thanks," I replied. "I'm at a good part in my book."

"It's the Grand Canyon!" says Mum. "You've got to come with us and look!"

"You've seen one canyon you've seen them all," says I, the seasoned blasé traveller of eight. At which point Mum kind of freaked out and yelled, "Lenore Elizabeth! You get out of the car this instant! One day you'll thank me for this!" My dad opened the door, and they dragged me out.

I don't remember much about the Grand Canyon, but I did draw a picture of it later on when we got to a hotel. In the drawing there is our little family of three gazing out over a large canyon, and there's another man reaching frantically for a black hat that has clearly blown off his head and is disappearing over the cliff. I found it last year in a little book of pictures I'd drawn of each of the places we visited on that trip and when I showed my parents Dad said, "Oh, yes! I remember – remember that, Jan? The bloke's hat blew off and he tried to catch it and almost fell over the cliff!"

So. There is that.

We were still a good distance from Regina – 1,451 miles – when we reached Las Vegas. And wouldn't you know it but our rental car's brakes failed just as we drove onto the main strip! Dad somehow managed to avoid a catastrophe, but it meant we ended up arriving in Regina ignominiously, by Greyhound bus, with all our stuff – a bit like the Beverly Hillbillies. We even got our first Canadian immigration cards stamped in Coutts, a village in southern Alberta that is a port of entry with the U.S. state of Montana. My immigration card is stamped July 27, 1968.

Once we arrived in Regina, we found an apartment and got settled in time to start the school year. We only stayed in Regina for one year before moving again, this time across the country.

However, our year in Saskatchewan was memorable for a few reasons.

A week before I was to start school, I broke my left arm and had to have a cast. So my first day of school in a new place where I didn't know anyone and had a very strange accent, of course I was asked what seemed like a million times by a million kids what happened to my arm.

"I fell off a wawl," I replied.

"You fell off a what?" they'd ask, incredulously.

"I fell off a wawwwl."

"A wawl? What's a wawl?"

"Oh, ya know. It's one of those big tawl things that you cloym up an' then ya fawl down."

The kids would either leave, still scratching their heads, or they'd get it and laugh. My self-deprecating sense of humour was appreciated by a few, although for many something was lost in the translation. Then they'd ask me what language we speak in Australia.

"Austrylian," I'd say. And that seemed to satisfy their curiosity and explained the whole "strynge" situation.

Yep. Welcome to Canada.

Dad discovered football (as we were used to soccer, cricket, and rugby), so we became ardent fans of the Saskatchewan Roughriders. Dad also discovered country music and we soon became fans of Charley Pride, George Jones, Tammy Wynette, Loretta Lynn, and the "Man in Black" himself, Johnny Cash.

At an unveiling of a statue of Métis hero Louis Riel, we met Prime Minister Trudeau (Senior) and Mum and Dad were able to thank him for inviting us to Canada. And once again, they had no way of knowing then that half a century later their daughter would be working with another Prime Minister Trudeau – Pierre's son, Justin – as an elected member of Canada's parliament in Ottawa. An immigrant's dream come true.

In Regina we saw snow for the first time, and when the first flakes started lazily falling, we ran out into the yard and started trying to catch them, just as I'd tried to catch the little golden finches in Karuah. Only these ones melted and disappeared in front of our eyes. All three of us kept turning around in the yard, saying, "Look at this one! And this one! And that one!" It was an incredibly magical experience.

Pretty soon the snowbanks were taller than me. And once I got my tongue stuck to the car door. I thought the lacy ice patterns on the silver metal looked so pretty – and they looked a bit like popsicles. So I went for a big lick. Oh-oh. Big mistake.

I started crying. My mum didn't know what to do and kept saying, "Just pull your tongue in!"

Easy for you to say, is what I was thinking but, alas, could not speak.

In the end Mum went to the next-door neighbour, who was Polish and told her to put warm water on it. And thank God that did the trick, although there was lots of blood. Not to mention embarrassment. But I quickly learned what not to do in a Canadian winter.

Mum also had her own lesson about Canadian winters when she wore a miniskirt to school at minus thirty degrees. While she was at a bus stop her legs turned blue.

Something I will never forget took place in the late spring of 1969. Dad had brought a boomerang with him from Australia. And although living in the city as we did in Sydney, he had never tried throwing one. But now that we were in the flat Prairies, he thought that would be a great place to throw the boomerang and get it to come back to him as we'd seen in the movies.

So one weekend we drove out to a spot along the highway, with a flat field for miles around, and Mum packed us a picnic with a blanket from which to watch. Well, before too long there was a lineup of cars and pickup trucks parked along the highway with people out watching this crazy fellow with a huge boomerang in his hand, staking out the land: pacing back and forth, wetting his fingers and sticking them up in the air as if testing the wind. He likely even looked like a professional boomerang-thrower.

And I have to say, looking back at it now, Dad likely realized he had an audience so he milked the attention for all it was worth. A real ham if ever there was one. I guess I come by my acting skills honestly, and as we've discovered more recently, there's an artistic gene that runs in Dad's side of the family too.

However, on this day in spite of the intense buildup, try as he might, poor Dad just couldn't get that boomerang to do his bidding. It takes a special skill. And culturally, it's an ancient hunting practice of Australia's Indigenous people. So it should be left to them.

The folks in Saskatchewan left disappointed that day, but we enjoyed our picnic anyway.

By the end of the school year Mum and Dad had decided to check out another region in Canada and they'd heard the East Coast was very beautiful. They applied for teaching positions and again both were offered good jobs immediately. That following summer of 1969 they bought a small camper trailer, hitched it onto our car, and we drove and camped right across Canada to our next new home: Truro, Nova Scotia, where Dad would remain a professor at the Nova Scotia Teachers' College and Mum would teach at the Truro Junior High School until their retirement.

By the time I started junior high my parents bought a small house in a village called Belmont, outside Truro. Coincidentally, Mummy Marshall's family owned a cottage in a place called Belmont in New South Wales, so perhaps the name appealed to her. In any case during these junior high years, I bused to school while Mum and Dad drove the short distance to Truro to teach.

In 1972 when I was twelve, Mum and Dad gave me the exciting news that we'd be welcoming a new member of the family. After years of pleading for a little sister she was finally coming. They named her Tamara, and because she was the first Nova Scotian born in the family, they gave her Evangeline as her middle name after the Longfellow poem that tells the sad tale of the Acadians of the region.

Mum and Dad gave me the honour of choosing a third name for my sister. So, again due to my love of mythology, I chose the name "Dione," meaning "Divine One" or God (Dios). Dione was a Titan goddess and the mother of Aphrodite by Zeus. I thought that befitted a little goddess. And I loved dressing her up and reading her stories, and bundling her up in the winter to take her for little sled rides and tobogganing.

In Grade Eight, I decided to enter the Earl Grey Public Speaking Contest. My speech was entitled "My New Home" and it was about the trip from Australia, saying goodbye to the life we knew and coming to a land full of new possibility. I won first prize. That was pretty exciting for our little family and again it was a step towards performance.

By this time, I was also writing poetry and short stories and even began "publishing" a little monthly magazine with my friends, Andrea and Hans Budgey. I was the editor and we filled it with short stories, poems, recipes, and drawings. Before long I also took up an instrument, thanks to the excellent school band system established by music teacher Ron MacKay. My instrument of choice was, of course, something loud – trumpet – which for some reason Mum preferred me to practise outside. Go figure. I regularly entertained the local cows in the fields around our home.

One day Dad gave me a book to read by Carlos Castaneda. This was the first book I'd read about spiritualism and I loved it. I asked him, "Dad, is this real? Did all of this really happen or is it just in his imagination?" My father simply replied, "Anything is possible." I love Dad for saying that. It gave me the encouragement to remain open-minded and to keep seeking spiritual enlightenment from many sources. Around this time Dad also introduced me to Zen Buddhism and writers like Alan Watts and Joseph Campbell.

At fifteen, in Grade Ten, I auditioned for my first musical, *Guys and Dolls*. Mum and Dad suggested that I should wait a year or two as they were worried I'd be disappointed, given I had no musical training and they said the older girls who had been taking singing lessons and lived in Truro their whole lives would be cast in the show – and, after all, Truro is home to the third-oldest music festival in North America.

I said, "I don't care. I have just as good a chance at getting a role as anyone else. And if I don't try, I'll never know." So I went ahead and auditioned along with three hundred other girls. After a couple of months, we heard that the cast would be announced.

One day after school I was sitting in a popular Chinese restaurant with my best friend Cheryll Sickles when our friend Frank Lambert came rushing in, out of breath and so excited to tell us that I'd landed one of the two leads: Adelaide, the "harlot with a heart of gold." We were ecstatic. And, to be honest, it felt like justification for my decision to take the plunge and do something I'd been warned was impossible. I'll always be grateful to guidance counsellor Norman Hines for casting and directing me, and to music teacher Margaret Dill for coaching my songs.

When the show finally opened to a fully packed thousand-seat auditorium at the Cobequid Educational Centre in the spring of 1975, my mother told me that she and Dad got the shock of their lives. When I walked out on stage with the confidence, swagger, and stage presence of a pro to belt out "I Love You a Bushel and a Peck" and "Adelaide's Lament," they learned that their daughter could act and sing naturally – without years of training. Mum also said that when she watched me onstage it was as if I was a different person and she couldn't believe that person came from her. I guess that's the epitome of what a good actor tries to do.

Because I was now rehearsing in band and the musicals, Mum and Dad decided it was best to move into town since they were both teaching there anyway. Other high school and community theatre productions followed, including a number of musicals produced and directed by Jack Sheriff for the Kipawo Theatre Company in Wolfville, Nova Scotia. Dad would drive me the ninety-seven miles after school on a Friday and pick me up on Sunday night. What an amazingly great father he was. I will always be grateful for the many incredible opportunities my parents gave me growing up.

It was at the Kipawo Theatre that I met the first love of my life – Charles Page Fletcher from Bass River, another small village near Truro. Charlie had played Tony in *West Side Story* at my high school several years before I got there. He could sing like an angel, was as lovely as Adonis – and he was a rebel like James Dean, with denim bell bottoms, a black leather jacket, long curly hair, and flashing green eyes. And a temper to match Hades. What more can I say?

As rehearsals for *Jesus Christ Superstar*, my first show with Kipawo, got underway I had a bit of a crush on both Jesus *and* Judas. Guess who I picked? Sigh. In any case Charlie and I became an item and soon we were hitchhiking the hundred miles to Wolfville every Friday, while Dad would pick us up on Sundays.

Soon after this I talked Charlie into doing an audition with me for the largest professional theatre company in Nova Scotia, Halifax's Neptune Theatre. Although he scoffed at me, saying, "You think they'd hire us? You're crazy!" I assured him that I wasn't crazy and that I felt we both had the talent to become professional actors.

We auditioned for artistic director John Wood in the basement of a local church in Truro with a Shakespearean monologue for our classical piece, and I wrote out a scene between Adelaide and Nathan Detroit from *Guys and Dolls*, which we performed together for our modern piece. I figured nobody else would do that.

After our audition there was a momentary silence before John Wood booked us both on the spot for their summer production of the musical *Gypsy*. I was sixteen and just finishing Grade Eleven. Neptune's Daughter was on her way.

CHAPTER 3

AN ACTOR PREPARES

My Grade Twelve year at the Cobequid Educational Centre High School in Truro, Nova Scotia, was much like any other sixteen-year-old's routine. Life for me at the time was all about schoolwork, cheerleading, performing in the musical (*Fiddler on the Roof* – I played Yente), and playing trumpet in the school band. And partying with friends on the weekends. I was so in love with my boyfriend Charlie that I wrote poetry to him continually when we were not together, including my first love poem, "For Charlie So He'll Learn to Love Poems."

But as soon as the school year finished, I began rehearsals in Halifax for our first professional show, the musical *Gypsy*. We both had several small roles and made $75.00 a week. Not much, but hey, we were in showbiz!

I was sixteen and in heaven. Charlie and I shared a rental apartment for the summer at our Kipawo Theatre Company pianist's home in Halifax. Everyone was older than me except for Katt Evans, The Balloon Girl, and the lead actors were fantastic. My only wish was that I had said yes to director John Wood's question "Can you do pointe ballet?" He didn't cast me as Baby June, who went up on pointes once, and I learned from that experience never to say no again to those kinds of questions.

Many of the cast members remained good friends over the years, in particular rock and roll singer Frank MacKay, who also played small roles in his first theatrical production, and our very first stage manager,

Paul Shaw ("Pshaw"), who taught me much about the etiquette of theatre and rehearsals. One important non-official rule, for instance: "When you are in a rehearsal room and not performing, DO NOT read a book or magazine. PAY ATTENTION to your fellow actors! It is RUDE and DISRESPECTFUL not to give them your full attention!" These days the same can be said for reading one's cell phone, as I can attest as a director myself now to the annoyance of actors paying more attention to their phones than the action on stage or rehearsal.

I guess you could say that playing Adelaide in *Guys and Dolls* at fifteen was when the acting bug "bit" me, and the community shows after that continued to whet my appetite. It was the summer I spent performing in professional theatre at the Neptune in 1976 that cemented my determination to create a career as a professional actor and singer and travel the world.

And I did.

When I had talked Charlie into auditioning with me for Neptune Theatre, I had guaranteed him that we would both become professional actors in spite of his lack of belief. He was twenty-four, living with his parents in Bass River, Nova Scotia, doing construction work and selling marijuana for a living (we didn't call it cannabis back then, and it was illegal). Several years later after becoming a professional actor with me that summer, Charlie (appearing as Page Fletcher) would be cast as the mysterious drifter, The Hitchhiker, in the very successful TV series of the same name, followed by playing the lead, Alex J. Murphy/Robo Cop, in the also popular *Robo Cop: Prime Directives* series. What can I say? I know talent when I see it.

After *Gypsy* ended that summer, it was time for me to head to Toronto for university. I had first asked John Wood to take me to perform in Ottawa as he had been offered the position of artistic director of the National Arts Centre (NAC) there. He had already invited many of the Neptune company actors to go with him, including Charlie, and I was not keen to continue my studies. I had a raw hunger to simply keep performing. But John turned me down, saying, "You're too young. Go to university." I was crushed.

Undaunted, the following year after John and the company left for Ottawa, I immediately contacted John Neville, the new artistic director of Neptune Theatre, and asked him if I could audition for him. I said, "I know I'm only sixteen, but I want to be an actor and I'm ready to work really hard." He agreed to meet with me.

I met with John at the Neptune administrative offices in the spring of 1977. Although I offered to audition, he said, "No, that's okay. I'm happy to just sit down with you and talk. I can tell more about a person that way."

We got along extremely well and talked about everything, including my early beginnings in Australia. John was British and had performed as a young man in the West End in London as Romeo to Claire Bloom's Juliet, Hamlet to (Dame) Judi Dench's Ophelia, and shared the stage with Peter O'Toole and Richard Burton. In 1989, he also starred in the Terry Gilliam fantasy film, *The Adventures of Baron Munchausen*, with Uma Thurman, Oliver Reed, and a young Sarah Polley.

At the end of our meeting, John said he was in the middle of planning his first season of shows but would contact me at my parents' place in Truro if there were any roles I could play.

Four days later John Neville called to offer me small roles in two Noel Coward plays: *Tonight at 8:30* and *Hands Across the Sea*, which he planned to direct the following summer. I was thus able to continue working in professional theatre the summer after I graduated high school. This also meant that once that summer season ended, because I had performed in three professional productions in the past couple of years, I qualified to join the theatrical union, Canadian Actors Equity, thus becoming a professional actor at age seventeen.

I remember the pride I felt in joining the union, particularly because my family has always been staunch union members with the Teachers Union in both Sydney and later Nova Scotia. In fact, my mother's grandfather, Thomas Marshall of Glasgow, Scotland, a coal miner, had immigrated to Australia and helped establish the first Coal Miners Federation of New South Wales.

The summer productions were once again extremely enjoyable and although I was the youngest member of the company, I felt at home with the adults both onstage and off. John Neville was an incredible human being who cared passionately about not just the theatre but about people. He made us all feel like a family; the cast and crew would get together after each show upstairs in the Neptune bar to talk, laugh, sing, and in general make merry, just as thespians have done throughout the ages.

I'll never forget those wonderful days of camaraderie and the feeling of finally finding my real "tribe" or community with those of like mind. It was an exciting world full of promise. The theatre community is a special one which really encourages people to be their authentic selves, to get in touch with their emotions, to take chances, and say "yes" to life in order to create something of beauty for the world to enjoy.

By the time the Neptune plays closed that summer, I had been accepted to the drama program at York University to study theatre for four years, culminating in a Fine Arts degree. My electives included political science and philosophy, which, in hindsight, also "set the stage" for my second career, as my passion for politics and social justice was strong even at that age.

Looking back, I realize that if the little girl I was did not put aside her doubts and fears and push back against those who tried to convince her not to follow her heart and her own instincts, none of this would have happened at all. I was willing to take the risks that may have resulted in "failure." That is why I tell people if they have a dream to go for it.

Once the Neptune Theatre summer season had closed in 1977, I said my farewell to Mum, baby sister Tamara, and to my boyfriend Charlie, who would soon be going to back to work in the Actors Company at the NAC in Ottawa. Then Dad and I took the train from Truro to Toronto as he wanted to help get me settled into my new on-campus residence at York.

If my first day on campus is a reflection of what was to come in the next few years, it was captured in the hot air balloon taking people for rides far above the "madding crowd" for a bird's-eye view of Toronto and the land stretched out beyond. As usual, I was game for the challenge, and Dad encouraged me to go, but he remained with feet firmly planted on the ground.

Once aloft it seemed like the world below me stretched on forever. I was not afraid. No indeed. I was excited. And looking forward to whatever other challenges and experiences lay in store.

I was off!

And as we rose, I remember belting out the song "Up – Up and Away" by Jimmy Webb, which had been a huge pop hit when I was a kid. It was produced by rock and roll legend Johnny Rivers in 1967 for the band The 5th Dimension. Little did I know it then but, as fate would have it, years later I would meet Johnny and live in his mansion that had been built by Greta Garbo as an escape from Hollywood back in the 1920s.

When I met him, Johnny had risen to fame in the '60s and '70s with three gold albums and numerous top ten hits, including "Tracks of My Tears," "Poor Side of Town," "Memphis," "Mountain of Love," and "Baby I Need Your Lovin'." Also among his top ten songs are "Swayin' to the Music (Slow Dancin')" in 1977, which earned him his second gold record, and "Secret Agent Man," which he famously recorded live at the Whisky a Go Go in 1966.

Johnny and I bonded over music, politics, and life in general. I remember his words of advice when it came to how to have a successful career: "There are two kinds of people in the world," he'd say, "The ones who make it happen, and the ones who say, "'What happened?'"

But that was much later.

Meanwhile, on my first day as a freshman on campus, I was high above the world and still ascending … with just one song on my lips as we rose in my beautiful balloon. I could feel it: something good was on the way!

CHAPTER 4

WAITING IN THE WINGS

In my first year in the drama program at York University, I learned a great deal about the history of theatre, the need to stay in shape physically and mentally, and that we would never be ready for the "real world" until York was through with us. I'm sure that's the mantra of most training programs. And perhaps I was lucky to have bucked the trend, but I did not take my earlier professional theatre experience for granted nor did I let it go to my head, as I've never been one to think I cannot learn more and improve my craft. Life is a series of learning experiences and, if we are lucky, we get to live long enough to become masters of our craft.

I quickly settled into university life and made a few great friends with whom I'm glad to say I am still in touch. It was with delight I discovered that two other drama students also had last names beginning with the letter "Z," a precious experience for a kid from Australia with a weird last name and no extended family on the same continent. It was a joyous experience to meet Miriam (Mimi) Zucker from Cleveland, Ohio, and Dan Zagrosek from Toronto, and almost immediately we three became an inseparable triad. And within a short time, Mimi became a best friend and remained so.

Many of our friends in that program have done well in the years since our training. Djanet Sears has become an award-winning playwright (*Harlem Duet, Da Kink in My Hair*); Jim Milan is an award-winning theatre director (who I later worked with in two plays); Mimi, Dan Lett, Charlotte Moore, Alan C. Peterson (Alar), Albert Schultz, Tony Elwand,

Geraint Wynn Davies, and Stuart Hughes have become actors. And Mimi eventually even became the owner and director of The Children's Acting Academy of New York, where I have at times taught.

Meanwhile, though, at the time, I buckled down to my studies and for the most part enjoyed the theatre program as well as courses in dance, English, philosophy, and political science. At one point the Three Zs got together and consulted after hours and agreed we were all sick to death of spending the first two months being an "egg" in Movement class: for weeks we were supposed to embody a regular, untouched egg, then another few weeks we had to be an egg being cracked against the side of a bowl, and the final weeks of those first two months we were an egg being poured into the bowl and scrambled.

Yup.

I don't know about you, and I'm not an expert on Movement for the theatre, but that was the most boring and unenlightening exercise I've ever experienced. I'm not sure of the reason behind it, but I have never found it useful in any show I've ever been cast in or any performance I've ever given. And I've never been offered the role of an egg – nor would I accept it if I were!

However, I was cast as a different inanimate object in my second year at York. And that was an experience I will never forget.

Neil Dainard was another of our professors who taught a course in film, which was great in that it introduced me to many of the great European directors. This in turn has given me a taste and tolerance for long, slow movies without any car chases or violence, and instead subtle stories and emotions. I'm grateful for that.

Neil was also the director of one of the annual plays the drama program produced in our second year, *The Caucasian Chalk Circle* by Bertolt Brecht. Third- and fourth-year students were cast in the lead roles, which was to be expected, so the Three Zs agreed. What Mimi I were not expecting, though, was to be both cast as "rocks," which we were to perform under a burlap sack, pushing a heavy wooden platform around the stage, upon which the lead, Grusha, would deliver her lines.

I ended up getting booted out of the show by Professor Dainard because of the need to miss one rehearsal due to the fact that I had managed to land an audition in Ottawa for director John Wood at the National Arts Centre.

When I reminded the stage manager that I would not be in rehearsal the following day, she said, "Oh dear. Does Neil know this?" I reminded her that I had told her about it the first day of rehearsals and included it in the form they'd sent around. But she said, "Well, I'll have to tell Neil." And the next thing I knew he came storming over to me, saying, "What's this? No! You *must* be in rehearsal tomorrow! No excuses!"

Since I was already familiar with the rules and protocol in a professional theatre production, I tried to explain I'd done everything an actor must do if one has a prior commitment, including telling the stage manager ahead of time. But Neil would not listen and I began to realize he was making an example of me in front of my classmates: "I have had to make sacrifices for York University so *you* must make sacrifices for York University too!" he fumed.

"Neil, I've had this booked for a couple of months now and I told the stage manager our very first day of rehearsals when we were asked if there were any days we could not attend rehearsals. I also wrote it down on the form you sent around that day."

Neil still insisted.

Finally, I said, "But, Neil, I can get any new blocking I might miss from my friend Mimi, who is there doing the same thing as me. I mean, let's be honest, I'm just playing a rock!"

At that Neil Dainard let out a bloodcurdling yell like a wounded animal. It was enough to blow you into the next room. *"That's your job! It's your job to be a rock! Either you're in rehearsal tomorrow or you're out of the show!"*

After that, when I went outside the building, my classmates came out and surrounded me. And I remember Andy LeWarren saying, on behalf of the group, "Listen, Lenore, we don't know what that was all about back there. Neil had no right to talk to you that way! But we all agree on this: if you show up at rehearsal tomorrow, we will all be really disappointed. You just go and get on the bus tonight and do that audition for the NAC. We'd all give our right arm to have that opportunity – and so would Neil too, I suspect. So just go out and do your thing in Ottawa – and to hell with Neil!"

After a bit more reassurance from the group that I would not be letting them down by missing one rehearsal, I agreed to stick to my original plan.

Upon my return to class the following day I was informed that I was fired from *The Caucasian Chalk Circle*. And then subsequently, when each student had our annual year-end review in a room with all the drama profs, I was told that they had made the decision that York University was not the place for me, so I would not be asked to return the following year to continue the program. I agreed.

A few years later I ran into one of the professors in the room that day, who told me that as soon as I'd left the meeting, they had all turned to each other and someone said, "That girl will be making more money and be more famous than any of us in the next few years." They were right. In any case, I was free and able to do professional auditions without further fear of any backlash.

Before I could do anything, however, I received an urgent message to call home. As it turned out, my first director of high school musicals, CEC guidance counsellor Norman Hines, had a request for me to fly home and immediately step in for the female lead of the school's annual musical, in this case *L'il Abner*.

Now, at a time before emails, computers, or internet, Mr. Hines told me that he could pay to have me fly home the next day. I would have only two days to learn the entire show in time for opening night. If I said no, he would have to shut down production and cancel the musical for the first time in the school's history. But if I agreed to give it a try, we could save the show for the hundreds of kids, their teachers, and parent volunteers involved.

I said yes. How could I not? My hometown and alma mater needed me. After agreeing to do the show, I went downtown to the Theatre Store and bought the book and score for *L'il Abner*. In this way I was able to study my lines all the way on the plane home to Nova Scotia that night.

The next day I met my co-stars Kevin MacLeod and Peter Ettinger and the three of us became inseparable. Rob Denton, who played Pappy, became a close friend as well. These students were in Grade Twelve and I had graduated two years before. They'd been rehearsing for months and knew the show really well, so all I needed to do was step in.

Mr. Hines gave me directions and blocking, and music teacher Mrs. Dill taught me Daisy Mae's songs as well as those of the ensemble. I also learned the basic choreography. The rest of every waking moment was spent memorizing, memorizing, memorizing.

We had prompters opening night and indeed every night of the week-long run. Obviously, excitement was high within the cast, but faced with the sheer necessity of having to prepare for a live audience in such a short amount of time, I was beyond excitement, beyond fear or doubt, as I knew exactly what I must do. Nothing else mattered but the show. I don't remember anything about that week in my life other than the feeling of being completely "in the zone" as if preparing to do battle, and the feeling that I was deeply needed, that I had a clear purpose, and would do anything it took not to let any of the people down.

Recently I was contacted on Facebook by a woman who says she was one of the prompters and that while they had been instructed to be ready to feed me any lines should I need them, they were not called upon at all as I did not falter once.

It's hard to think of this now since two of these lovely young men passed away recently. Rob Denton became a cartoonist skilled at caricatures and Peter Ettinger went on to become a great rock singer with his band Ettinger in Alaska.

It turned out *L'il Abner* was a huge hit for the school and I did have to chuckle at the thought that instead of playing a rock beneath a burlap sack I was able to be out in the open, starring in a musical to end off my second year of university. In any case it was an amazing experience and I'm glad I was able to help my community in its time of need.

Once back in Toronto after *L'il Abner*, the first professional audition I managed to secure was for the Charlottetown Festival, a summer theatre in Prince Edward Island, renowned as the only theatre in Canada to produce original Canadian musicals. I was excited at this prospect because the main production of the festival each year was *Anne of Green Gables: The Musical*, which I had seen a number of times in P.E.I. with my parents during summer vacations.

When I was twelve, my parents took me to see both *Anne* and *Kronborg: 1582* (later retitled *Rockabye Hamlet* for Broadway), a rock opera based on Shakespeare's *Hamlet* by Toronto writer-composer Cliff

Jones, starring Cal Dodd as Hamlet, Beverly D'Angelo as Ophelia, and Rudy Webb as Claudius. That show and these actors were all, in a word, breathtaking. The cast of that 1972 production showed me what I wanted to be when I grew up. I wanted to do *that*. It's interesting to note that seven years later I'd be working with Cliff Jones myself, doing exactly that – and twenty years later I'd be working with Cal Dodd in Toronto, in *X-Men: The Animated Series*, with Cal as Wolverine and me as Rogue. Looking back now I can see all the breadcrumbs leading from one turning point in my life to the next. It's amazing. As Hamlet says, "There are more things in heaven and earth … than are dreamt of …" and I've found that to be true.

Anne of Green Gables: The Musical has always been enormously popular with tourists, who flock to Prince Edward Island every summer to see the show and visit the house that served as the setting for Lucy Maud Montgomery's novels about the young Anne. The musical is based on Montgomery's first book in the series. It had been adapted into a musical by Canadian writers/composers Don Harron, and Norman and Elaine Campbell. The global popularity made the show the longest-running musical in Canada. So by the time I was old enough to actually audition for the summer season, I felt instinctively that I was destined to perform at the Charlottetown Festival.

I showed up for the audition with my waist-length blonde hair the colour of bright orange carrots. The night before I had decided to dye my hair with henna into a reddish-golden colour in order to look a little more like the character of Anne. The henna was supposed to simply give my hair a warm light reddish tint, creating the illusion of the red hair for which Anne herself was famous. In the play, Anne is teased mercilessly for her bright orange hair, so she tried to dye it a "beautiful raven black" in order to look more like her best friend Diana. Instead, her hair turned a bright "bottle green."

Now stuck with bright orange hair myself for the audition, I braided it into two long plaits like Anne. And once I was in the room with artistic director Alan Lund and the creative team it gave me a funny, and one could say "colourful," story to share. In fact, this crazy stunt – or, on the other hand, dedication to my craft – was so much like something the character Anne would have done herself that the creators of the show immediately saw my affinity for the role. And before long we were all laughing and swapping tales as if we'd known each other for years.

I booked the job. As well as understudying Anne, the Festival also offered me a small role of Cobweb the Fairy in *On A Summer's Night* by Jim Betts, starring Dougie Chamberlain as Oberon, Wanda Canon as Titania, and Stan Lesk as Puck. Patrick Young, Brian McKay, Michelle Fisk, and a fellow student from York University, Charlotte Moore, were cast as the pairs of mortal lovers. Charlotte was two years ahead of me at York, having graduated in the spring. We decided to rent a house together in Charlottetown for the summer to save on costs. We were both excited for this new adventure.

Little did I know then, starting off the summer as a kid who had just been kicked out of university and now understudying a role I would never get to play, that by summer's end something extraordinary would happen to catapult my career into the stratosphere overnight. The time of "waiting in the wings" to take my place centre stage would soon be over. The magic that is timing and destiny was afoot. And the rebirth of a sex symbol was about to begin. You see, Marilyn Monroe was calling my name – in sweet, alluring, velvet tones so soft that there was nothing for a young woman to do but to subconsciously follow her siren song.

CHAPTER 5

HEY MARILYN!: THE GOOD, THE BAD, AND THE UGLY

The summer of 1979 began quietly enough, but with a simmering excitement. Ensconced once again in Truro in my old upstairs room at 111 Willow Street, with its slanted ceiling and starched white cotton curtains, I began to prepare for my role of Cobweb the Fairy for the Charlottetown Festival's upcoming production of *On A Summer's Night* by Jim Betts. As I lay in bed reading all of the library books I could find about fairies and their temperaments, it seemed like my childhood love of fairies and anything magical was being rewarded. I also reread Shakespeare's *A Midsummer Night's Dream*, upon which the musical was based. Each afternoon I would venture downstairs to our living room to rehearse the songs from *Anne of Green Gables* by listening to the original cast album on Dad's record player, singing along with Gracie Finley, the original Anne, over and over again until I knew them note for note.

Soon enough, it was time to take the ferry to Prince Edward Island from Pictou, Nova Scotia, to begin rehearsals for both shows and, with the help of our parents, my new flatmate Charlotte Moore and I moved into the small bungalow we were to share for the summer. We got along really well and after rehearsals would go for dinner and drinks with our fellow company members and on trips on our days off to the beautiful white sand beaches of the Island.

As the understudy for Anne, I took copious notes of the blocking for her scenes, meaning where Anne moved onstage and when, as well as the choreography that accompanied her songs. By the time the show opened I was ready to replace Anne (played by Susie Cuthbert that summer) at a moment's notice.

My boyfriend Charlie visited every other weekend as he was on a summer break from Ottawa's National Arts Centre. His movie star looks always slayed me and he made a huge impression on the other members of the company, who welcomed him into our circle whenever he came over.

Little did we know then that Charlie, who made his film debut as Tom Rice in the horror film *Humongous*, would star in *The Hitchhiker* and later *Robo Cop: Prime Directives*, for which I would also become a guest star. But the summer of '79 was the first time Charlie experienced having to stand aside and watch for the entire summer season while I performed, instead of me being "the girlfriend" while he performed with the NAC.

I have always called that time "the golden summer" because the weather was for the most part gloriously sunny, the nights full of starry skies were exquisite, and it felt so good to be part of a professional theatre company full of young people closer to my age, all with the same goal. We were performing and entertaining people and having a really good time doing it.

At the end of the play on opening night, a serendipitous event occurred when the designer of the show, Werner Russold, came over to me and said, "Hey, Lenore, a very dear friend of mine from Toronto is here. He lives on the Island during the summer, and he was just smitten by your performance tonight and thought you stood out – and he would love to meet you!" Intrigued but already feeling rather sorry for the guy, thinking, "I didn't do *that* much in the small role. How on earth would I stand out?" I said, "Sure, I'd love to meet your friend. Where is he?"

Werner brought me over to a man who looked to be in his thirties who was sipping a drink in the corner quietly observing the party, and it did not take long to discern that his friend was extremely shy and not good at small talk. It was hard at first to get him to say anything at all. I introduced myself and said, "I hear that you enjoyed the show."

"Oh yes, yes, I really loved the show!" he managed to blurt while blinking and blushing profusely.

"Ahh ... That's great. I love the music," I replied.

"I ... umm ... I thought you were really terrific and I couldn't take my eyes off you!" he continued.

"Wow. That's amazing. Thank you!"

Then I asked him his name and, still blushing and now looking intently at something on the floor, he replied, "Uhh ... Uhh ... It's David."

"Okay. And, David, so you stay here in the Island in the summers, do you?"

"Yes."

"Uh-huh. And ... you live in Toronto the rest of the year?"

"Yes."

"Great! So ... if you don't mind me asking, what do you do, David?"

David turned even more red at what I meant as an innocent question, and looked down at his feet before managing to stammer out the words, "Well ... Ahhh ... Uhhh ... I write."

I took a deep breath as I continued to draw out what appeared to be a painful confession of some sort. "I see ... Well, that's great, David. That must be really interesting work."

I waited. But nothing else was forthcoming. I continued the line of questioning, feeling guilty that I was putting this poor soul through his paces in attempting to answer the simplest of questions at what was becoming a very loud and "happening" party.

"So ... What kinds of things do you write, David?"

Now time seemed to stand still for an eternity before his reply, which he uttered in an admittance that he seemed almost embarrassed to share.

"Uhh, well I, uh, uh ... I write plays."

At that point, with a sudden intake of breath, I stepped backwards as something inside me clicked and a wild thought flashed across my mind about who this unassuming man before me may be. I took a chance, and said, rather gently, trying to make eye contact, "So your name is David, and you write plays?"

"Yes."

"You wouldn't happen to be David French, would you?"

At that he blushed again but for the first time looked up at me directly with a flabbergasted expression as he managed to spit out, "Why, yes. Yes I am!" at which point I let out a little squeal of excitement and said,

"Oh my God! I can't believe it! David French, you are my very favourite playwright in the whole world, along with Chekhov and Shakespeare! I've been studying your plays at university, and I simply love every single one of them!"

At this point, David's look of fear completely disappeared and his blue eyes and face, while still blushing, absolutely beamed. I could tell he didn't know what to say but he was very pleased. It didn't matter. We were on the same team.

After this encounter, David French and I became firm friends – for life. He would often invite me to his cottage in Cable Head, Prince Edward Island, where he wrote his plays during the summer months, and I would spend my day off either alone, or with my boyfriend, or I'd bring many of my cast members – all beautiful young women and men in their prime and full of life, laughter, and excitement. We would drive out to David's place by the carloads, bringing picnic baskets, wine, and beer, and we'd all hit the beach. We'd have races and play games and dear David was in the middle of it all, thrilled at being part of this spectacular private party. And he quickly got over his shyness as we all treated him like one of our own. David was in his glory! We often spoke about that time as our "golden summer," as indeed they are rare. Several years later, he wrote *That Summer*, a play he told me came to him while thinking back about that special time in both our lives.

When Charlie Page Fletcher came out with me to meet David the two men became good friends as well. And we had many a great laugh about pretty well anything. We were good for David, and he knew it.

At one point he admitted to me that he'd been having writer's block until we met and as he got to know me – and Charlie – better, he confided that a new play idea had come to him and his writer's "block" was broken. *Salt Water Moon* was the name of his new play, and it was a two-hander, with just two actors in it: a young woman and her ex-boyfriend who has come home to their small hometown to try to win back her love and her hand in marriage. The two are pretty high-spirited and some fireworks explode between them in the course of the play. David told me he got that from spending time with us too. Small wonder.

The two characters of Mary Snow and Jacob Mercer were also based on David's parents, and the play was written as a precursor to his existing

Mercer family dramas about the same characters when they're older. These include two of my favourites, *Of the Fields, Lately* and *Leaving Home*, which I had discovered at York University. But David was clear in telling me that he was modelling the young Mary Snow (age seventeen in the play) after me and his mother. I was honoured. And still am.

I also introduced David to my family that summer and we had a number of meals together. He particularly loved meeting my little sister, Tamara, who was then eight, and it's worth mentioning that the character of Mary in his new play talks about her younger sister as I often did, with a sadness that they were forced to be apart and a wistful longing to be reunited.

Funnily enough, one time when Tamara wanted to get David's autograph, this great writer hesitated for so long over what to write and asked for an extra week to figure out what to say. Such was the humble nature of this sweet soul who, although he is sadly deceased, I still feel honoured to call one of my best friends.

Towards the end of the summer I heard that there was a production of *Dracula* playing at a small theatre company in Victoria, P.E.I., and I invited Charlie and David to attend with me on a day off. I have to say it was the funniest production of *Dracula* we could ever have seen – not because it was supposed to be but because of several things that happened throughout what was essentially an amateur production, and it was with great strength that I managed to prevent David and Charlie from both falling into the aisles with laughter whenever something went wrong.

The merriment began when an obviously fake plastic bat went "flying" through the air from one side of the stage to the other on a very obvious string and once it got to the other side you could hear it splat against the wall offstage. The next mishap occurred because the character of Renfrew was wearing a pair of trousers that unhappily exactly matched the couch upon which he (also unhappily) often had to deliver his monologues about eating flies and whatnot, so his bottom half completely disappeared and he appeared to be a disembodied torso and head. Again this was, I doubt, what the production intended. However, that's what we got.

Finally, at the very end of the show when the curtains came together and the stage went dark, a time when the actors can leave the stage to return triumphantly for their curtain call, the same actor got stuck onstage after everybody else had left. And when the lights came up, he was caught frantically clawing at the curtains, unable to find his way offstage.

Now, of course, this would be an embarrassing moment for any actor, but by this time Charlie and David were barely able to control their hysterical laughter. After we left the theatre to climb into our "getaway" car, we saw the same actor in back of the theatre kicking his poor dog. Well, that was it. I couldn't control either of them any longer and while feeling sorry for the poor dog, we pulled away from the theatre with the two of them absolutely howling and crying with laughter. Events such as this kept our summer wildly entertaining.

Meanwhile, my work at the Charlottetown Festival proceeded, and I was eventually asked to step in on very short notice to play another small role, that of Prissy Andrews in the musical *Anne of Green Gables.* As it turned out, it was to replace my roommate, Charlotte, who had unfortunately broken her leg onstage tripping over a tree which was part of the set.

While the circumstance of Charlotte's injury was unfortunate, it was nice to become part of the *Anne* company onstage for the first time. Although I had been understudying "Anne" by watching from the wings all summer, it had become apparent that the actress playing her was determined to perform in sickness as well as in health. So I never was able to go on as Anne.

Instead, I spent the summer enjoying the gorgeous weather and camaraderie of the company – and since Charlie and I were madly in love, we had a great summer. Remembering Charlie now as the handsome young man he was always reminds me of the song "Nature Boy." He was carefree and wild with a rather enchanting quality and as beautiful as Michelangelo's famous statue of David. But he also liked to drink. A lot. And he loved his weed too. This would soon become a major problem in our relationship.

When the summer season winds down each year, the Charlottetown Festival puts on a concert called the Maud Whitmore Scholarship Concert. The entire theatre company is encouraged to perform songs or skits that they feel show their performing abilities, so it's a particularly good opportunity for those playing smaller roles who didn't get a chance to do so in the shows that summer.

I decided to do a song from the musical *Funny Girl*, originally starring Barbra Streisand. It was my favourite show at the time, based on hearing her 1968 album, though I had never seen the show performed. The song I chose was "Cornet Man," which I liked not only because I played the trumpet throughout my school years, directed by the inimitable school band maestro Ron MacKay, but also because the song was a raunchy torch song that was completely different from anything in *Anne of Green Gables*. This number would enable me to show off my vocal range and my budding sexuality.

It was not enough of a challenge for me to perform it simply as Barbra Streisand had done, however. Since I like to give my characters a little more complication and unexpected twists, I decided to do the song as a character reminiscent of Marlene Dietrich, so I put on a German accent, used my deeper, sultry tones to begin the song, and put finger waves in my blonde hair, balanced off with a sparkly black beret. For the rest of the ensemble, I chose a grey trench coat covering up a sexy little number underneath, with fishnet stockings and high heels.

Artistic director Alan Lund loved the song and my performance during rehearsals and decided to place the song as the finale for the first act of the concert, ending the first half with a bang.

The night of the concert as I prepared for my number, I felt butterflies in my stomach, but also a certainty that this song would truly show an audience – and any visiting directors – just what kind of stuff I was made of as a lead performer if given the chance. As it turned out I was not wrong. And neither was Alan Lund, the consummate musical theatre impresario that he was.

As the song began the audience was quiet. Who was this girl? A new kid in town whom they had not really noticed all summer because I'd done nothing that would make me stand out in a crowd (other than to David French and, of course, Charlie and my family). However, as the song progressed and I reached the moment where I changed from a sultry, trench-coat-wearing Marlene Dietrich into her role as a sexy bombshell in *The Blue Angel*, I peeled off the trench coat, threw my shapely fishnet-stockinged leg over a chair directly in a spotlight centre stage, and belted out the rest of the song with sexy moves in a, shall we say, highly energetic fashion.

And *voilá*! I was immediately transformed into a performer who appeared to have been doing this all her life – and, really, I had been since I was fifteen and playing Miss Adelaide, the "harlot with a heart of gold," in my Grade Ten high school year and during all the rehearsals to my dad's record player in our living room in Truro.

While giving it everything I had in this razzmatazz section of the song, I could feel the energy pulsating in the audience. There was a connection between them and me that gave me a feeling of strength and power that I had only ever felt before as Adelaide back home in Truro. But this time, it was even stronger.

The Confederation Centre Theatre is large and wide, seating around a thousand people, and on this hot summer night it was packed. And as I performed solo publicly for the first time onstage, I could feel the audience was breathlessly eating out of my hand, watching every move and savouring every note and thrust of my hips.

I had not experienced anything quite like this and as the curtain came down, a roar of approval came up from the audience almost as one voice, with people jumping to their feet to give me my first standing ovation. And wow. They say that this kind of response can be so addictive, as it's such an obvious public statement of approval, that most actors (who, deep down, for some reason are actually searching for approval) find it like ambrosia from the gods. I was no different.

Little Lenore had found her temple, her altar, and her magic circle and from that moment she was hooked.

When the curtains had closed after my song, the rumbling sound of approval ringing in my ears, I peeked through the curtains at the side of the stage to see and listen to individual reactions to my performance. I will never forget the sound of that buzz of the crowd, people asking, "What's her name?" and "How come we haven't seen her before?" and "That girl will go far!" and "What a knockout!" These were all very heady things for me to hear, and I enjoyed the feeling that my instincts had been correct in choosing that particular song and simply hoped that perhaps the next season I would be offered larger roles. Unbeknownst to me, however, there were two people in the audience that night whose presence would change the trajectory of not only my career but my life.

They were Cliff Jones, a musical theatre writer and composer from Toronto, and his wife, Eve. Cliff had written *Kronborg*, the rock opera based on *Hamlet* that I had loved so much just a few years before and had made me decide I wanted to be a musical theatre performer. What I also didn't know was that, like David French, Cliff and Eve also spent their summers in Keppoch, Prince Edward Island. Cliff had recently written a new rock opera, this time about the tragic and complicated sex symbol Marilyn Monroe. *Hey Marilyn!* was the name of the show, and while the CBC (Canadian Broadcasting Corporation) had already produced a radio version of the musical starring Beverly D'Angelo and Cal Dodd in the roles of Narrator and Johnny Hyde, Cliff and Peter Coe, an experienced theatre director from England, had been searching for an entire year for the right actress to play Marilyn in their upcoming theatrical premiere.

Peter Coe had directed the musical *Oliver!* in the West End in London and also on Broadway to great success, and he had recently taken over from John Neville as artistic director of the Citadel Theatre in Edmonton. The show was slated to open in just five months, in January of 1980, and after searching across Canada and the U.S. they still had not found the right actress to play Marilyn.

In an interesting twist to this turn of events, Cliff had broken his leg the very day of the Maud Whitmore Scholarship Concert while playing tennis and, although he had tickets, he did not feel like going to the concert owing to the warm night and the pain of his injury.

This is when a strange thing occurred. And I've heard it from both Cliff and Eve a number of times over the years. Eve can't explain why, but says her women's intuition started firing off on all cylinders. And they say she told him emphatically, "No, Cliff, you are coming to the theatre with me come hell or high water. I don't know why, but something is telling me we both have to go and there's some reason you have to be there."

Cliff, like a good partner, took her advice and accompanied her to the concert complaining all the way. That is, until they saw my number. As Cliff and Eve both tell the story, as soon as I had finished my number, with the applause still ringing wildly about them, they turned to each other and said, "That's Marilyn!" I still get chills when I think of that story, as it makes one wonder what in the world is really going on and if there is truly such a thing as destiny or karma.

I have to say I will always be grateful to Eve for bringing Cliff to the theatre that night because later that night Cliff sought out Alan Lund and asked him about me and requested my number. And, broken leg or not, he called the house where Charlotte and I were staying and asked if I could meet him at the theatre to go over a few songs from a "new show" he'd written.

I dutifully showed up at the theatre that very afternoon and Cliff proceeded to run through some of the numbers from the show. I picked them up very easily and even without having ever seen any Marilyn Monroe movies, I could sing them in a breathy quality he said was eerily similar to Marilyn. Cliff was sold on the spot.

But now he needed to convince the director that this unknown nineteen-year-old from Truro, Nova Scotia, had what it took to play Marilyn Monroe. It was arranged that as soon as the summer season was over, I would be flown out to Edmonton to meet Peter Coe at the Citadel Theatre to audition for the role. The day after our last show I flew to Edmonton and was put up in a hotel for a night.

The next day I went to the theatre to meet Peter and his musical director, who got on the piano to take me through scales and arpeggios to get an idea of my vocal range, which, in spite of having no vocal training, was wide. I could belt up to a high D, although C and B-flat were my strongest high notes, and my lower range was good as well. After that was established they proceeded to get me to sing some songs from *Hey Marilyn!* which by now I knew by heart, Cliff having given me a tape of the CBC version with which to practise. After I'd done the songs from the show, Peter Coe asked if I could do any other songs to give them a better idea of my range. I'd luckily brought a songbook of Broadway musicals, so I did a number of those as well.

Finally, Peter Coe, looking rather perplexed, said, "Well, is there anything else we can get her to do?"

And after getting a response of, "Not really. She's done everything we've asked her to do," Peter turned back to me, saying, "Well, Lenore, you're perfect for this role. However, I'm a little hesitant to offer it to you because you're so young. You'd have carry this play. She's in almost every scene and you've never starred in a professional production before. So I'm going to need some time to think about this."

Now, this was September, and I knew the show was to open in January, with rehearsals starting in November, which, by the way, was when I would turn twenty. And while most young actors in my position at the time would likely have simply agreed and flown back home to wait by the phone for a response from the big man, I was not most young actors. I'd already been tossed out of university because I was not most young actors. I didn't even have an agent to represent me yet. But I had a card up my sleeve.

As it turned out, in the time since I'd finished the summer season I had already received an offer from John Neville at Neptune Theatre in Halifax to do his fall and early winter season. I'd been offered the part of Bianca in Shakespeare's *The Taming of the Shrew* as well as the female lead in John Gray's new musical *Eighteen Wheels*, and another role in Henry Ibsen's *The Master Builder*. And the season was going to begin rehearsing in a few weeks' time.

I very calmly explained this to Mr Coe, and then said, "So I'm very sorry, but I feel an obligation to John Neville, who got me my Actors Equity, and if I'm going to bail on his offer, I need to tell him right away so that he can replace me for all of those roles. I'm heading back to Nova Scotia tonight at 9 p.m., so I'll need to know before I catch my flight."

I thought Peter Coe's jaw was going to drop right onto the ground. He didn't know what to say.

And when he could finally talk, he turned to the musical director, scratching his head, and said, "I can't believe that I'm in negotiations with a nineteen-year-old girl for the starring role of my big musical this season."

Peter Coe looked at me again with wide-open eyes, still scratching his head, then his beard, and said, "My God. I can't believe this is happening. But all right, if you must have an answer, then ... okay, you've got it! I'd like you to play my leading lady in *Hey Marilyn!* Will you accept?"

To which I replied, "With pleasure. Thank you." And I held out my hand, looking him straight in the eyes. And then I left to get ready to catch my plane.

As soon as I returned home I called Neptune Theatre and spoke to John Neville, and it was one of the hardest conversations I've had in my life, having to tell someone who believed in me that I was sorry but I could not do his season after all. John did not take it well. In fact, he was furious. I was unaware at the time but found out later that there was some kind of rivalry and animosity between John Neville and Peter Coe. Both were British directors, and Peter Coe had just replaced John Neville at the Citadel Theatre, after John had left to become AD at the Neptune.

John tried to talk me out of it, but I said, "I'm really sorry, but I have to take this role as it's a once-in-a-lifetime opportunity." Which it was. Later that night I even had a call from John and the actress Susan Wright, from the Neptune bar. Susan was to play the lead role of Kate in *The Taming of the Shrew* and both clearly had been drinking. They were angry at my decision, and Susan basically said in her inimitable way, "Who do you think you are to turn this down, you little cunt?" But I stuck to my guns. I knew instinctively that I had to do *Hey Marilyn!* And, to be honest, it was a feeling that Marilyn had chosen me to play her. I didn't want to let her down.

A fallout of turning down the Neptune offer was that since one of the productions would soon have started rehearsals, I was now without a job for the fall. So I called Peter Coe to ask if he had any other roles I could do before rehearsals began. As it turned out, the only thing he had was a small role in *The Trojan Women*, which would be done in mask, with Barbara Chilcott playing the lead. I said okay and was grateful to be working.

Around about this time I also finally received word back from my National Arts Centre audition in Ottawa that I'd done before the summer, the one that got me fired from *The Caucasian Chalk Circle*. The message I received was that NAC's artistic director John Wood would like me to play Miranda in Shakespeare's *The Tempest*. This news thrilled me to no end, but, alas, the production overlapped with *Hey Marilyn!* and there was no way I could do both. I had to reject the offer.

That was hard to do too. While my decision was already made to do the play about Marilyn, I would have loved to finally be with Charlie and his fellow NAC company members, who had also become my friends over the past couple of years. But I'd be lying if I didn't admit there was a little feeling of satisfaction at having to turn down the offer too. I still felt a little raw about John Wood telling me I was too young to take to Ottawa with Charlie and many other actors from the Neptune company after performing in *Gypsy*.

"If you snooze you lose!" I thought.

The Trojan Women was an interesting show and I enjoyed being part of another company, and even though I was once again playing a small role, it gave me time to prepare mentally for my upcoming role as Marilyn. However, something was "rotten in the state of Denmark," and I would soon face an even greater challenge than any I had faced before.

When I arrived in Edmonton it was arranged for me to have an apartment at Edmonton House, in which most of the performers from out of town stayed while working at the Citadel Theatre. Mr. Coe lived upstairs in a penthouse suite with his wife, who was a beautiful designer and pregnant at the time.

One day shortly after my arrival Mr. Coe called to say, "Listen, I'm going down for a swim in the pool. Can you meet me there and we can have a swim and talk about the show?"

I thought, "How exciting! The director wants to get to know me and become friends. This is really cool!" So I agreed.

Coincidentally, one of the songs from the show included the lines,

"Oh, won't you take a swim
In my swimming pool.
I had it built for all my friends
And I'll feel foolish
If no one comes to swim
In my swimming pool
That I had built just for you."

Marilyn does this song towards the end of her life after she buys a house in Santa Monica. She was apparently always trying to call people up and ask them to come swimming, which never happened because she really didn't have many close friends she could trust and rely on, so she was feeling really lonely. I always related to her about this for some reason, although funnily enough I now have a swimming pool myself and often feel the same way as Marilyn did.

In any case, in the fall of 1979 I went down to the swimming pool at Edmonton House excitedly thinking my director and I were going to bond over swimming and talking about our show. But to my dismay, it soon became apparent that Mr. Coe had other ideas.

CHAPTER 6

A STAR IS BORN

Almost as soon as I had slipped into the water of the Edmonton House pool in my one-piece bathing suit, Mr. Coe swam up close – too close – and cornered me against the side of the pool, putting his arms on either side of my body, trapping me. It all happened so fast, I was completely taken aback.

He tried to kiss me – and I froze. I had never had something like that happen to me before, and so many things went flying through my mind in a jumble. I instinctively did what many women do when they find themselves in a compromised position like that. You don't want to admit even to yourself that it's really happening and perhaps we feel the need to buy some time to figure it out and sort out our thoughts and feelings.

But then, why should we even have to?

In any case, I just wanted to get out of the situation as quickly as possible as it was overwhelmingly uncomfortable, so I giggled coyly and pretended that I thought he was just joking. Then I suddenly saw my chance to escape and swam under one of his arms to get away from him.

He tried to pursue me in the pool and continued with some affectionate words, but once free of him, I knew I didn't want to continue the charade. So I made an excuse about having to leave, saying I was expecting a phone call from my boyfriend Charlie and I had to get back to my room.

Little did I know it then, but this was just the beginning of a pattern of sexual harassment that began in the swimming pool at Edmonton House with his wife pregnant upstairs in the same building and it continued almost until opening night.

Mr. Coe would often phone me and ask me what I was doing. I would say, "I'm studying my lines," but he would ask me to come meet him to talk or for a coffee or drink or whatever and I would always come up with excuses about why I couldn't meet him. It even reached the point where he was calling me and saying how much he missed me and had to see me. Again, I would come up with a million excuses as to why I could not.

I was completely flummoxed as to what to do about the situation and felt terrified about standing up to this man who was much older than me and reminded me of the Sheriff of Nottingham with his little goatee. I did not find him attractive at all.

And here he was, a married man! I wanted to tell him off. But I was terrified thinking that maybe the only reason he had brought me here to Edmonton in the first place was because he wanted to go to bed with me and if I refused him outright and told him off, he would send me packing with my suitcase back to Truro, Nova Scotia. It was a terrible predicament for a young woman to find herself in, away from home and with no close friends in whom to confide. I still did not even have an agent at the time to explain what was happening.

It got so bad that I went out to Hudson's Bay Company one weekend and bought myself a diamond engagement ring with my $500 weekly salary; I blew my whole paycheque on the ring to show up at rehearsal the next day wearing it. I lied and told everybody how excited I was that my boyfriend Charlie had sent me an engagement ring in the mail, asking me to marry him, and that I had agreed. I hoped that this would dissuade the sexual harassment by my director but again it really did nothing to curtail his behaviour. I was naïve not to realize that if a pregnant wife on the premises didn't deter him, a long-distance fiancé wasn't likely to.

Finally, one day after rehearsal I found myself walking home with Mr. Coe from the theatre to Edmonton House and I decided to bite the bullet. I said, "You know, Peter, I'm extremely grateful for this incredible opportunity you've given me, and while you're very attractive [I lied], please understand that I need to focus all my energy on our show. I have a huge job to do and surely you understand that I can't be distracted. That all of my time and energy need to be directed towards the show."

As with most abusers, his reaction was one of complete surprise and denial, saying he had no idea what I was talking about.

Undaunted, I said, "Come on, Peter, you know exactly what I mean. I just can't engage in any kind of relationship at this time. I already have a boyfriend. And I need to focus on doing the best job I can to play Marilyn Monroe. There's a lot of pressure on me and I really need your support to do the best job I can. There's no room for any sexual dalliances."

Again, Mr. Coe professed he knew nothing about what I was saying.

I have to say that at the time I felt really, really lonely for the first time in my life – full of shame and guilt because I didn't have the courage to call him out in public or even report him to someone who could come to my defence. I didn't mention it in my weekly phone calls home to my parents, nor did I mention it to Charlie in Ottawa because I thought he might show up and knock the guy out. And then what would happen?

Looking back now with the wisdom of my years, I feel deep sadness for the young teenage girl who had nobody to turn to for help while dealing with a predator who was so selfish, he would risk the success of an entire show to satisfy his own sexual desires.

Opening night was getting closer and the pressure on me and on the rest of the cast was mounting. Now it became clear that Mr. Coe had received my rejection of his advances loud and clear, as his behaviour now changed from one of pursuer to punisher. In rehearsals he mostly gave me the cold, silent treatment while the rest of the time he humiliated and embarrassed me. If I had to go to the bathroom during a rehearsal, I would tell the stage manager, as one does, but whenever I came back, Mr. Coe made a point of drawing attention to the fact that I had been to the bathroom, asking me questions like, "What were you doing in there? What was taking you so long?" He made comments like this while at the same time he refused to direct me.

He did not block my scenes. He was directing everybody around me; everyone else was getting daily notes. Yet I had none. For an actor with all the experience I have now, having no direction would seem weird, but I would be fine with that and have enough confidence to just do my own thing. But I was used to having directors who directed you. They'd give you blocking in rehearsal and then you would take it from there and make it your own.

That did not happen in *Hey Marilyn!* Instead, Mr. Coe left me entirely alone to the point that after one rehearsal as we got closer to our first preview performance, the choreographer, who was from New York, made an announcement, saying, "Okay, everybody, listen up. I know there are still some scenes that have not yet been blocked, but don't panic. Just stand and sing and focus on the songs – and trust me that we will get to you to block your scenes." He seemed to be looking at me as he said it. So that's what I did. I stood and I sang the entire show, focusing on making sure that I got all the vocal licks I wanted to and working with the musical director to perfect it.

Meanwhile, under all this pressure, I turned twenty. I did not tell anyone it was my birthday because I wanted to be brave and grown-up and not call attention to the fact. That night I began studying my script and reading books about Marilyn again as I did every night. Early on I had decided I did not want to simply do an impersonation of Marilyn; I wanted to portray and express her "essence."

I started crying. The weight of not telling anyone what had happened with Mr. Coe was taking a toll. I felt so lonely. But I suddenly had a strange feeling – that Marilyn Monroe was there with me trying to tell me something. She had suffered at the hands of abusive men too as a young girl.

I had a book about Marilyn in front of me, reading every little detail I could find about her. I closed the book and said to the empty room, "Marilyn, if you're here, and if you chose me to portray who you really are, is there something important you want me to know?" And with eyes still closed, I threw the book open and pointed two fingers at different spots on both pages.

When I opened my eyes, my tears immediately turned to laughter, as no words at all were written on the pages. Instead, there was a huge black and white photo of Marilyn that spread across the two pages. She was laughing at the camera, and in front of her was a huge birthday cake. It was a photo taken at her thirty-sixth birthday – her last. Her birthday was in June, and she looked so vibrant and gorgeous, and yet two months later, on August 4, 1962, she would be dead. I got chills. But it seemed like such a strong, positive sign that all Marilyn wanted to say was to wish me a Happy Birthday. That meant I was on the right track in my portrayal. And I was not alone.

Someone in the cast had figured out it was my birthday, and since leaving your teens and turning twenty is a special one, my fellow actors presented me with a cake and had a little party after the next rehearsal.

Peter Coe did not attend, nor was he invited. But most of the cast came to celebrate, including Sam Moses and Rudy Webb (who had blown me away as a kid at the Charlottetown Festival with his riveting performance as King Claudius in Cliff Jones' *Kronborg 1582*). Rudy was now playing the role of our show's Narrator, and Sam was Johnny Hyde, Marilyn's agent.

That night the cast brought out a birthday cake and many shared that they were shocked by Peter Coe's behaviour towards me. But I couldn't get past a feeling of shame – as if his bad behaviour was my fault somehow. I was also concerned that if I told anyone the truth it might get back to him, and possibly create an even worse situation. So I continued to say nothing and instead shrugged it off, saying I hoped he would at least block my scenes before opening night.

I realize now that I should have told one of the more experienced performers, or the stage manager, what had happened. But at nineteen, just turning twenty, I just didn't have the courage.

As our first preview loomed in January, after one rehearsal during which yet again none of my scenes were blocked, Peter Coe called the entire cast to come on stage for notes. He usually had the lights turned down in the theatre where he sat holding a large megaphone like the ones I'd seen in old black and white movies about directors on film sets. Then, with the lights onstage turned up bright, Mr. Coe would call out his directions and questions to the actors and orchestra through the megaphone from out of the darkness of the house. Looking back now I see that as another sign of a rather insecure man who needs to have power over others – in this case an entire theatre company.

In the play, there were close to twenty-five people all on stage. And we had a fantastic large live orchestra as well. That seemed to be usual back in those days, which was fantastic, but over the years with cutbacks the live orchestras in regional theatres have dwindled. I still miss a full orchestra to this day.

On this particular night Mr. Coe called the full company to the stage, and there we were under full lights while he went through the entire show telling people to do this or that, to cut this number or that number, to move this song here, and cut that dance routine or comic schtick. He kept calling out different characters' names and went through the entire show calling out his notes and directions through his big ol' megaphone from the darkness of the house.

And then he got to me. He asked me to come to centre stage, then said loudly into the megaphone: "Lenore. For God's sake! What on earth are you doing up there? Are you just going to stand there like a block of wood through the whole show? Aren't you going to move around or anything?"

I felt like I had been slapped across the face with a wet mackerel. Tears of humiliation sprang to my eyes, and I blinked them back as I said, "Well, the choreographer told us that if you hadn't blocked our scenes yet to just stand and sing. So that's what I've been doing."

There was an ominous silence; you could hear a pin drop. Then Peter Coe roared through the megaphone, and I remember his words as if it happened yesterday, they are so ingrained in my mind and on my soul: "Listen, sweetheart, if Liza Minnelli were here, she'd be telling me what to do!"

Uh … yeah. She likely would have. But here I was, a barely-turned-twenty-year-old whom he had hired for her very first starring role. And newspapers across the country had been writing stories about our show for months, with sentences like this one which is also seared in my memory: "Marilyn Monroe is the sexual icon of the century. Yet on the main stage of Edmonton's Citadel Theatre an unknown girl from Truro, Nova Scotia, is going to attempt to re-create 'The Great MM.'"

The pressure was on all right.

Meanwhile, all eyes were upon me. Everyone in that theatre was waiting to hear how I'd respond to what was for all intents and purposes a public humiliation. I did what any self-respecting actor would do in the situation. I held back the tears that by now were ready to pour down my cheeks, and I took a cue from characters I'd seen in the movies in similar situations … I said nothing, turned on my heels, and, with my head held high, walked off the stage.

I kept walking, stopping only long enough to get my coat from my dressing room. And without waiting for anyone, I walked all the way home to Edmonton House. As soon as I got to the safety of my own room, I let the tears flow. And then I got to work.

Furious that I had had to put up with his bad behaviour, his sexual harassment, his abuse, his constant humiliation for months now, I took my script out once more. And this time I went through it and blocked the entire show myself. I worked well into the night and into the wee small hours of the morning.

And when I returned to the theatre the next day for another run-through of the show, I made a point of first going to every dressing room to speak to my fellow actors, who were still shocked from what they'd witnessed the night before and feeling really, really bad for me, saying things like, "Oh my God, Lenore! I can't believe he did that to you. Why is he treating you this way?"

Yet I still did not tell them what had been going on. I kept that humiliating secret and instead I said, "It doesn't matter why he did it. Let's not worry about that right now. We have a show to do. Just please do me a favour today – I'm asking you for just one thing. Tonight, Marilyn is going to move. Please just move with her!"

And they all got it. Every one of my cast mates said, "We're with you, Lenore, we're with you 100 percent. You do whatever you need to do, and we will be right there to support you."

Just writing these words forty years later brings tears to my eyes as I remember the pain of that young woman having to deal with something no young person should have to deal with on her own, and then being punished and publicly humiliated for standing up for herself. But the support that my cast members gave me that night and from then on during the run of the show was healing balm to my soul. And I guess it still is.

Next, I went to my dressing room and for the first time put on my Marilyn Monroe makeup and wig, and dressed in the long red sequined dress designed for me by the inimitable theatre designer Larry Schaffer. And when I walked out of that dressing room, I was Marilyn Monroe.

And that night Marilyn Monroe moved.

I had decided that I would portray Marilyn in such a way that when the cameras were upon her (and we had a full dolly and movie camera onstage) or if she was speaking to a man she wanted to impress, she became the breathy, sexy Marilyn Monroe of Hollywood fame, as if she herself was putting on the character of "Marilyn," which is, of course, what many people who knew her in her lifetime said she did. But for the rest of my performance, Marilyn behaved and sounded "normal." My Marilyn actually became Marilyn Monroe herself under certain circumstances of her choosing, while the rest of the time she was an entirely different person.

For the most part I sang the show mainly using my own natural singing voice, which is clear and strong and determined, except at the end of the show when Marilyn was messed up from pills and booze. It was important to me that I portrayed Marilyn as an extremely intelligent woman, who had great vulnerability and was also an alcoholic and addict but who knew how to play to the crowd. Unfortunately, she became trapped in the persona she had created.

After the rehearsal that day, Peter Coe came up to the stage with tears streaming down his face and embraced me in front of everybody (how magnanimous of him!), saying, "Oh my dear, that was a brilliant performance!" I would have liked to have said, "No thanks to *you*!" But I did not. I continued to rise above the abuse I'd suffered.

That was the performance I proceeded to give night after night and on opening night with the huge mainstage theatre at capacity, it was the performance I gave. I still had no idea what people would think. But when the curtain came down, and I walked out onstage for my bow as star of the show, it became clear. A roar of approval came from the crowd, and the entire audience sprang to their feet in a standing ovation. I was amazed, overwhelmed, and truly grateful for the response, particularly after all I'd been through.

Once the curtain had closed, and I was back in my dressing room still giddy and sipping champagne with the designer whom he had brought to celebrate, Mr. Coe arrived to congratulate me. With him was an American producer, David Merrick, a famed Broadway impresario at the time, and he immediately said, "My dear, you are at the beginning of a brilliant career!" The following day when reviews came out in the newspapers, Keith Ashby, of the *Edmonton Journal*, quoted him as saying, "The girl? She's brilliant!" The headline on the front page of the paper with a huge full-page photo of me as Marilyn Monroe read, "A Star is Born!" That opinion was shared in reviews across the country.

Little did they or anybody, including my family until now, know the true story behind my first portrayal of Marilyn Monroe (as there would be several others in the years to come) and the truth behind the rock opera *Hey Marilyn!*

It's funny, looking back at this turning point in my life, when I think of the times since that people have said to me that "everything has come easily to you" as if I had never known the feeling of loss, inadequacy, or disappointment. Nothing could be further from the truth. It's my sincere hope that by sharing this experience now it may give some support to others to call out sexual misconduct and abuse while it's happening instead of waiting forty years as I did, because I've discovered that this kind of wound can fester if left to remain in the shadows.

All in all, *Hey Marilyn!* was a personal triumph despite extremely challenging circumstances. You could say it was in this first challenge that I discovered my inner strength as a kind of superpower to overcome an immediate threat to my safety and personal dignity. A baptism by fire, if you will. While the experience was a difficult one, it set me up at a very young age as an actor – and a woman – to be able to deal with almost any situation that would later come up, with the skills and confidence to perform with grace under pressure. And, like Liza Minnelli, to know where and how to move, and to "move" an audience.

After this huge first splash at age twenty, it seemed like everyone suddenly wanted a piece of me – offers began coming in fast and furious. Now I really needed to find an agent to represent me.

CHAPTER 7

"YOU GOTTA GET A GIMMICK!"

During the final week of performing in *Hey Marilyn!* I was offered my first film role by a director who had seen the show. Shortly after the final night I was whisked off to Wilcox, Saskatchewan, to play Lila Petrie, a young teacher in *The Hounds of Notre Dame* directed by Zale Dalen, in which I co-starred with several wonderful actors, including Barry Morse (*The Fugitive*), Frances Hyland (*The Ecstasy of Rita Joe)*, award-winning theatre director and actor David Ferry, and Thomas Peacock, who would win a Genie Award for Best Actor for his role as Father Athol Murray.

The film is a true story about a Canadian priest, Father Murray, who in 1927 was assigned to St. Augustine's parish in Wilcox, Saskatchewan, where he enrolled fifteen troubled boys in the Notre Dame Residential School run by the Sisters of Charity of St. Louis. Murray was the inspirational force behind the famous Notre Dame Hounds hockey team. Known as Père, he would never refuse a deserving student an education, even if that meant tuition was paid in potatoes and wheat rather than dollars and cents. Leading the college until his death, he influenced generations of Canadians and the development of Canadian hockey. More than one hundred former Hounds have been drafted by the National Hockey League, including Wendel Clark, Curtis Joseph, Rod Brind'Amour, Brad Richards, and Vincent Lecavalier. Hockey Saskatchewan's Athol Murray

Trophy is named in his honour. Père Murray said of his allegiances, "I love God, Canada and hockey – not always in that order."

Once the film was done, I was off to Toronto as I was invited by the CBC to perform as Marilyn Monroe once more at the first Canadian film awards – the Genies – on national TV.

It was here that I met Craig Russell, an incredible female impersonator and gay icon across North America and Europe. Craig had starred in the film *Outrageous* and had been president of the Mae West Fan Club, eventually becoming her personal assistant. Craig and I had been asked to perform songs at the awards show, me as Marilyn Monroe and Craig as Judy Garland. And once we met, we bonded and became lifelong friends. He invited me to visit him in Hollywood. I accepted his invitation, and we agreed I would stop off in L.A. after an upcoming trip home to Australia to see my family in Sydney on my way back to Canada.

Once I landed in Sydney, my aunt Cecily suggested we contact the *John Singleton With a Lot of Help from his Friends Show*, a TV variety show that showcased performers with musical talent. The show's producers were keen to introduce an Australian girl who had just played Marilyn Monroe to acclaim in North America, and after my first appearance on the show, the response was so good that they brought me back a few more times. I performed not only as Marilyn Monroe but as Marlene Dietrich and performed songs just as myself. The audiences lapped it up as everyone loves to see a kid from the hometown do well. My Zann family aunties Cecily, Moira, Lynn, and Helen and cousins Jacquelin, Veronica, Vince, Peter, Michael, Natalie, Luke, and Lisa all loved seeing me, a relative, become a TV sensation. And Mum's best friend, Paula Bloch, a talented visual artist and Teachers Union rep, was so tickled by this turn of events that from then on "Auntie Paula" became a close confidante and staunch supporter of all my artistic endeavours. I ended up staying in her beautiful home nestled between Bondi and Bronte Beaches for many years whenever I returned home to Australia.

Andrew Lloyd Webber also gave me his personal phone number to call if I was ever going to England and mentioned that his new one-woman show, *Tell Me on a Sunday,* would be a good one for me to perform. I'll always regret not calling him when I got back to Canada, but truthfully, I was in complete awe of the composer of *Jesus Christ Superstar* and

Cats, and I didn't have the courage to phone him. Fortunately, my film and TV career really took off that year upon my return to North America.

In the meantime, though, while performing on the *John Singleton Show*, Tiny Tim and I were also getting along really well backstage, and we'd sing songs together in the dressing rooms while waiting to go on camera. Most people don't know that as well as being a singer Tiny Tim was a musical archivist and he had a photographic memory when it came to pieces of music. He could tell you the names of musical pieces all the way back, and even sing and play them on his ukulele. Years after his early fame in 1967 when his hit song "Tiptoe Through the Tulips" became a worldwide sensation, he was travelling around the world doing "music marathons" where he would ask the audience to yell out a song and he'd perform it and just continue for hours. He was truly amazing, and the Australian audiences loved him.

Finally, one night we decided to perform a song together on camera and when we suggested it to John Singleton and his producers they were delighted. I'll never forget that performance as Tiny Tim played his customary ukulele while I sat on his knee dressed as Marilyn, and we sang "I Wanna Be Loved By You" to each other as a duet. Classic. Sure wish I had a copy of that!

Tiny Tim also invited me to perform in a documentary movie that was being made about his life. Called *Street of Dreams*, it was currently being shot in an old mansion in the heart of Sydney by Australian film-maker and avant-guarde artist Martin Sharpe. As we tried to figure out a time when we could shoot my scene, it became apparent that that very night after taping the *John Singleton Show*, this was the only night we'd both be available before I flew to L.A. So, like true renegade indie art filmmakers, Martin Sharpe called his volunteer crew and asked them to meet us at midnight at the old mansion – and all of them turned up.

For my role in the film Tiny Tim taught me a song from the featured film noir classic *Gilda* called "Put the Blame on Mame, Boys." In the scene he played a grand piano while I moved around the piano singing to him and to the camera. And for the duration of the film and our encounters in real life Tiny always called me "Miss Lenore," as he called all the women in his life, including the women he married: Miss Vicky, Miss Susan, etc. He said it was a mark of his respect.

Tiny Tim taught me several important lessons about show business in the brief period I knew him in Sydney, and also later when he was back in New York where he lived, for he would often call me just to chat. One of the intriguing things he told me was his belief that to achieve fame one had to do what a song in the musical *Gypsy* talks about: "You Gotta Get a Gimmick."

I was fascinated by this concept, especially when he explained what his own "gimmick" was. He told me the attention grabber he had hit upon that had made him a star in the late 1960s and early '70s was his image as a long-haired, falsetto-singing "troubadour" who played the ukulele and wore far-out, colourful clothes. He also famously married his then girlfriend Miss Vicky on *The Ed Sullivan Show*, which was a first as well. That was another "gimmick," but it sure did attract a lot of eyeballs, which was good for Ed Sullivan as well as for him.

But what Tiny Tim explained to me was that although long hair was a new fad at the time he became a sensation, he was really modelling himself after the early Renaissance troubadours who wandered from town to town in Renaissance Europe, composing and performing songs with a mandolin and "singing for their supper" in a high falsetto. And, he explained, the important thing to note was that the songs they composed were usually love songs of unrequited love since it was considered the ultimate height of romantic love to fall in love with a woman who was unattainable.

Consequently, Tiny explained, most often their song was about and directed to a married woman under whose bedroom window they would stand and sing, hoping she would grant them an appearance in her window or on her balcony. The lady of the house may then reward their song with a favour of some sort: she might drop a perfumed handkerchief or maybe a small monetary reward for their song, or offer a meal in the kitchen with the servants. Of course, she could tell her friends about it and they'd all think, "How romantic!" I don't know what the husbands thought of this, but Tiny assured me that if it ever came to blows or a duel it was a grand way to die for love.

Tiny further explained that, in this way, the object of desire would always remain "perfect," due to her very unattainability. In any case Tiny Tim told me that he wrote the song "Tiptoe Through the Tulips" because it was based on this idea of a perfect love, and of complete respect for the woman. The singer tells her that he will be waiting by the window for her. He asks for her pardon if he was to kiss her and expresses his desire for her to tiptoe away with him. I thought that was a beautiful concept.

However, Tiny also shared with me that his "gimmick" changed over the years as there were a lot of people who "hated" him and loved to make fun of him. Once a tall, very skinny man, he started to put on a lot of weight and by the time I met him in 1980, he was huge and unhealthy. People would make fun of him for that as well. "So," he sighed, "my gimmick became being an object of ridicule and people's hatred." And he realized that he was now considered an oddity, almost like a freaky circus performer, which is likely why Martin Sharpe filmed parts of the documentary *Street of Dreams* at Luna Park in Sydney Harbour, a very old but classic amusement park.

I made sure to tell my friend that he was a beautiful human being who was deserving of love and kindness and affection. And that I felt he would find his soulmate someday. It was not me – that I made clear! But I told him to call me and that Christmas was a good time to get me at home in Nova Scotia.

Tiny also confided in me that his biggest dream was to die onstage to the sound of applause, with the woman he loved waiting for him off-stage in the wings. Years later, he eventually got to live out (or die out?) that dream when, on November 30, 1996, he had a massive heart attack onstage at the end of a live performance. I was told by his agent at the time that he held the last note of the song for as long as he could, clutching his heart (which, of course, people just thought was part of the act). Then he staggered offstage and fell into the arms of the woman he loved, Miss Susan, with the sound of applause in his ears just as he had always wished. I can't think of a more fitting ending to my friend Tiny Tim's life story, and I feel blessed to have known and performed with him.

Before he passed, occasionally he used to call my parents' place at Christmas and my dad said they always had very thought-provoking conversations. When he first started calling, Dad had no idea who he was, as he'd say his real name and just say that we were friends. But when I got home and Dad told me a guy named Herbert Khaury had called from New York, I told him, "Oh my God, Dad! That's Tiny Tim!" After that they'd have even more interesting conversations whenever "Herbert" rang. My dad was a great conversationalist and could have a stimulating discussion with anyone, but he hit the jackpot with Tiny Tim.

CHAPTER 8

HOLLYWOOD: CRAIG RUSSELL AND THE GAY '80s

Back in 1980 after I left Australia, I flew to Los Angeles where, as planned, I took a taxi straight to Craig Russell's bungalow as he wanted to be the first person to show me around Hollywood.

I was excited! Still only twenty years old, I was introduced to a very different Hollywood than the one most people imagine. I got to see the real LGBTQ2SIA+ world that was happening in the early (pre-AIDS) 1980s. It was a fun, exciting world that sizzled – and partied all night with the help of a ton of booze and pretty much any drug you could name.

When I arrived at his home, the first thing to greet me was a message Craig had taped on the door: "Welcome Home to My Star, Lenore!" along with a picture of me performing as Marilyn that he'd cut from the *Toronto Star*. As soon as I had rung the bell, Craig threw open the door breathlessly and ushered me in to his home. I noticed that Craig had cut his hair short and dyed it platinum blonde – like mine, he gushed. He had also bought us two matching mink coats which he insisted we wear to all of his shows and when we arrived, he'd tell everyone I was his daughter, which amused me to no end.

We had limousines to take us everywhere, lots of champagne, and lineups of young men excitedly waiting for Craig after his shows, all wanting to party with us – and, well, what's a young gal in Hollywood for the first time to do?

I must admit that it was at this time I was introduced to cocaine for the first time as well. Honest to God, though, we had so much fun it oughta be against the law! Well, actually, I guess some of it was, but when in Rome … Or Los Angeles … What can I say? We stayed up all night and slept all day. We had people staying overnight and dancing in the pool until dawn. We wore sequins and feather boas galore and never regretted a thing. Craig told me stories about his time living with Mae West as her personal assistant, and how she'd invite a bunch of gorgeous young body builders to her house and let them hang in her pool. She'd just touch their muscles (and other parts) but never slept with any of them because, Craig said, "She felt that just having them around helped her keep a strong level of vitality and built up her sexual drive, which in turn made her vibrant for her nightly shows. Not to mention it kept her 'reputation' intact. For as Mae often said herself, 'A hard man is good to find.'"

Craig explained that he had been a hairdresser in Toronto and worshipped Mae West as a young man, so he formed a Mae West fan club and named himself its president. He studied her films and Mae was therefore the first famous female star he began impersonating. He often wrote letters to her as the president of the fan club and finally, he said, she replied to him and included a one-way Greyhound bus ticket to Hollywood with her address. He took it.

And that's how Craig Russell first got to L.A. He ended up staying there for a time and said he talked to all kinds of famous people who called her, including Marlene Dietrich, Tallulah Bankhead, and Judy Garland, who all became part of his entourage of twenty-six women he claimed were "inside him."

It was not all fun and games, though. I once witnessed Craig crying in his dressing room after a highly successful show where men had thrown hundreds of roses on the stage during his curtain call, and a string of waiting, would-be suitors were lined up outside his dressing room door. When I told him, "Craig, they love you," and asked why he was crying, he looked up at me through mascara-smeared eyes, howling, "They don't love *me*! They love *her*! They love *them*! They love the women I portray – they don't love *me*!" It broke my heart, and it was a real eye-opener to experience someone famous, at the height of their game, feeling unworthy, unloved – and unlovable. It was just like Marilyn Monroe, whom I had portrayed only a few months earlier.

It gave me a lot to think about and has stayed with me to this day. Once again, like I had done for Tiny Tim before him, I was adamant with Craig Russell that he was a talented, wonderful, kind, and loving human being who deserved love and kindness in return – and whom I personally loved very much. I told Craig I didn't need to see any of his "ladies," that it was *him* I loved. And always would. We remained very close friends for many years and whenever he performed in Toronto, usually at the Royal York Hotel, I would stay in his suite with him. We had many a great night with many wonderful friends and, of course, some hangers-on as well. I met Lady Iris Mountbatten at one of his soirées in the suite after a show. She asked if she could borrow my feather boa (a black one this time, given to me by Tiny Tim when I performed the song from *Gilda* in his movie). I said, "Sure!" And the next thing we knew she was singing a little ditty she'd made up in a very low, husky, slurring, drunken voice, "It's better to have been a has-been, than never to have been at all ..." I'll never forget that one!

Another time I had brought my boyfriend Charlie over to meet Craig and I left them alone for a few hours as I thought it would be good for Charlie to get to know someone like Craig to get over his occasional toxic masculinity. And I wanted Craig to get to know Charlie without me there.

I came back and knocked on the suite door. I heard Craig's voice on the other side. "What's the secret password?"

"It's me, Lenore," I said. And the door magically flew open.

I don't know what I was expecting to see, but there was Craig, with his Mae West wig on crooked, wearing his Judy Garland little black sexy number with fishnets and high heels, garish red lipstick with his makeup totally peeling off his face, and dark glasses. I glanced across the room to see Charlie, barefoot and shirtless, passed out on the floor. There were empty bottles of booze everywhere.

Here at the door Craig was smiling at me and in one hand holding the biggest bag of cocaine I had ever seen, while with his other hand (which had long red nails) he dipped his forefinger into the bag to scoop up a nail full of coke, which he held out to me with a sly smile, crowing, "Here, little girl!"

And so. Again. What's a girl to do? When in Rome ...

And those were the good days!

Eventually, Craig's drinking and drug use overtook his talent and his health as well. Some of his last performances were sad and I'm glad I missed them. He told me himself that he had showed up drunk and high at a show in Vancouver with his head shaved and carrying a Japanese parasol and proceeded to swear and throw things at the audience. And at a gig in Carnegie Hall, he apparently made his entrance onstage but then sat under the piano for the whole show, with most people walking out and demanding their money back.

Later, in Toronto once more, he would call me in the middle of the night and beg me to come and keep him company. He was lonely, he said. And so, I did. I never turned him down. But I also never drank or did drugs with him again as I could see he needed an intervention. And when I arrived in the middle of the night by taxi, he would come outside in a little pink negligee and furry pink slippers to greet me, take me inside, and proceed to show me all the empty booze bottles lining his cupboards and tell me what a hard life he had had and how "I wish I had tits like yours!" I tried to get him to go to AA, but he wanted none of it.

On January 11, 1982, Craig married a young woman named Lori Jenkins, a fan, at Toronto's City Hall. They wore the same matching fur coats Craig had bought for my visit to L.A. And Craig tastefully wore red high-heeled pumps along with a man's tailored suit. I heard about the wedding after the fact as I was not in town at the time. Craig later confided that it was a publicity stunt because by now, like Tiny Tim, he too figured that "You Gotta Get a Gimmick" to get publicity and attention, especially after his professional reputation had been badly hurt by his alcohol and drug consumption. Never a good reason to get married. But who am I to judge?

Craig also told me that shortly after they married, he had accepted a three-month tour in Germany and while he took Lori with him as his dresser as well as his wife, he had met a cute guy over there and sent her back home to Canada. She didn't hear from him for four years. But it was Lori who looked after Craig when his health was severely failing, and she stayed with him until the end. On October 30, 1990, the day before

Halloween (Craig's favourite day of the year and a traditional celebration for Toronto's gay community) dear Craig, only forty-two, died of a stroke resulting from AIDS at Toronto Western Hospital.

Craig was funny, talented, larger-than-life, and the most totally outrageous character I've ever met. He accepted me completely and when we hung out during his good days, the two of us were like little kids who had been let loose in a carnival. I don't think I've ever had quite as much fun with anyone ever since. But over time I saw his demons come out and take over and that was not something I was willing to encourage. I gave him the sincere love and respect that I had for him no matter what. But I also knew when I needed to bow out from his journey of self-destruction.

I would say that both Tiny Tim and Craig Russell were two of the most talented and interesting people I've ever had the good fortune to meet.

But as a young actor at the beginning of my own career I knew my destiny was unfolding in another direction and I had to be on top of my game. That's why in the spring of 1980 it was time for me to go back home to Canada after my trip to Australia and L.A. to find a talent agent who could help me begin the serious search for acting work. Almost as soon as I'd arrived back in Toronto, however, I received an invitation to New York to meet with a businessman, a Mr. Russo, who said he was interested in representing me in the U.S.

Mr. Russo told me explicitly not to sign with an agent in Canada until I'd met with him and that he'd send me a plane ticket to New York. After my experience with Peter Coe in Edmonton, I was reticent to go by myself and insisted that my boyfriend Charlie come with me. Reluctantly, Mr. Russo agreed and sent us two return tickets to New York.

Charlie was still doing theatre at the National Arts Centre in Ottawa but agreed to come with me to New York for the weekend. It was exciting as neither of us had ever been to the Big Apple. And here we were, suddenly being thrust into the high-stakes game of show business in one of the most cutthroat cities on the planet. What's not to love in that scenario?

Charlie and I arrived by taxi at the magnificent Waldorf Astoria hotel in the heart of Manhattan where Mr. Russo was waiting for us in the lobby. Upon our arrival, he took one look at me simply dressed in jeans and a jacket, my long hair loose down to my waist, and with obvious concern said, "Where's Marilyn? I have a ton of important business associates coming here in a couple of hours, and they're expecting to see Marilyn!"

I looked at Charlie and let him do the talking. "Listen, buddy," said Charlie, a born brawler from Bass River, Nova Scotia, "don't get your knickers all in a knot! Marilyn will be here. She just needs to get ready. So where does she do that?"

Mr. Russo took us up by elevator to an incredible suite. It was a suite fit for a queen. There were chandeliers and a fireplace, and a huge table laden with an assortment of delicious lobster tails and shrimp, oysters, and other finger foods, wine, champagne, and beer, all in silver containers, full of ice. Charlie beelined straight for the champagne and poured us a couple of glasses. Then, as I disappeared into the bedroom to get ready, I saw Charlie whip out some marijuana he had brought along (Don't ask me how he got through customs with that!) and he proceeded to sit down and roll a fat joint on the table. "Oh, well," I thought. "That's Charlie for you!"

While he was occupied with that, I proceeded to "turn into" Marilyn Monroe, which I had by now perfected and could do in half an hour. When I walked out into the main room in my long red sequined gown, with white gloves and wig, looking immaculate – a total professional – Mr. Russo let out a low whistle.

"Well, how do you do, fellas? Let's get the party started, shall we?" I said in my low purr as Marilyn, giving him and Charlie a little wink and a shrug of my shoulders, bare under the sequined halter top of the gown.

And that's how the night began.

Soon there were all kinds of people knocking at the door and coming in to meet "Marilyn," and one after the other, they all shook their heads with amazement, and said, "Wow!" or "Yep, that's Marilyn all right." I stayed in character all evening, talking with people individually or in groups, and after a while, Mr. Russo said, "Okay, people, let's put our heads together and think of how we can best use this opportunity."

And then before I knew it, he was telling people they better get going because Marilyn needed her beauty sleep. Once all the people had left, and it was just Mr. Russo, Charlie, and myself, I asked Mr. Russo what he had in mind as a business deal. He responded that it was simple really, and that all he would want is 30 percent of everything I ever made. I looked at him and said, "Well, agents usually take between 10 and 15 percent so why would you take 30?" He looked directly at me, shrugged, and said, "What's 30 percent when you're making millions?"

I then asked him, "How many other people do you represent?" and he told me one, a pianist. Confused, I said, "So what do you do for a living then?"

He told me, "I'm in the import and export business."

When I asked what immediate plans he had for me if I was to sign with him, he replied, "Well, we want to make money from this Marilyn thing, right? Like we'll make a 'Fonzie' thing outta it," alluding to Henry Winkler's rise to fame as Arthur "Fonzie" Fonzarelli on the American television series *Happy Days*.

"A Fonzie thing?" I repeated innocently.

Mr. Russo blithely continued, "Yeah, Fonzie! I can make a call to Jerry Lewis and Frank Sinatra and get them to have you show up as Marilyn on Jerry's telethon and maybe onstage in Vegas with Sinatra to do a song with him – you know, like a gimmick!"

My mind immediately went to Tiny Tim's advice. But I thought, "Well, this girl isn't interested in becoming anyone's gimmick!" So I said, "Mr. Russo ... You do realize that Marilyn is just one of the many characters I play? I am a serious actress. I am not a Marilyn Monroe look-alike. She's just one of my characters."

"Yeah, yeah," he replied. "Don't worry! We're gonna make you famous, kid! Now get some sleep. You're gonna need it. I'll call you tomorrow and we'll get to work." And with that he was gone.

As soon as the door clicked shut Charlie and I – James Dean and Marilyn Monroe – looked at each other, looked up at the chandeliers and the remainder of the spread on the table, then back to each other, and fell down laughing, splitting our sides. I mean, the incongruity of it all: these kids from Truro and Bass River, Nova Scotia, here in this room after the night we had just had.

And then we said, "Okay, let's hit the town!" So we did. We got a limo (our first) to take us to Sardis, then The Russian Tea Room and after a truly great night out on the town we headed back to the Waldorf Astoria and decided that we had seen enough for now and were headed home the next day to think over Mr. Russo's offer.

We weren't convinced it was the best move. And besides, Charlie said some Italian guy he'd been talking to in the corner all night had told him, "You know, kid, you can get more done with a smile – and a gun – in this town than you can with anything else."

Yeah. We needed to really think about what we might be getting into.

Back in Toronto I was offered a guest role on *The Phoenix Team*, a popular Canadian TV series starring Elizabeth Shepherd and Don Francks, who had risen to fame in the States playing the lead role in *Finian's Rainbow*, a musical in which he starred on Broadway as well as the feature film of the same name. I was to appear in two episodes of the series. Don and I immediately became good friends.

When I learned about Don's experience in show business in New York and Hollywood, I asked his advice regarding Mr. Russo's offer of representation. Don asked me to tell him the entire story in detail and when I said that Mr. Russo had told me he and his colleagues were "in the import and export business," Don snorted, laughing. I'll never forget his response. Looking me directly in the eyes, he said, "And so we are talking about a group of Italian businessmen, who represent only one other performer – a female pianist/singer – who are self-described as being in 'the import and export business' and whose first thought is to turn you into a Fonzie-like character and appear with Frank Sinatra and Jerry Lewis? And they want to sign you for life and take 30 percent of everything you will ever make?"

I nodded. That was about it.

"Well, my dear, I'd advise you to stay clear away from it as possible. These guys could very likely be involved with the Mafia, who are still extremely involved in show business, and the last thing you want is to be owned – and to *owe* – the Mafia. You would sign your life away on the dotted line and they might call you one day to say, 'Hey, honey, so-and-so is in town and we want you to go over to his hotel, have dinner with him, and keep him company for the evening.' And if you say no, they tell you just how grateful you should be to them as they got you some gigs and now want you to do them a favour too. Next thing you know you're doing favours all over the place, drugs are offered, and you're hooked, in more ways than one. No, sweetheart, I do not advise you to take an offer from these guys, 'cause once you're involved with the Mafia you'll be owned for *life*."

That gave me a lot to think about. Besides, I had already been turned off by the idea that someone only wanted to see me play Marilyn all the time, instead of creating opportunities for my entire breadth of talent.

I thought of everything I'd learned from the memorable characters I had been lucky to meet in the past few months. Craig Russell, while being feted as a star, was deeply miserable because he felt it was not for himself that he was receiving public attention and love but for the famous women he impersonated. Then I thought of Tiny Tim, who had advised me to embrace this kind of opportunity because one needed to "get a gimmick" to become a star. And at this point Marilyn Monroe had become a kind of gimmick, but I didn't want to spend my life trying to recreate that, especially as I got older. I wanted to constantly stretch myself and apply my acting skills to continually different roles and not get stuck being seen only as one type of character.

And then I thought of young Norma Jean Baker, who had been stuck in a persona she herself had created, that of Marilyn Monroe, the world's most famous sex symbol, who died naked and alone at the age of just thirty-six being told by an uncaring, unforgiving industry that she was over the hill. A woman whom all the world loved but who was unable to love herself. And who knows who told her she "owed" them?

No. My mind was clear. I didn't want to owe anyone or to be owned by anyone. I didn't want to be a star so badly that I was willing to "get a gimmick" or *be* a gimmick. I wanted to do this on my own and have a long, illustrious career which would hopefully touch many people's lives around the world and make them think about the important things in life, like loving and caring about others and the planet. And I didn't care if it took a lifetime instead of having instant success. And *that* was the only "gimmick" that interested me.

So I took Don Francks' advice, and funnily enough it would be years later before we would work together again. Next time it was on the show that has touched millions of lives around the world, for Don Francks is the original voice of Sabretooth in *X-Men: The Animated Series,* and it was an honour to work with him on this great project from 1992 to 1996. Don passed away in 2016. May he rest in peace.

CHAPTER 9

"READY FOR MY CLOSE-UP"

As soon as I arrived back in Toronto I met with talent agent Bill Boyle, who had been referred by friends in the business, including actor Sam Moses, who had played Marilyn Monroe's agent, Johnny Hyde, in *Hey Marilyn!*

Bill Boyle was pleasant, he was well-regarded by people I knew and trusted, and I liked his business partner Norah Taylor, whom I also met in his office. After talking briefly, Bill wanted to sign me right away as he said there were many film and TV projects currently casting in Toronto and that there was no time to lose. He wanted to get me work for which he would take 15 percent of my earnings, which was the going rate for agents. It was music to my ears.

I signed that same day. And true to his word I was immediately presented with several screen roles that kept me busy during the spring, summer, and fall. First was a film, *That's My Baby*. This was followed by CBC's *Hangin' In*, starring Lally Cadeau and David Eisner. David was also soon working with me on another feature in Montreal, the horror film classic *Happy Birthday to Me*. Directed by J. Lee Thompson (*The Guns of Navarone*, *Cape Fear*), it featured Melissa Sue Anderson (known for her role as Mary Ingalls in the NBC drama series *Little House on the Prairie*), Tracey Bregman (best known for the CBS soap operas *The Young and the Restless* and *The Bold and the Beautiful*), and Canadian-American film star Glenn Ford, who had starred in *Gilda* (1946) and *Blackboard Jungle* (1955).

Although neither Glenn nor Melissa talked much to the cast, preferring to stay in their trailers, there were a few fireworks on set one day when Glenn, who was clearly drunk, decided to deck the second AD, Charles Braive, over some perceived slight. It was also sad to see the crew having to put large signs up just off camera with Glenn's lines on them because he often had trouble remembering them.

J. Lee Thompson was a hoot, though. He was on set from dawn to dusk and very pleasant to the cast; I just remember his main direction on set was "More blood! More blood!" whenever there was a murder scene.

I was happy to be left alone; I knew my lines and seemed to have a natural feeling for the camera. And with a large cast of great young burgeoning Canadian talent, we had a lot of fun. I especially liked working with the French-Canadian crew. They were lovely, and it gave me an excellent chance to practise the French I'd learned in school as well as learn more conversational French. I met Pierre Charpentier, a key grip, who at age thirty was ten years older than me, but absolutely stunning.

The first time we connected was during a scene set at an outdoor motocross event. I was sitting in the grass on a hill overlooking the scene and Pierre came up behind me and gently placed a daisy in my long hair. I was smitten. We began chatting during film breaks after that and to my surprise Pierre told me that he had once been in a film himself when he was just a young boy. He told me it had been a short film for the National Film Board of Canada (NFB) and was about a young boy in Montreal who roller-skated through the city, with music and breathtaking scenic shots but no dialogue.

This was unbelievable to hear because as it turned out I had been shown that very film in high school back in Truro, Nova Scotia, during my Grade Twelve film course. I had thought the boy in the film was simply beautiful – and it made me want to learn how to roller-skate some day.

The next thing I knew, Pierre invited me to go roller-skating up on top of the hill for which Montreal is named (Mount Royal) and I agreed to go with him to learn how to roller-skate on one of our weekends off.

First, I'll tell you why that was a bad idea. Well … you don't just throw on a pair of roller skates and skate elegantly around without a bit of practice. Secondly, it was on top of a mountain. And thirdly, I was in the middle of shooting a movie, and taking part in a sport that could be physically dangerous is not encouraged and in fact frowned upon because if anything happens to you it could affect your performance, looks, or shooting schedule.

After a while, both Pierre and I were thinking that I now had the knack to try skating alone without Pierre to lean on. Imagine our chagrin (and my pain) when my legs suddenly went up into the air in front of me. I quickly put out my left arm to stop my fall – and *snap*! I heard and felt something break.

"Shit!" I said.

"Merde!" agreed Pierre.

"I think it's broken," I continued. "And I'm back on set shooting tomorrow!"

We were both worried: me for what I would say to the producers and Pierre because he would be blamed and might even lose his job. But then Pierre had an idea. "Listen, my roommate François is a doctor. Let's go to him and he can look at it and tell us what's what."

I agreed. My wrist was beginning to swell like a balloon, which was not a good look on camera.

We found François at home, and he ushered us to the hospital where he worked. After some X-rays he had the verdict. "It's broken."

"Merde!" I said. (I'm a fast learner.)

"Yeah, you're going to need a cast," said François.

"But I can't! It will look incredibly weird if my character suddenly shows up in a cast halfway through the movie! Is there anything else we can do?"

François thought for a minute then said slowly, "Well, we could try a plastic mold that could be wrapped on with bandages and wrapped off when you're shooting. You'd have to be careful not to bump your arm on anything, though."

The three of us looked at each other.

"Yep! Oui! Allons-y!" I said. "Let's go!"

And that's what we did.

I finished the film that way. The film producers never found out. Pierre kept his job. And we bonded even more over our shared secret.

Our mutual attraction was becoming irresistible, and by the end of the summer I knew I would have to make a decision about my relationship with Charlie. When I came home to Toronto at one point that summer and found another woman's clothes rolled up into a ball and stuffed into the corner of my closet, I knew it was time for both of us to let go.

With Charlie based in Toronto mainly doing plays (with women falling all over him) and me in Montreal shooting movies back to back (with a sexy Frenchman just waiting for the cue to become my lover), we agreed to give our relationship a break. So between films I began staying with Pierre in his Montreal apartment. And I loved it. I loved the French: their lifestyle, language, culture, music, food, and joie de vivre. Pierre was also expanding my concept of relationships – introducing me to the very notion that a person does not have to be tied down to one partner for their whole life, or as Pierre put it, "Who says we have to have one mother and one father?"

The next film I booked in Montreal that summer of 1980 was *Visiting Hours*, which starred the fabulous American actress Lee Grant, Linda Purl, and Canadian actors William Shatner, Michael Ironside (in his first starring role), and me. Montreal's Jean-Claude Lord was the director of this psychological thriller about a guy who hates feminists and decides to kill an outspoken feminist broadcast journalist (Lee Grant). She survives his attack, so he goes on a killing spree in the hospital where she's recovering. Hence the title.

I play a tough street girl the psycho invites to his apartment and brutally rapes (in her underwear, of course) but doesn't kill, then she gets her revenge by tailing him and turning him in to the cops. It's actually not a bad film. Especially thanks to the performances of Lee Grant and Michael Ironside.

Meanwhile, I was often being attacked or murdered by psychos in my underwear in those days. "Tax write-offs for dentists," I used to call these films, as that's basically who the investors were back then. There were tons of horror films shooting in Canada in the early '80s because they were not that expensive to make, but would turn in a pretty good profit on one's investment. And, being young, buxom, blonde, and unafraid to doff my clothes, I was cast in quite a few of them.

Although I would have preferred to be cast in more mainstream fare, becoming a Canadian "scream queen" in my twenties did provide the invaluable experience of working on a film set, hitting your mark, finding your light, learning the film industry pecking order, and dealing with the myriad of egos on and off set. Horror films also gave me the opportunity to perfect my now-infamous scream, which I was able to put to good use a decade later in *X-Men: The Animated Series*. #roguescreams is actually a video online that someone created using all of the times I screamed in the series. Check it out. It's hilarious.

This time, before I began shooting *Visiting Hours*, I made sure to tell our producer and director about my broken wrist as it was still in the part-time cast and I knew it could become an issue in the upcoming rape scene. When we came to set to rehearse it first, I warned Michael Ironside not to grab my broken left arm, only my right. He stuck to our arrangement like a pro.

Once again I found myself in my underwear. I had asked for a closed set this time so there weren't a ton of people standing around gawking. But when it came time to shoot the real climax of the scene, the director and producer stopped production and called for a quick break while they took me aside and said, seriously, "Look, Lenore, we know that you asked for no nudity in this scene and we signed a rider to the contract agreeing to that, but we find ourselves in a dilemma here now that we are actually shooting the scene."

"Uh-huh … What's the dilemma?" I responded warily. I already had an idea of what they were going to say next.

"Well, here we have the killer on top of you and he's got a knife and is threatening you. We're not going to show him raping you, but we want to let the audience know that's what's going to happen. He has the knife in his hand, and he's going to cut down your top …" (which was pink – and very tight).

"Uh-huh," I said again with even more wariness.

"Well, so the dilemma is that when he cuts down your top, the camera is going to pan down and see your breasts. So we'd like to know if you can give us your permission to show them."

Now I don't know what you would have done in a situation like this. And I don't know what other twenty-year-old actresses would do. But it made me angry because I felt the nudity would be gratuitous, and in spite of my contract saying "no nudity," they just assumed they could pressure a young actress into doing this on the spur of the moment, without her agent around to speak up for her.

Well, not this young actress.

I said, slowly, measuring every word, "So you're wondering what the camera will see when he cuts her top open, eh? That's the dilemma?"

"Yes! Yes, exactly!" they said excitedly, thinking that I was sympathetic to their view of the problem.

"Okay. Well, as I see it you have two choices. Following the knife and showing my breasts is one. But why don't you pan up and show my face instead? Show the audience what she's *feeling*? After all, it's a movie about a feminist, right? That's what I suggest we do."

To say these guys were surprised by my response is an understatement. They were shocked. And ashamed too, I'd bet, because why hadn't they thought of it? But I stuck to my guns and that's exactly what you see in that scene in *Visiting Hours*. Thank God they'd cast a feminist in the role or it would be just another sad slasher scene we've all seen a million times.

In any case, after *Visiting Hours,* I was still on a roll and the next film I was cast in that summer was called *The Black Mirror,* or *The Miroir Noir*, a film by Parisian director Pierre-Alain Jolivet and shot at Le Petit Bastille, a former federal prison, in Quebec City. Based on a play by French playwright Jean Genet, it was set in a women's prison, and I was cast as one of the three leads along with Louise Marleau and Alberta Watson. For some reason they thought I was too young and inexperienced to play the role, but Pierre-Alain told them I was perfect for it and that was that.

This film would be shooting for several months so it took me almost to the end of the year. And Pierre Charpentier was back as grip, so we had the opportunity to spend some quality time together both on and off set. I felt safe knowing Pierre was there as it was an emotionally harrowing piece, with several very physical scenes as well. It felt good to know his watchful eye was there behind the camera and a few times he would give me advice about where to move or stand to get the best light and camera angles.

Shooting was intense but fun. I loved every minute and really got into my character, for which I had to sacrifice my long hair for the first time as the director wanted my head shorn to show she was a new prisoner. I also loved being part of the French production and always insisted the crew speak to me in French so that I could learn the language better. By now it was no secret that Pierre and I were an item, so the crew treated me like I was family.

During lunch breaks a sumptuous feast would be set up on long tables all the way down the hallway where condemned prisoners had once walked to the gallows. That was grisly history, but with the hallway transformed with candlelight and piles of food with bottles of wine being cracked open even for lunch, it became a place of merriment and warmth. There was a real feeling of family. That was the best time I ever had on a set. And I'll always be grateful to both Pierres for that incredible experience.

My dressing room was one of the rooms where prisoners were locked up for solitary confinement, but there was a barred window overlooking the trees which by the end of shooting were turning gold and orange. And my friend Pierre Charpentier would sneak away when he could to keep me company while I was waiting to be called to set.

Making love in that room was pretty wild, and I hoped that filling that room full of love may have dispelled some of the sadness in those old stones. In any case it was Pierre's and my secret at the time. And we enjoyed every minute.

Unfortunately, *The Black Mirror* never received a public release. I was told there was a disagreement between producers in France and Canada and it was locked away in a vault somewhere in France. Maybe it's still there. I don't know.

By the end of shooting, I had booked another horror film, this time in Toronto. Titled *Bells* at the time, it would star Richard Chamberlain, and once again I'd be murdered in my underwear, this time blown up by a psycho who could kill people over the phone. But bit by bit, film by film, I was learning the craft of screen acting, making good money, travelling, and loving the life I was living. I felt blessed.

That would continue for the next few years. But by the time I turned twenty-one, I was also ready to go back to Los Angeles to find an agent there and hopefully break into the American market.

CHAPTER 10

SHADOW DANCING WITH ANDY GIBB, SPIELBERG, ALEXA, AND THE MORAL MAJORITY

Early in 1981 I flew back to L.A. where, much to my surprise, I met Stephen Spielberg. He was already casting *Indiana Jones and the Temple of Doom*, the second film in the franchise, and had heard about me from a casting director he knew. I got the call one afternoon while I was having drinks with friends at the famed Polo Lounge in the Beverly Hills Hotel. Norah Taylor, the business partner of my agent, Bill Boyle, was with me, as well as our good friend, actor, and publicist Dawna Shuman from Lighthouse PR. I thought it was a prank at first. But it was real. The phone call came through, and I heard "Phone call for Miss Lenore Zann regarding meeting with Stephen Spielberg."

As it turned out, back at Dawna's cozy Hollywood pad on Cheremoya Avenue, where Norah and I were crashing, her neighbour Shelby Gregory had answered the phone and got the message. He couldn't wait to tell us and, knowing we were at the Polo Lounge, made the call. So off to Paramount Studios I went later that afternoon to meet Mr. Spielberg in his office.

After I was approved by security and started up the stairs to his office, a good-looking guy was rapidly descending the stairs at the same time. He seemed to be in a hurry and certainly his mind was elsewhere. After crashing into me he quickly apologized and suddenly I realized,

"Oh my God! Mel Gibson!" My next thought was, "Gee, he's a lot shorter than I thought he was!" Then a bit later when I was waiting to go into the office another short man came out the door. I did another double take: Sylvester Stallone! I realized then that these high-profile A-list actors would be taking meetings with Mr. Spielberg about all sorts of projects. Who wouldn't want to work with him? This was my first experience with the other side of Hollywood – the work side rather than the party side. And I have to say for someone my age from Truro, Nova Scotia, it was truly exciting.

In the end I had a great meeting with Mr. Spielberg. I liked him immediately, finding him to be kind, curious, and funny. We had a nice chat, and I gave him a marketing package Norah Taylor had put together for me and showed him still pictures from *The Black Mirror*. It turned out he had seen the outtakes from the film, which had piqued his interest in me. He told me he was looking for a young woman to play a role in *The Temple of Doom*; the character works in a bar and takes up with Indiana Jones. I can't remember who brought up the idea of the character singing at the bar as well. But I remember showing him stills of me performing as Marilyn Monroe in my long red sequined dress and said, "If you need someone who is also a singer in the bar, I can do that too."

We spent about forty minutes together and it was pleasant. But I did not get the role of Willie Scott, an American nightclub singer and performer Indy meets performing at Club Obi Wan. When the film came out, I thought it noteworthy that Spielberg had asked Kate Capshaw to dye her brown hair blonde, and her costume is a red and gold sequined gown. Spielberg later married her.

Although I did not get the role, Mr. Spielberg did suggest me to two New York casting agents, Jeremy Ritzer and Howard Furer, who were looking for a young woman to star in a new NBC sitcom called *Love, Sidney* opposite longtime star Tony Randall. I did my first audition for the role in L.A. and was subsequently flown to New York to do a screen test with Tony Randall himself and meet the producers and director. So suddenly I found myself in a New York taxi heading into Manhattan for the second time in my life.

I got the role.

However, another offer – for a regular role on *Saturday Night Live*, which was already a popular series on NBC – came through. It turned out producer Lorne Michaels (another Canadian) had just seen my screen test for *Love, Sidney* and wanted to sign me to an annual contract as "the sexy blonde" type on the show.

I turned it down.

I had already agreed to do *Love, Sidney* and I really preferred to do a show which included both drama and comedy. Besides, we were finalizing the contract. I had also been warned by Tony Rosatto, a Canadian comedian who was already performing on *SNL*, that it was tough going on the set with high pressure to be funny and write and make up comedy on the spot – and that a lot of cocaine was being imbibed by the cast.

SNL was offering $4,000 a week, which would have been fabulous, but Tony's description scared the shit out of me. I had already seen what coke can do to people and I knew myself well enough by then to know it would not be a healthy place for me to be. I wanted to hold out for *Love, Sidney.* And Norah Taylor, who had become my new manager, had negotiated a hefty deal whereby I would be paid $11,000 per week the first year, $16,000 per week the second year, $40,000 per week the third and fourth years, and $60,000 per week if the show continued after that. The final touches were just being put on the contract.

NBC's plan was to do the first series ever about a gay man and a young woman who become roommates out of necessity in New York, and when the young woman becomes pregnant from a boyfriend and wants to have an abortion, Sidney says, "Oh no, don't do that. I've always wanted a child. How about you have the baby and I'll help support you? We can bring it up together."

However, unbeknownst to us, the premise of the show had come to the attention of Reverend Jerry Falwell and his Moral Majority, who were totally against the major plot points of the show (a gay man, a pregnancy out of wedlock, discussion of abortion, and said gay man and young woman bringing up the baby together). So Falwell and his Moral Majority threatened NBC with a major campaign against the show, including boycotts by advertisers if NBC went ahead with it.

By now both parties had signed the contract for the series, and I was preparing to move indefinitely to New York. But suddenly I had a call from Norah, who had just received a call from the president of NBC himself, Grant Tinker (Mary Tyler Moore's husband). Norah was in shock as she relayed their conversation. Apparently, Grant Tinker had said something like this: "This show is my baby. I'm so sorry, but we have come up against a brick wall against the show. Jerry Falwell is threatening NBC, saying that they'll get advertisers to boycott the show if we go ahead with it as planned. I'm being overpowered by others, and I just can't make the wheels turn. I wish I could. But if we are to do the series at all we have to completely rewrite it and unfortunately Lenore's role will need to be written out. I'm so sorry." Norah told me Grant Tinker was crying on the phone. I have no reason not to believe her.

"What about the signed contract?" you might ask. Good question. We discovered, much to our chagrin, that Hollywood contracts usually have a line somewhere saying the producers can get out of the contract if need be, without having to pay the performer a penny.

NBC ended up rewriting the entire show. My role changed from a naive young actress who gets pregnant and has a baby to an older woman with an eight-year-old daughter. The show's focus changed to the relationship between the older man and the child. *Love, Sidney* aired for just two seasons on NBC, from October 28, 1981, to June 6, 1983. It starred Tony Randall as Sidney Shorr, Swoosie Kurtz as Laurie Morgan, and Kaleena Kiff as Patricia "Patti" Morgan.

Although Sidney was clearly a gay man, his homosexuality was downplayed throughout the series' forty episodes. It would take a long while – seventeen years – before NBC would produce *Will and Grace*, which introduced a gay character as the leading role, played beautifully by Eric McCormack, another Canadian. The storyline sounds familiar: Will, a gay lawyer, allows his best friend, Grace, an interior designer, to stay in his house for a temporary period after her marriage falls apart. But she ends up being his permanent roommate.

There you go. Welcome to showbiz.

The bottom line for me back in 1981 was that I had my first taste of real, deep disappointment. At the ripe age of twenty-one, I was already feeling jaded by the experience and the industry in general.

Interestingly, the following year, in 1982, Norah received a call from the series asking me to do a guest role that might become a regular or returning role. She was told that ratings weren't great for the series, so they hoped introducing my character might perk up the show. However, I had already signed a contract to perform in a musical special for Showtime, called *Something's Afoot*; I would be co-starring with Andy Gibb and Jean Stapleton. So I was unavailable.

Later that same year in 1982, NBC contacted us again about another new show and I was flown to New York for a third time to audition for the role of Diane Chambers in a series called *Cheers*.

It came down to a final screen test between me and Shelley Long, who was thirty-three at the time and had much more professional experience than I did. That show would have been a good one! I loved the script because James Burrows and Glen and Les Charles were involved as executive producers. I could just tell it would be a hit show. And it was. *Cheers* justifiably ran on NBC from September 30, 1982, to May 20, 1993.

In 1982, I returned to live in Toronto. After a couple of years I was once again performing in *Something's Afoot*, directed by Broadway director/choreographer Tony Tanner. I co-starred with Jean Stapleton (*All in the Family*) and Andy Gibb, along with a large and exceptional Canadian cast that included friends from the Charlottetown Festival (Charlotte Moore and Brian McKay) as well as other musical theatre performers from across the country. I played Andy's love interest. And, as often happens with performers in showbiz, we ended up dating for several weeks while rehearsing and performing in the show.

Andy and I stayed up most nights going to parties across Toronto and singing Bee Gees songs together, with him playing the piano and both of us singing harmonies. When we were alone, he would tell me about how he always wanted to be a Bee Gee with his older brothers, but they would never let him because they said they didn't need another Bee Gee. So they set him up for his solo career.

One day Andy mentioned before he was to go and get an overall health check (for the production for insurance purposes) that he was concerned about his heart. He was only twenty-four.

While he was driving me home to my place in his limousine, as he was counting out his wads of American money (because it was in his contract to get paid in cash every week), he looked up at me and said, "You know, when I was your age I was making a million dollars a week off *Shadow Dancing*" (his solo album that his brothers paid for). And I remember looking at him in the back of that limo and seeing the lines of anxiety etched across his forehead and around his eyes and remembering all the cocaine I'd seen him consume over the past number of weeks and I thought to myself, "Well, I would rather be who I am, where I am, buddy." And it crossed my mind that this handsome and talented young guy could easily be dead by the age of thirty. But I didn't say it out loud. I would never be that cruel.

Andy Gibb died of myocarditis five days after his thirtieth birthday.

Soon after completing the show and several other films throughout 1982, I accepted an offer to perform at the Charlottetown Festival again in Prince Edward Island in Alan Lund's *Singing and Dancing Tonight*. I thought a summer of clean living, performing onstage in musicals eight shows a week while hitting the beach with the cast and other friends would be good for me. It was a nice job and steady paycheque, and close to home so my family could come to visit. It was a lovely respite after the roller-coaster ride that was showbiz in Hollywood and New York.

Over the next several years I appeared in a number of film and TV episodes and also accepted some theatre roles at Neptune Theatre where artistic director John Neville first introduced me to politician Alexa McDonough in Halifax. Alexa was leader of the New Democratic Party of Nova Scotia, Canada's left-of-centre social democratic party. She and I hit it off immediately and she invited me to job-shadow her on International Women's Day. It was the first time I had attended a government session and it shocked me to see Alexa McDonough, the only woman elected to government at the time, and the only New Democratic member, on her feet giving speeches on the floor of the House of Assembly while the men around her talked and laughed and threw paper airplanes at each other. I'll never forget it. And for the first time I thought, "Alexa needs some help down there. We need more women in government. Maybe someday I should join her."

After some time in the House of Assembly Alexa signalled to me to meet her outside. We quickly jumped into a waiting cab and drove to Mount Saint Vincent University where she was to give a speech about how far women had come. Alexa was in tears. She said, "You saw what it's like. That's what we have to contend with. No respect. And I'm supposed to give a speech about how far we've come? I have absolutely no idea what I'm going to say."

Later, when we reached the university and I was once more sitting in the huge crowds who had come to hear her, Alexa showed me what grace under fire really looks like. She was able to give an extemporaneous speech that had the whole auditorium on their feet cheering.

I learned a lot about politics and performance that day from a real pro. And I decided then and there that at some point when I was much older with more experience, I might indeed turn my hand to politics.

Now Alexa too has passed and I miss her to this day. But I will always be grateful to Alexa McDonough, who first told me I'd make a great politician and encouraged me to consider running for office. When I was finally ready to take the plunge in 2009, she was the one I called. I'll never forget her response: "Ahhh, good. Finally! I've been waiting for you. I'm getting ready to retire now myself ... So yes, I think it's your time to step up. And, God, I always wished I had the one thing you've got that I don't have: theatricality!"

CHAPTER 11

A CUBAN ROMEO AND JULIET

Throughout 1982 and '83, I continued to perform in TV, film, and theatre – including the title role in *The Lady from Maxim's* at the Saint Laurence Centre in Toronto, and Alan Lund's *Singing and Dancing Tonight* and *Anne of Green Gables* at the Charlottetown Festival. But by now I was also shooting productions in Toronto as well as Montreal, so I stayed with Pierre when shooting in Montreal and with Charlie in our little apartment in the Beaches when shooting in Toronto.

It was during this time that I shot the horror flicks *Bells* (starring Richard Chamberlain) and *American Nightmare* directed by Don McBrearty in Toronto. More blood. More gore. More underwear. And more nudity.

American Nightmare is about a pianist (Lawrence S. Day) and a dancer (Lora Staley) who are searching bars and strip joints for his missing sister, with a razor killer on the loose who is murdering strippers. I play Tina, a stripper. And Charlie (Page Fletcher) was cast as my boyfriend who wants me to stop stripping.

Did I want to do another film like this? No. But our rent needed to be paid.

Charlie and I had a huge fight one night because, like Joe DiMaggio who happened to be on hand for the scene in *The Seven Year Itch* where his wife Marilyn Monroe stood over the subway grate (and her white dress billowed up showing her legs and panties), Charlie happened to be standing at the back of the set when my strip scene was being shot and, like Joe DiMaggio, became furious at all the catcalls and whistles of the guys who were watching. Charlie took it out on me, just as Joe DiMaggio had done to Marilyn. Which begs the question: Does art imitate life or does life imitate art?

Also, in another bizarre twist of fate, my former York University professor, Neil Dainard, played the psycho killer who was murdering strippers in the film. This meant that he ended up slitting my throat, which, who knows, he may have secretly enjoyed after our *Caucasian Chalk Circle* experience of a few years back.

And then came a role in a feature called *One Night Only*, billed as a "sexy romp." It was a cheap, raunchy film dressed up to look like a female version of the much better (and more successful) American film *Risky Business*. We shot the entire film in Montreal in just fourteen days, largely because most of the cast, crew, and producers were all high on coke and just kept working through the nights.

To tell the truth, through the '80s we were all partying our brains out in the film world back then. Coke was easy to get, and everyone had film money to acquire it. I even heard at the time that certain producers were making it available for everyone. But who am I to judge? I was right there partying along with everyone else.

After shooting *One Night Only*, I I needed a break, both from working and from the accessibility of cocaine. So, early in 1984, I decided to "defect" to Cuba where I knew there'd be lots of sun, sand, and surf – and no drugs.

Actually, I just went there for a two-week vacation with my French lover, Pierre Charpentier from Montreal. But after Pierre returned to Montreal when our two weeks were up, I decided to stay longer. I ended up staying for several months, this time having fallen in love with a Cuban bass player named Reynaldo, who couldn't speak a word of English. No problemo: I learned Spanish, and we taught each other the "universal language" – of love. The best way to learn any language!

I managed to talk a local apartment manager into renting me a place in Varadero for $8 Canadian per month. It housed mainly Cuban performers, many of whom became friends and would take me with them to their shows. I met dancers, singers, and musicians this way and got to see some amazing shows night after night. In return, I taught them English and told them about life in Canada, the U.S., and Australia. I also agreed to sell them my clothes since I had a suitcase full of many outfits and accessories that were simply impossible to get in Cuba due to the American embargo that had been in place since the 1959 revolution.

My apartment had two beautiful white sandy beaches on either side, a cold-water shower, no glass in the windows, and graffiti covering the white stucco walls outside. I didn't care. It was my own pad in Paradise.

This was a time when I learned about socialism and fell in love with Ché Guevara. I read as much as I could about his life and why he gave up a promising medical career to become one of the most famous and revered revolutionaries in the world. Personally I was blown away by his life story, his charisma, his chutzpah – not to mention that he was gorgeous – and he greatly inspired my political beliefs and increased my existing desire to change the world to make it a fairer and more equitable place for all. This desire for social justice I had first learned from my mother and grandmother, and later Alexa McDonough.

It was while visiting friends in Matanzas with Reynaldo that the difference between socialism and capitalism was made clearer. The little home of Reynaldo's friend was full of musicians, and between playing guitars and drinking Havana Club with cola (called a Cuba Libre in that country) we watched Fidel Castro deliver a long speech on TV. From time to time the gang would give a cheer and wave their fists or musical instruments in the air in agreement with their president. I could understand some of what Fidel was saying, but he was also fond of speaking in a rapid-fire manner which was impossible for me to catch.

Finally, though, as Fidel was wrapping up his speech with one last passionate encore, my friends started whooping and hollering excitedly, pounding their hands on the mismatched chairs and couches strewn around the room, slapping each other on the back, and clapping in a long applause while nodding excitedly in agreement with him. I asked Reynaldo what Fidel had said that got them so fired up. I'll never forget the response: "Leonor! Esta es muy, muy importante! It is very important to our country! Fidel, he say, los Americanos, they make fun of our poverty. They laugh at our old cars and our capital city of Havana with its ancient buildings with their paint peeling down and no money yet to fix them. But he says, 'In Cuba, first comes penicillin, *then* comes paint!'"

I had read about how, after Cuba's revolution, President Castro and his government focused their limited financial capital on training doctors, nurses, and teachers as their number one priority was the health and education of the people. Before 1959, the Cuban people had one of the lowest rates of literacy in Latin America, but in time Cuba achieved the highest rate. The country also went from having very few Cuban doctors to graduating more than 200,000, many of whom they sent to other, even more impoverished countries, gratis.

I learned much about the politics and culture of this unique little island in the time I spent there. First, I fell in love with the beaches and the music – and I'd be lying if I didn't admit at that time, I loved the rum too – and the country's beautiful poets like José Marti, the National Poet of Cuba. But before I knew it, I had fallen head over heels in love with the heart and soul of its people. And that feeling has never left me.

Reynaldo and I soon became inseparable; he'd pick me up on his motorbike and we'd zip around visiting all of the beautiful spots where tourists did not go: beaches, hidden vistas, and great concerts and dances with only Cubanos present. And since everyone in Cuba loves dancing, I had the opportunity to learn salsa and meringue with many dance partners as Reynaldo's band played.

We soon became known among our Cuban friends as "the Cuban Romeo and Juliet." Nobody could see how we could make this love affair last when neither of our countries saw eye-to-eye or wanted us to be together. Cuba's leaders didn't like Cubans fraternizing with Westerners outside of the tourist hotels, and the West (in particular the United States) frowned upon Westerners fraternizing with socialists. Canada was not so bad, but I'd been warned before my trip not to get my passport stamped in Cuba as it could lead to problems at the border when I wished to return to the States. Like Romeo and Juliet, we belonged to two completely different worlds:

"Two houses both alike in dignity, …
From ancient grudge break to new mutiny,
Where civil blood makes civil hands unclean."

Inevitably, after several months of constantly postponing my return airline ticket and selling outfits to finance my extended stay, my suitcase was empty. And the last thing I had to sell was my watch. That bought me a few more weeks. But once the watch went, I knew it was "time" to go.

The last thing I bought before Reynaldo drove me to the Varadero Airport (by motorcycle since I ditched the now-empty suitcase) was a bright red Ché Guevara T-shirt, which I wore home to Canada long before that image and those T-shirts became de rigueur for any serious rebel with a cause.

Reynaldo and I cried when we parted, and I left a piece of my heart in Cuba for him and for his proud people. But I said I'd be back some day and years later I did go back and looked him up in Havana where he still worked as a musician and now had a beautiful family. It was wonderful to visit them and meet his wife and kids.

Once I got back to Montreal, I told Pierre that we needed to break off our relationship as I knew I would never be satisfied just buying a little home in Montreal and staying there together. I was now on fire and wanted to put my newfound political knowledge and curiosity into further world travel to see what other countries were using as their political systems of governance. My wanderlust was ignited.

Upon returning to L.A., I had several auditions but nothing was quite clicking. Then one afternoon I went with a couple of friends to one of my favourite haunts, Venice Beach, to go roller-skating. Wouldn't you know it, I was just doing a final spin on the boardwalk at sunset taking in the mirage-like crazy carnival atmosphere that is Venice – with snake charmers and dreadlocked drummers, girls skating by in bikinis, sidewalk artists, a musical cacophony, and huge roller-skating dance parties ... No sooner had the words "It's Babylon!" escaped my lips when suddenly *whoosh*! My feet slid out from under me, I put out my hand behind me to stop my fall, and *crack*. My wrist. Oh God, not again!

When I finally found a doctor who would agree to see me (for $500 US), he just shrugged and said, "Yep. It's broken. What do you want me to do?" I said, "I suppose I'd need a cast on it," to which he replied, "Well, that's gonna be another $1,200." It was 1984. I didn't have $1,200. I didn't have a credit card back then. I said, "What would you do if I was dying?" He just shrugged and said, "You're in America, honey! If you got the money, I got the time!"

And that's when it hit me. If Cuba's motto was "First comes penicillin, then comes paint," then in America with its millionaires, mansions, and perfectly manicured lawns, with fake sets and false fronts hiding the poverty and desperation that lay behind them, the motto must be "First comes paint – and forget the penicillin."

Yes. I was now a rebel with a cause, and it decidedly affected my life's trajectory. I decided then and there that some day I would get involved with politics and try to change the world.

CHAPTER 12

BACK IN THE U.S.S.R.

By the late fall of 1984 I was becoming disillusioned with the entertainment industry. I had come really close to a number of great roles in film and TV in L.A., but each time they had slipped through my fingers and I had not landed anything big.

And because I did not hold an American work permit back then, each time my funds ran out, I had to return to Canada (where I was better known) to secure more acting work. I was even beginning to wonder if acting was enough to feed my spirit anymore, let alone to fulfil a deep desire to make a difference in the world. I also found myself missing my family. So I flew home to Nova Scotia to spend time with them while I tried to figure out what to do.

Mummy Marshall and Daddy Pop, by now octogenarians, had recently come over from Australia to live with the family for a while. So one day I asked Mummy Marshall plaintively, "How does one get to be eighty-four anyway – without giving up?" She told me, "Never give up hope." While mulling this over I decided to walk to a local graveyard on the top of a small hill overlooking the town of Truro. I always liked to go up there to think and put things in perspective. When you're sitting in a graveyard looking out at the world below, sometimes things come to you that they wouldn't any other place.

On this particular fall day, I threw myself on the ground, asking the universe to send me some kind of sign if I should keep going as an actor, or give up and become a revolutionary like my hero Ché and go fight the Contras in Nicaragua.

After pounding the ground with my fists and crying tears of pure frustration into the grass, I rolled over on my back and looked up at the sky. I imagined I was becoming one with the earth and that I was there for eternity – that I was connected to the trees and their roots, and I imagined my connection flowing over the hill to my family and friends and community, and then down through the earth to the other side of the world where I was born, to Australia and my family there and all the generations before them.

My heart rate slowed down and a state of peace came over me and I began to see that I was okay, that the only thing that mattered was right now – that very moment. And then the next and the next. And as I pictured this web of connections – the web of creation – I realized that I could trust the Universe to look after me and that I'd be all right. And then I realized I felt cold. I'd been lying in the graveyard for a while and the sun was setting. And that's when a sudden rush of gratitude came to me as the thought dawned that I could still get up and walk away from that graveyard while the others buried there could not.

A great flood of energy traversed through me then and I felt like I could fly down that hill. I was excited to be going home to my parents' beautiful old heritage house on Willow Street that looks so much like Green Gables from the Anne books. And I'd be able to see them all again – my parents and grandparents and my sister Tamara, now an inquisitive, funny twelve-year-old whom I didn't know very well. I'd been gone from home since I left for university in Toronto when she was just five.

But already I got the feeling that while my little sister was happy to see me when I came home, she often seemed to be embarrassed by me. I guess I was considered rather outlandish in a small country town, wearing my long blonde hair in Bo Derek braids and roller-skating down the street along with her while she was riding her bike.

But on this particular day, when I walked down the hill from the graveyard and into my parents' yard, Mummy Marshall came flying out of the back door. I'd never seen her move so fast. She was calling me to come quickly as she said she had answered a phone call from my agent in L.A. – with good news. It turned out I had finally booked my first gig in the States, a film called *Return*, starring Frederic Forrest. So after asking the Universe on top of the graveyard to show me a sign about my future, here I had my answer. I was to return to L.A. to start shooting, followed by final scenes in Salem, Massachusetts.

Once I'd finished shooting *Return* in Massachusetts, I flew home to Nova Scotia, since Mummy Marshall and I had decided to go on a trip together before the year ended and at her age I was always worried about losing her. Mummy Marshall was my best friend and confidante; she was the one person in the family who best understood me, having once been a professional performer herself.

Since my grandmother was a socialist at heart with a deep love for Tolstoy and Russian history, she confided that, at eighty-four, her lifelong desire was to see Russia before she died. And I wanted to help fulfil her dream.

"You're on!" I told her.

So off we went on the trip of a lifetime, touring what was then the U.S.S.R. for three weeks – my grandmother at eighty-four and me just twenty-four. And what a great adventure-loving team we were! For three weeks we toured Moscow, Kiev (in the Ukraine), St. Petersburg (called Leningrad at the time), and Yalta on the Black Sea before returning to Moscow once more. And in that time we got to see many museums and historic places.

There were lovely Russian and Ukrainian tour guides, of course, but Mummy Marshall proved she knew even more of the history. It was like I had my own private tour guide. We visited churches and villages, markets and libraries, statues and palaces, art galleries and museums. And she walked so fast on these tours the rest of the group could barely keep up with her. We had a blast meeting many young people, attending concerts and the Bolshoi Ballet (which we had both always wanted to see). We also visited both the Summer and Winter Palaces, where I learned firsthand what the words "opulent decadence" really mean.

There is wealth in Los Angeles as all the multimillion-dollar mansions in Beverly Hills will attest, but what do you make of a solid gold life-sized peacock clock with a golden tail that fans open every hour encrusted with thousands of multicoloured precious gems, while a bunch of little woodland creatures with sapphire and emerald eyes circle around its feet? Catherine the Great sure loved her bling, that was clear.

And while she was a very interesting, clever woman, and a patron of the arts, most Russian citizens – peasants – were barely able to feed their families let alone have golden peacock clocks to tell the time. No wonder there was a revolution.

Being an odd-looking duo, we attracted some attention, so young men flocked around us at our nightly dinners out, asking us to come and dance with them. They were very smart about it, however, because one of them would always first ask the "chaperone," Mummy Marshall, to dance before they'd ask me. They'd hold out their arms and say, "Babushka, Babushka – with the white hair – come dance with me!" Mummy Marshall never said no, and her chorus girl dancing legs would remember steps she thought she'd long forgotten. The next thing you know she was whirling around the dance floor. Then the next young man would step over to me and hold out his arm.

What's a gal to say? Well, when in Moscow … she says, "Da!"

I was invited to a number of private parties in Moscow by young folks I met, and unfailingly I'd come back to our hotel shoeless because someone had admired my shoes and said they couldn't buy fashion like that in Russia. I'd give them away and walk back to the hotel barefoot.

People have always asked me how I was able to get out away from the hotel and group tours to mingle casually with Russian citizens like that without being stopped or followed by police or the KGB. They have an idea that foreigners were always monitored. But I can honestly say if I was under surveillance nobody ever stopped to ask me where I was going or where I'd been. I moved about freely and talked to many regular citizens who loved their country and their system of governance there – but also a number of young people who wished they had a political system more like Canada. And they wanted to have a larger variety of things to buy, as we currently do in the West.

Sometimes children would hear me speaking English and ask if I was from America and when I'd say, "No, Canadian," their eyes would light up and they'd say excitedly, "Ahhh! Canadienski! Wayne Gretsky! Montreal Canadiens! Yeahhhhh!" Proving that hockey is a universal language too.

Which brings me to another great lesson I learned in Russia: people all over the world have much more in common than their differences. Human beings from all nationalities just want to live and be happy, and provide for their children and grandkids. The more we try to paint an entire people with the same brush, the less human they seem and it is easier to hate and fear them. Sadly, some world leaders take advantage of this basic misunderstanding and use it to create divides and friction between people in order to have power over them. My motto has always been to operate with an open heart in the world and be willing to learn about other people's culture, customs, and language in order to create better understanding between us. It breaks my heart now to look back at this time of peace while war is raging in the Ukraine, with all of the suffering it causes.

Mummy Marshall and I absolutely loved Kiev, in particular the market where older ladies were selling bouquets of raspberries wrapped in newspaper to eat fresh, and we would often go for walks on the promenade together along the Dnieper River, which runs north to south through the city, flowing into the Black Sea. In the early evening we would join in the ritual of whole families out walking along the banks of the river. And as we walked arm in arm, we would run into people who wanted to speak English with us as for some reason they seemed to know we were tourists. Most of the people we met right across the U.S.S.R. were very well educated because post-secondary education was free. It's been my belief ever since that both health care and lifelong education should be provided by governments of every nation to all citizens no matter their financial or social status. After all, I have seen the benefits firsthand.

Yalta was the final stop on our tour. Located on the Black Sea, it was a very peaceful, beautiful seaside community with numerous public spas and private sanitariums. Long considered a place to go to improve one's health, it was interesting to learn that many Russian workers were given two weeks family vacation in Yalta each year fully covered by the government.

I also learned in Yalta that one of my favourite playwrights, Anton Chekhov, had owned a home there and that he was not only a fabulous playwright, but also a doctor who was known for treating people for free. When he was home there'd be long lineups at his front door each morning. And he'd work on his plays at night.

He had a second home in Moscow which was known affectionately as "Chekhov's little house" where he did most of his writing. I made sure to visit it when we returned to Moscow at the end of our trip. And since one of my favourite Chekov plays is *The Cherry Orchard*, I ate a cherry from one of the trees in his courtyard and brought the cherry pit home with me as a keepsake.

I also bought a couple of prints by Russian artists, including one of the god Pan as an aged man, looking rather forlorn, with an orange crescent moon setting behind him. It seemed to capture the melancholy that permeates Russian history and music. I bought a Chekhov poster for my friend David French, and a poster for my mother's home classroom at Truro Junior High School that featured a group of young kids grinning at the camera, wearing hockey gear and CCCP helmets. I figured if Canadian kids saw the poster, they'd be able to see that Russian kids were no different than themselves.

Just before our trip came to an end, I had an experience in Moscow that I was not expecting but will definitely remember for the rest of my life. It was nighttime, and my grandmother had just gone to bed upstairs in the huge old hotel where we were staying, but I had decided to stay up for another drink and a little reading before bed. There were two lovely young Greek men who wanted to chat. They told me they were studying at the Moscow State University. For free. They were both handsome and engaging, so when they invited me up to their room in the hotel for a nightcap, I was not about to say no.

A pretty wild night ensued which included copious amounts of Greek (Metaxa) brandy. And the Metaxa wasn't just in our glasses. It was all over our bodies. It was the first (and only) "threesome" I've ever experienced – and I have to say if you're going to try something like that, it really helps if they both have the same name. I got lucky that night (in more ways than one). My two guys were both Aries ... and not the star sign either. *Both* of them happened to have the *same first name*! What are the odds?

We must have exchanged addresses at some point that night during our Greek Bacchanalian festivities, but I really don't remember. They both wrote me letters and postcards for a long time afterwards begging me to come visit them on the two different Greek islands where they returned to live. I never did. Once was enough. But "We'll always have Moscow." Ahhh ... What can I say? A Rogue by any other name ...

CHAPTER 13

KEANU, NELLIE, AND AN OFFICER AND A GENTLEMAN

Early in 1985 I travelled to Toronto once more for film work. During this time, I met many interesting people, including Keanu Reeves and Lou Gossett Jr. and I spent time with both.

Keanu and I met at a film audition, which neither of us ended up getting. However, we went for a drink which turned into a romantic weekend. As it turned out, Keanu had performed in the Brad Fraser play *Wolfboy* in Winnipeg and a friend of mine, actor Bob Collins, had played his father. Bob had spoken highly of him but said he was pretty insecure back then. I did not know it at the time but in a few years I was also to perform in Fraser's play *Unidentified Human Remains and the True Nature of Love* in Winnipeg, Toronto, Chicago, New York, and Mexico City. At the time we met, Keanu and I were both in our early twenties. I remember him as being a very sweet guy – and a great kisser. I can't remember too many details due to the haze of margaritas and wine, but I do know we rarely left my executive suite that weekend.

When Monday came, he had to catch his return flight back to L.A. and we said goodbye. I remember saying, "I will miss you," as I had enjoyed his company so much. From this short time together, Keanu seemed a lovely human being who made a positive impression on me. I have been happy to see him grow as an actor over the years, and his well-deserved success.

Lou Gosset Jr. and I met at a popular restaurant in the centre of Toronto. I had seen him play Sergeant Emil Foley in the 1982 feature film *An Officer and a Gentleman* and thought he was a spellbinding actor. He was also the first Black man to win an Oscar for Best Supporting Actor. So when he asked me for my number, awestruck, I gave it to him and he called later that day. We spent a couple of weeks hanging out together at night after we'd finished shooting our films for the day. He was doing *The Guardian* at the time. He was extremely charismatic, handsome, and charming, and we would talk until the wee hours about his life experiences. He told me about making his debut on Broadway at the age of seventeen and the racism he had faced in the U.S. and consequently meeting people like Dr. Martin Luther King, Jr. and Malcolm X.

However, after a while I began to realize that he also had a cocaine habit at the time which was hard to ignore. He would be okay 'til about 10 p.m., then he'd get a little antsy and would make a phone call. Shortly after, someone would come to his hotel door with a delivery in a brown paper package. Each time this happened he would excuse himself and disappear into his bedroom. A few minutes later he'd come out into the living room area resplendent in African robes carrying an ornate tray with a small pipe on it. The first time this happened I was fascinated with the ritualistic element. And when he offered me a puff of the pipe I accepted, thinking it was hashish, which I'd done before as it was readily available in Nova Scotia.

I went back to my own suite after that first date and was so high I didn't come down for about three days. When I saw him the next time, I said, "Wow, that hash you got last time was really strong!"

He looked at me with a raised eyebrow and said, "Hashish? Girl, that was no hashish. That was cocaine!"

I said, "What do you mean? We were smoking cocaine, then?"

And he said with an incredulous look, as if I was a country gal who had just fallen off the turnip truck, "Yeah! It's called freebasing."

Well, I had heard of *that*. And it scared me. But I still continued to see him because he had a star power that was mesmerizing and I loved his stories. We bonded discussing social injustices and he taught me a lot about the civil rights movement. We'd have dinner and talk and laugh, and he'd be his charming self. But then later on, during each date, he would get restless around the same time and make that damn phone call.

With each night that passed, it was as if he became a different person – switching from a funny, charming, effusive, and affectionate gentleman to someone frantically combing through the carpet for coke crumbs or pulling the couch apart to try to find his stash. And at over six feet, and a Hapkido aficionado, he could be frightening in his intensity.

For some reason I never really worried for my safety, but the final straw came one night when he accused *me* of hiding his drugs (because he'd either forgotten where he put them or had already used them up). I realized then that this was not a relationship that could continue, and I told him so. It made me feel sad to see such a talented, intelligent man clearly bent on a path that was so destructive.

For more than a decade before his death in March 2024, he was very public about his battle with drugs and said that racism and depression contributed to his drug and alcohol addiction, which he battled through a stint in rehab in 2004. I'm so glad this talented and brilliant man found sobriety and was able to help others with his honesty.

My own drinking days were not yet over back then either, and with many after-hour speakeasies in full swing where the Toronto film community hung out, I was riding high as a young actor, booking a lot of TV and film roles, but was dissatisfied with the roles I was getting. I was also very torn between wanting to learn more about politics and acting and curious about what kind of governance systems around the world worked best for the benefit of the people.

Therefore, when a dear friend, Tu-Fu, invited me to spend Christmas of 1985 in Scandinavia, which was governed by a social democratic system, I jumped at the chance, wanting to see for myself how that system worked with its social program of a guaranteed annual income. Actor friends Ray Jewers and Nicola Lipman were living in England at that time and I thought perhaps I could visit them and take some voice classes in London. So that December I flew to Aarhus, Denmark.

Tu-Fu Gandhi Yo is South African, with dreadlocks and a smile that lights up the world. A former African National Congress activist and Cessna pilot, Tu-Fu was late to meet me at the small airport. However, once he arrived the reason for his tardiness became apparent as it turned out he'd had an accident earlier that day and cut off his thumb. This meant he could not drive the stick-shift car he had rented for our trip through Denmark to Sweden. So he gave me a quick lesson and by necessity I learned how to drive stick in Copenhagen, which has crazy roundabouts and tons of traffic. But I soon realized that, not having driven much before, if I could drive there I could drive anywhere.

After an amazing first European Christmas and New Year in Sweden, we made our way to England where we parted ways, as Nicola, who I had performed with in productions at Neptune Theatre, had invited me to stay with her for a few weeks. Ray had also heard I was in Europe and had sent word via Nicola to tell me he wanted to "discuss a proposition." Needless to say, I was intrigued.

It turned out that Ray was performing in London's West End in a new musical about Elvis and Priscilla Presley called *Are You Lonesome Tonight?* Ray was understudying Elvis and invited me to see the show the night he was to play the role. (I didn't know it at the time, but a year later I would be playing Priscilla in the Canadian premiere of the same play back home at the Charlottetown Festival.) Ray took me out for dinner after the play and asked me if I could do him "a big favour" and stay with his wife and two children in the English countryside in their house in Farnham, Surrey, rather like an unofficial au pair because he was planning on leaving his wife for another (younger) woman who was also performing in his play.

While I was surprised and rather taken aback by his request, Ray was adamant, and begged me to stay in England for a few months at least because he felt I was "a positive person" who could help his wife Philippa (Pippa) deal with the break-up of their marriage, and help with the kids. I said I'd obviously need to meet his wife and kids first, to see if that was something they would want, but since I'd been thinking of taking voice classes in England in any case, I agreed to meet Ray at Waterloo Station on his next day off and take the train to Farnham to meet the family.

Ray invited another friend, Hugh Quarshie, to come with us since Hugh and Philippa had always gotten along well, and Ray no doubt wanted to avoid a confrontation. Hugh was a marvellous actor who I had just seen give a dynamic performance as Tybalt in the Royal

Shakespeare Theatre production of *Romeo and Juliet*, arriving onstage in a red convertible.

The four of us went for a pleasant walk around Farnham Castle, and Ray took us for lunch, and indeed I got along extremely well with both Pippa and Hugh, so she invited me to stay with her and the kids Rosie and Jack at their country home. I took weekly voice lessons in London from a recommended teacher, and Hugh and I ended up going on several dates.

After a couple of months Philippa introduced me to her theatrical agent, who asked right away if I could do a New York accent. Of course, I could. So he asked if he could send me out for an audition. I immediately booked the role, performing in the play *Two for the Seesaw* (which had been originally performed on Broadway by Anne Bancroft and Henry Fonda). I began rehearsals almost straight away at the Old Vic Theatre in London, then performed it in Guilford at the Yves Arneau Theatre, after which we were booked for an open-ended run at the Regina Teatern, the only English-speaking theatre in Stockholm, Sweden, where it ran for several months. This meant that I found myself headed back to Scandinavia again, exactly where my European adventure had begun. But this time I was put up in a lovely apartment in the Old Town and paid two thousand kronors a week.

Just before we arrived in Stockholm, the Swedish prime minister, Olof Palme, was shot outside a movie theatre, which shocked the nation as political violence of that kind was unheard of in that country. Sweden was plunged into mourning.

During the run of the play in Stockholm I found out I'd been nominated for an ACTRA, a national acting award back home in Canada, for the role of Mary in the CBC Radio production of David French's play *Salt Water Moon*, the play he'd told me I had inspired when he first met me at age nineteen at the Charlottetown Festival. In this two-hander play, I had been lucky to work with the incredible Newfoundland actor Robert Joy as "Jacob."

In order to attend the awards ceremony in Toronto, however, I needed to get time off from my theatrical engagement in Stockholm. To do that, I was told I would have to buy out the entire theatre for two nights, the equivalent to one month's pay. Since we were doing an open-ended run, and it looked like we'd be running the show for some time, I took the chance, given that, if I won, it was an important moment for me. Not only was it the first time I'd been nominated for anything as a professional actor, but for the first time the industry was recognizing my work. So I flew to Toronto for one night.

Lo and behold, I won, receiving the award for Best Actress on national TV, with a beaming David French by my side. We stayed up celebrating with many Toronto friends all night, then I flew back to Stockholm with the ACTRA award (then called a Nellie, a bronze statue of a lovely rotund dancing woman) in my hand. Upon arrival in Stockholm, I took a taxi from the airport straight to the theatre to perform. The newspapers in Stockholm lapped up this story and my statue was proudly displayed in the front of house for the remainder of the run.

A few months later, I had a very different and rather frightening experience in Stockholm when, on May 1, a rather strange rain began to fall as I was coming out of an after-show party with friends. The rain seemed fluorescent, and, on a whim, I did a little spin in the plaza, saying, "If this were a nuclear rain we could all be dead in ten years!"

A few days later the whole country awoke to find out that indeed the rain that night, and subsequently, turned out to be radioactive – the fallout from Chernobyl. The Swedes were the first to discover high radiation in their water supply, which led to Russia admitting that a nuclear plant in Chernobyl had suffered a meltdown. This affected the rains that fell upon neighbouring countries in Europe. The Swedish authorities advised us all to buy iodine pills from the pharmacies to counteract the radiation and said that if we were unable to get iodine (because the stores quickly ran out of stock) we should eat as much iodized salt as possible on our food. I began using "healthy" amounts of sea salt on my food at that time and joked for years afterwards that's the reason why I like salt. Well, it must have worked.

Two for the Seesaw continued to run until June of 1986 and I booked a film called *The Girl* after that which shot in Sweden and Croatia (the former Yugoslavia). Since our Zann family had originated in the tiny town of Starigrad on the island of Hvar in Croatia, before they immigrated to Australia in 1889, my curiosity about our family and what our people did for a living was ignited. Were any of them performers? Where did my ability as an actor and a singer come from? Why was I the way I was?

And where should I go from here? My long-held desire to know the answers to these questions was overwhelming.

At twenty-six I was still thirsty for adventure, and not ready to go back home. Since I was already in Europe and had no idea when I would get another chance like this, I figured why not head to Croatia for the summer to uncover the mystery of our family's past in order to find myself and figure out my future. Little did I know then that storm clouds were beginning to brew in the Balkan region, which would lead to a violent sectarian war – with darker things in store for me as well.

Winter wedding of great-grandfather Marino John Oreilia Zann (Zaninović) and great-grandmother Lucie Emelda Finigan, in Sydney, Australia, June 28, 1905. Left: seated, Manda Zann (Marino's twin sister); standing, Margery Emerton (Lucie's niece); Right: seated, Claire Finigan Hughes (Lucie's sister); standing, Ursula Marohnić (Marino's niece). Best man is Phil Bushell.

Maternal grandmother Elizabeth Gladys Rose (Mummy Marshall) as a young stage and radio chanteuse (c. 1922).

Maternal great-grandmother, successful hotelier, publican, racehorse owner and businesswoman Bridie Frances Walshe (c. 1900).

Mum and Dad's wedding in Sydney, Australia, May 10, 1958. I came along 18 months later.

Mummy Marshall, Mum, and "Little Lenore"(Karuah, NSW, c. 1962).

Lenore the ballerina at the Royal Sydney Ballet (Sydney, Australia, c. 1967).

Lenore and Mummy Marshall (Truro, Nova Scotia, c. 1987).

The Zann Family: Dad, Mum, and little sister Tamara (Zann family homestead, Truro, Nova Scotia, c. 1979).

Cobequid Educational Centre (CEC) high school guidance counsellor and director Norman Hines and boyfriend Charlie (Page Fletcher) toasting my soon-to-be starring role as Marilyn Monroe in Cliff Jones' new rock opera *Hey Marilyn!* (Zann family homestead, Truro, Nova Scotia, September 1979).

The Lady from Maxim's – starring in the title role as a cheeky young "guttersnipe" who tries to pass herself off as a high society "lady." Mum and Tamara visiting my dressing room after attending this Georges Feydeau farce (St. Lawrence Centre, early 1980s).

A star is born! As Marilyn Monroe in three theatrical productions: 1. in my dressing room opening night of *Hey Marilyn!* (Edmonton Citadel Theatre, January 1980) 2. *Anyone Can See I Love You* by Marilyn Bowering (Victoria Playhouse, Victoria, British Columbia, 1988) 3. *The Marilyn Tapes* (Santa Monica Beach, 2004).

Made up as Marlene Dietrich for the Charlottetown Festival's annual Maude Whitmore Scholarship Concert where playwright/composer Cliff Jones and wife Eve discovered me to play the role of "Marilyn Monroe" in his new rock opera (Charlottetown, PEI, August 1979).

With Charlie (Page Fletcher) celebrating our first trip to the Big Apple (Waldorf Astoria hotel, New York, 1980).

With Tony Award-winning actor Brent Carver in *Unidentified Human Remains and the True Nature of Love* (Crow's Theatre, Toronto, 1990).

With actor Danny Kash in *Unidentified Human Remains* (Orpheum Theatre, New York, 1991).

With Andy Gibb (*Something's Afoot*, Showtime TV, 1992).

A rock 'n' roll wedding: with new husband Ralph Dillon (First United Church, Truro, Nova Scotia, July 26, 1987).

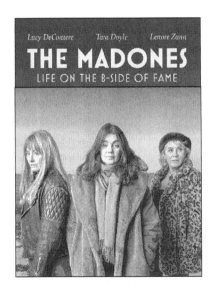

As Gladys Madone in *The Madones*, a film by Barrie Dunn, with Madone sisters actors Lucy DeCoutere and Tara Walsh (Halifax, Nova Scotia, 2022).

On the red carpet at *X-Men '97*'s official Hollywood premiere (El Capitan Cinema, Hollywood, Los Angeles, March 13, 2024).

With Mum and Dad after being sworn in as a Member of the Legislature (MLA) –
so happy to be making my parents proud with Mum pinning me with my MLA pin
(Province House, Halifax, Nova Scotia, June 2009).

With Mum and Dad in front of Canada's Parliament on our way to the swearing in
ceremony to represent Nova Scotia as a Member of Parliament (MP)
(Ottawa, November 26, 2019).

Signing the oath after being sworn in as the Member of Parliament (MP) for Cumberland-Colchester (House of Commons, Ottawa, November 26, 2019).

With Dr. Ingrid Waldron (right) and Green Party Leader and MP Elizabeth May after passage of our Bill C-226, National Strategy Respecting Environmental Racism and Environmental Justice (Senate of Canada, Ottawa, June 19, 2024).

"Shall we have tea?" As MLA with Her Honour Mayann Frances (Nova Scotia's first Black Lieutenant Governor) at the annual LG's Garden Party (Government House, Halifax, June 2009).

At the cottage with beloved niece Maia Li (Cape John, Nova Scotia, August 2012).

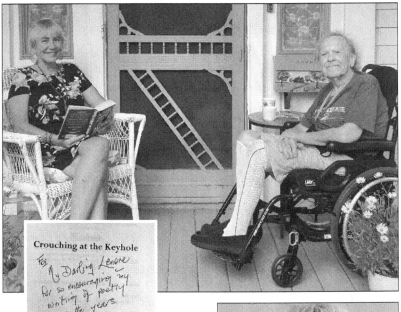

Crouching at the Keyhole

For My Darling Lenore for so encouraging my writing of poetry over the years. My Love Dad x April/2007

The author today.

Truro, Nova Scotia, July, 2023: Reading *The Last Devil to Die* (by Richard Osman) to my darling Dad on the front porch of the Zann family homestead on Dad's last day at home. I had made the decision that my main purpose during the summer of 2023 was to be of service to my father, to bring him joy, and do whatever I could to keep him company and make his final journey a peaceful one. What more can a loving daughter do for her father? He is gone. But his spirit is alive and well inside me.

Dad's personal inscription to me in his final book of poetry, *Crouching at the Keyhole*. The titular poem is about watching and waiting as a young boy for his grandfather to die.

CHAPTER 14

AN ACTOR'S GUIDE TO THE UNIVERSE (PART 1)

I believe sometimes you have to lose everything to find yourself.

The chestnut trees were in full bloom when I arrived in Zagreb, the warm June air filled with their fragrant, heady scent, abundant white blossoms lining the streets. In the summer of '86 I was feeling pretty heady myself – excited to explore the land of my forebears for the first time and keen to search for my Zaninović family roots.

Like many twenty-somethings, I had a burning desire to "find myself." The thought was, if I could figure out where I came from, I might better understand who I was and why I was the way I was (a performer, adventurer, seeker of knowledge) and hopefully the answers to these questions would help me figure out where I wanted to go from there.

Two for the Seesaw had just closed in Stockholm, after which I'd played a small role in the Swedish film *The Girl*, so I arrived with about $7,500 in cash. My plan was to open a bank account and travel and explore the country for three months, following any leads to determine where our family lived, what they did for a living, and why they left in 1889 to settle in Sydney, Australia.

That was the plan at least. But as the Scottish poet Robbie Burns once aptly wrote about plans going awry, "The best laid schemes o' mice an' men gang aft agley ..."

My three-month sojourn in "the Old Country" did come to pass, but not exactly as planned because I ended up getting robbed that very first night in Zagreb – by a giant and a dwarf (or Little Person, as we say today).

Yes, I know. It sounds like a Fellini movie, but it is what happened. It's my story and I'm sticking to it.

For my first week I had pre-booked a room in a beautiful old hotel in the heart of the Zagreb, at the time the capital of the former Yugoslavia (and now the capital of Croatia) to get my bearings before making my way to the town of Starigrad (Slavic for "Old City") on the island of Hvar in the Adriatic Sea. The name of the town and my great-great-grandfather Vincent (Vinko) Zaninović and his wife Ursula Garbati were the only things I knew for certain about our family's origin. These were the only two pieces of the puzzle. There were many more to find, though I didn't know where or how.

After checking in to the hotel, I took my cash to the nearest bank and asked to open an account. I was told, "Sorry. No can do." It was a socialist country and foreigners weren't allowed to open bank accounts.

I tried another bank. Then another. And got the same story each time.

"Now what?" I thought. Here I had all this money on me in cash, just ripe for the picking. How in hell was I to keep it safe for three months? As it turned out I didn't have to worry about that for too long.

After getting a bite to eat as twilight fell, I heard music coming from the local square, and followed it to discover a lively outdoor concert underway. The square was packed with people in high spirits singing along and dancing to the music. It wasn't long before a handsome young blond guy approached me for a dance and, well, what's a gal to do? When in Yugoslavia ...

It turned out that Petar spoke pretty good English and when he found out I was Canadian-Australian he immediately became excited and wanted to introduce me to his group of friends, who also spoke English well. They insisted on taking me to a popular café, then a bar and then another bar and wouldn't let me pay for anything, drinks or food. They were really sweet. As the night went on, we swapped many stories and laughs as we bar-hopped our way around the city. While I was aware that I was still carrying a lot of cash in my purse, I did not feel worried or threatened in any way.

Finally, we went to one last bar where two colourful and striking characters joined in our merriment. They told us they had worked for the circus for many years, one being extremely tall and the other extremely short. I don't remember their names, but they were full of fascinating stories about life in the circus.

You may recall I'd had this desire as a child to be ballerina in a circus, parading around the ring on my white horse and performing breathtaking moves on its back while the audience applauded me for my grace and skill. And here I was, years later, sitting down with circus performers. So it will come as no surprise to you that I was bedazzled by these two gents.

Not to mention that by this time I was feeling no pain as Petar and his friends had been generous with the drinks. I do remember holding onto my purse most of the night, but I put it down on the floor at the last stop. Big mistake.

That night I said goodbye to the guys, while Petar stayed overnight with me at the hotel. We slept in the next morning. But when I went to get cash from the purse to take us for breakfast, to my horror I realized the once-full purse was almost empty. The cash was all gone, except for $250. I woke Petar and told him what had happened, and he immediately said we should report the theft to the local police. So that's what we did.

My mind was racing, trying to retrace my steps from the night before, and as the reality of what this loss meant dawned upon me, I began to feel the full shock as I realized that with only $250 to my name I could no longer afford to stay in hotels if I was to remain in Croatia. And how would I survive for the entire summer in this foreign country?

At the police station we were taken in to meet an officer who Petar explained in a hushed voice was the chief detective inspector for the whole country. Detective Inspector Čopčić was young, dark-haired, brown-eyed, and very serious. He was fluent in English and listened intently as we told him of our movements the previous night, including the people we had met. When we got to the part about the final watering hole on our bar-hopping excursion, and I mentioned meeting "a giant and a dwarf" who were circus entertainers who had joined our table, his interest became even more pronounced and he asked for a full description of the two.

He then left the room for a few moments, returning quickly with a photo album.

Thumbing through the pages of the album he came to a spot and turned it around for us, asking if we saw the giant among the mugshots of this rogue's gallery. And indeed, there he was. We pointed him out immediately. The detective nodded, saying nothing, then presented another page and sure enough there was the dwarf. When we identified the latter, Detective Inspector Čopčić nodded again, this time saying dryly, "Uh-huh. We call him Quick-Fingered Luis. He is the snatcher. And the big guy is Jure the Hammer. They are well known to us. You're lucky you didn't get knocked out by Jure first before Luis snatched your entire purse, passport and all."

"They did work for a circus at one point in time," he told us, "but later fell into a life of crime which was simply much more lucrative. I'm afraid you have been swindled by two of the most notorious crooks in town. And while we will definitely search for them, I can bet my bottom dollar that we won't get your money back. But we will try. So I request that you not leave the city for a while to give us a chance to find them. Where will you be staying?"

At this point the initial shock of the theft was wearing off and I was beginning to feel overwhelmed. With only $250, I knew I could no longer afford the hotel but had no idea where I would be staying. But Petar spoke up and said that I'd be welcome to stay at his apartment where he lived with his parents and his sister Marina. We gave the detective their phone number and address and he said he'd be in touch. After we left the police station, Petar walked me back to the hotel as I needed to repack and check out while he went home to explain the situation to his parents, saying he would return for me later.

My mind was a jumble of thoughts and worries as I got back to my room and sadly repacked the things I had so happily unpacked just the day before. I wondered what this change of plans would mean with regards to my quest for identity. I decided the only thing to do was to accept what had happened as a lesson – albeit an incredibly expensive one – and simply live in the moment, taking whatever came day by day, learning whatever life lessons the Universe had in store for me while I searched for my past, in order to create a purposeful future.

Over the next few weeks, I got to know Petar's family pretty well. Although his parents could not speak English, both he and his sister could, and it turned out Marina had once visited Canada, so, far from being put out having an unexpected guest, the family was excited to have a visitor from abroad.

Not only did I get to experience the life and routines of regular everyday Croatian people, but great conversations ensued about life in both of our countries, and politics in general, including what worked and what didn't work under the socialist system introduced by their leader, Tito, who had brought many Slavic countries and religious ethnicities together to form the one country called Yugoslavia. And in their view, although nobody was rich, it was working.

Marina and her mother also told me many enthralling stories about gypsies and witchcraft and their own personal experiences with magic. One afternoon they invited an old Bacca (a gypsy fortune teller) they knew to come and do a reading of coffee beans for me over the kitchen table. She prophesied that she saw me in the near future among many boats and that a ship's captain would somehow come to my aid.

Since this was long before the internet, let alone Google or Wikipedia, had been invented, I decided to look up the name Zaninović in the phone book and discovered a Marin Zaninović, who was a professor of archaeology at the University of Zagreb. I went to his office and left a note pinned to his door explaining my quest and asking for his help.

A couple of days later, on a Friday morning, he called the flat, and Petar's mother answered the phone and put me on. Dr. Zaninović's English was very good and he told me that while his branch of the family was different from mine, he had written a book on the entire Zaninović clan. And that the following week he planned to travel to his summer home in the ancient town of Starigrad, on the island of Hvar, where the original homestead of my branch of the clan was still standing and in use by the family.

There was more that was even better. In order for him to tell me the whole story of our family history, he offered me the opportunity of travelling with him by train from Zagreb to the medieval coastal city of Split from whose port ferries depart for Starigrad on Hvar and all the other beautiful Croatian islands which dot the Adriatic. This was too good an offer to pass up, so I agreed to meet him at the train station on Monday morning.

Then I called Detective Inspector Čopčić to say I planned to leave Zagreb the following Monday, and he offered to pick me up at the flat to provide me with an update on my stolen money. That Friday afternoon Detective Inspector Čopčić came around to collect me as promised, saying that he was taking the afternoon off to show me the sites of the capital city that he loved and protected, while giving me the update on my case.

It was a beautiful, picture-perfect day. The stately buildings of Zagreb stood with dignified old-world grace against a blue sky, multicoloured flowers in bloom everywhere, and the warm air of early summer made the air shimmer with an effervescent light. Once more I felt transported to another time, or as if I had stepped into the frames of an old movie.

Detective Inspector Čopčić ("Call me Ivan") picked me up in his police cruiser. And, like his city, I found him fascinatingly old-fashioned in one sense, but modern and progressive in another. I felt safe with him, and, in spite of his status as a police officer, I felt us to be on the same level, as equals. After first telling me that he was a proud socialist and explaining a short history of the country that was Yugoslavia at that time, pointing out some of his favourite historic sites and landmarks, he turned on the car radio and began singing along with gusto as he drove his cruiser through the streets of Zagreb, then winding up, up, up a hill overlooking the city, pausing only once to exclaim, "What is life without art? Without music? Without poetry?"

When we arrived at a particularly pretty look-out spot where the city stretched out below us like a sleepy cat having an afternoon nap, he said, "And now, Miss Zann, let us discuss the situation at hand with regards to the petty thieves who took your money …" He proceeded to tell me that he had managed to track down the two suspects and that they had admitted to the theft and were now both incarcerated (yet again), but my money was gone. How they had spent it, or whether it had disappeared somewhere along the way after their detention by police I will never know, but the reality of the situation I now had to accept was that I would not be getting it back.

I suddenly realized that if I wanted to stay in the country, I would have to live on the $250 I had remaining, or find some way of making more money. And it popped into my head that perhaps I could sell some of my possessions and clothes as I had done in Cuba a few years before. No matter what, I knew I was not going to pass up the opportunity of taking the train to Split with Professor Zaninović, and there was also no question that I simply had to make my way to Starigrad at some point to get a feel for the place and hopefully find my family.

Detective Inspector Čopčić also had some sombre advice which has stayed with me ever since. He said, "Now, Miss Zann, it is obvious you love to travel, and you are very trusting of people you meet along the way, including young Petar, and even myself. However, in my policing career I have observed that crimes against people are more often committed when the victims have been *drinking alcohol* and are therefore more careless about whom they associate with, what areas they go to, and pay less attention to their belongings. Most crimes against tourists occur in this manner as well because there are some types of locals who, like the two men who stole your money, make a profession of watching for opportunities to take advantage of others, particularly in bars. We have a name for such individuals. We call them seagulls because they watch and wait to snatch up morsels that don't belong to them. So I feel it's my duty to caution you about this so that you don't run into the same problem in your future travels."

This was the first time my drinking had been brought to my attention by a stranger as a possible problem. Like many young people, I liked to drink. I liked to party. And I thought everyone did. I did not yet suspect that I might have inherited the disease of alcoholism, a genetic disorder I've since discovered existed on both sides of my family tree, particularly in the Irish factions.

My mother had always warned me about the dangers of imbibing too much, since she'd seen it firsthand in her two uncles, Mummy Marshall's brothers. But (also like most young people) I had not wanted to heed my mother's warnings. But now, at age twenty-six, Detective Inspector Čopčić's words hit home. And while I was not yet ready to quit drinking, this was a turning point as I began to become more aware of my actions and habits and their consequences.

By this time, still parked in the cruiser on the hilltop above the city, surrounded by luscious greenery, the once-sunny skies had begun clouding over and a soft rain began to fall. The sound of the drops softly falling on the roof and the way they stirred the leaves outside the car was very relaxing.

Detective Inspector Čopčić changed the subject, openly curious to know more about me and my life as an actor in North America. Like many European men, he also wanted to know why I was still single. "But you are a beautiful woman! Why do you not have a husband?" I explained I'd had a few long-term boyfriends but had not yet met one I wanted to marry.

Meanwhile, the skies outside had darkened and the rain became a sudden summer squall, thick drops thudding on the roof and bouncing off the hood of the cruiser. We quickly rolled up our windows, and, with no AC, the car soon became a stifling sauna, the moist heat producing a heavy sheen on both of us. It became impossible to converse over the loud din, and the louder we shouted, the harder the rain fell, as if it were trying to drown us out. We began to laugh at the absurdity of the situation, and as we continued to sweat, the rain outside looked more and more refreshing. The car radio was now playing some rhythmic Latino dance music. I leaned towards the detective's ear.

"Wanna get wet?" I asked with an impish grin.

I didn't have to ask twice. Throwing open the doors, we leapt outside, and immediately felt the embrace of the warm and sultry air mixed with cool rain. We didn't bother to close the car doors, and the music continued as we joined hands and danced to the salsa rhythm of the rain. Within minutes we were both soaked through to the skin.

Once more a strange feeling came over me as if I was in a movie – in a sensuous, velvety, slow-camera-dolly-move kind of scene. By now we were close to the front of the cruiser, and I lay back against it, arms wide, head back, and drank in the rain. He soon joined me, and we began to kiss passionately, gasping for air and drinking in the rainwater that was running in rivulets down our bodies. I began to climb up on the hood of the cruiser, reaching for him to join me ... And we kept on climbing 'til we were on top of the cruiser roof.

Now there's a popular song that talks about "making love in the afternoon" and "getting caught in the rain." Yeah. Well, all I've got left to say is ... that was a mighty fine rain!

When he dropped me off at the apartment building, I thanked Detective Inspector Čopčić ("Call me Ivan") for finding the culprits of the theft, for his sage words of advice for my future travels, and for taking the time to show me the "hotspots" of his beautiful city.

He had one more thing to say before he thanked me as well. "Miss Zann, I must say, really you are unforgettable. Just remember if you have any further trouble in our country, just call and I'll take care of it."

Little did I know at the time just how important these words would be.

On the Sunday evening before my train to Split, an intriguing yet unsettling experience occurred with Marina. We were alone in the apartment for once and she had insisted that she wanted to do an "energetic reading" for me since she claimed to be psychic and said the old gypsy Bacca had put a spell on her as a young child. She sat me down across from her at the small kitchen table, lighting a white candle on the table between us, which threw dancing shadows on the walls. She told me to stare into the candle and empty my mind. Then, after a time, she said to look up into her eyes and tell me what I saw.

Well, to begin with, as I looked into Marina's eyes, I saw her pupils suddenly contracted, becoming tiny little black pinpricks which seemed to bore into first my eyes and then my soul. I saw colours of purple and gold swirl around her face and head and as I continued gazing into the black pinpricks, they seemed to become malicious, determined to get inside of me and take over. I became frightened at the feeling of a powerful woman wanting to control me, possibly trying to cast a spell over me, and I gave a start and pulled back, refusing to let the energy in. Marina asked what was wrong, but I did not feel like telling her what I'd seen, so I described the colours but nothing more. It was intense.

The following morning Marina had said she would set an alarm and wake me up in time to catch my train. But she didn't wake me, and luckily, I woke with just enough time to get to the station to make my train. I quickly bade goodbye to the family in Zagreb, gave Marina's mother some money in gratitude for giving me a place to stay, grabbed my suitcase, and made it to the station without a second to spare.

I had no trouble spotting Professor Zaninović on the platform: a tall, imposing older gentleman carrying a briefcase. He looked rather like Merlin, or Gandalf, or the magician in one of my favourite books, C.S. Lewis's *The Magician's Nephew*, only with short, silver hair, tidily combed. I knew this train ride would be like no other I'd ever taken. And I was right. My journey to find my ancestors had finally begun.

CHAPTER 15

AN ACTOR'S GUIDE TO
THE UNIVERSE (PART 2)

"Leap and the net will appear." – John Burroughs

Professor Zaninović and I got along famously, and he taught me a lot about the history of our family, including the fact that according to his research, the name Zaninović has Hebrew, Italian, and Slavic roots – with the family originating south of Krakow, Poland, where the name was originally Yohan (meaning John, as in John the Baptist), but was later changed to Ivan (also meaning John).

Professor Z also believed the family migrated to the burgeoning city-state of Venice in the eleventh century, where the name changed once again to fit in with the Venetians, becoming Zani, Zanni, Zanini, or Zani-no – the Venetian form of Gianni (short form of Giovanni, and once again the equivalent of John). Zanni or Zani is also a trickster, or comedic figure in the ancient Italian theatre form of commedia dell'arte.

Around the twelfth century the family immigrated to the little island of Hvar off the coast of what is now called Croatia, and intermarried with locals. The name was changed once again – Slavicized this time – by adding a "vich" to the end, which means "son of." Thus the family name became Zaninovich (or Zaninović).

In the ensuing years due to raids on the small coastal villages of the region by the Turks, who burned villages and slaughtered the inhabitants, the Zaninović families moved up into the mountains away from the coast before finally returning to settle on the coast once more in the ancient town of Starigrad.

Starigrad itself, Professor Zaninović explained on the train, was founded by the Greeks in 384 BCE in an area that was already a highly prized and thriving agricultural region in a coastal kingdom once called Illyria, which was ruled by a pirate queen named Queen Teuta, whose Indigenous peoples were rather nomadic. These Illyrians were illiterate, but many of the remains of their stone fortresses can still be seen today.

The soil upon which Starigrad was built is extremely fertile and the area around the city, called the Starigrad Plain, is renowned as the oldest human-tended agricultural area in Europe, with a river flowing through it that keeps it both moist and aerated for growing during most months of the year. However, this also made it highly desirable to others.

The Greeks, who at first were good trading partners of the Illyrians, soon wanted more, and, as happens time and again, after the indigenous Illyrians gave them permission to build a small colony in the harbour, the Greeks built walls to keep the Illyrians out.

Angered at this insult, the Illyrians attacked the colony from the sea. But the Greeks sent for reinforcements and thousands of triremes, ships with three sails that were much larger and faster than the boats of the Illyrians, were sent to quell the attack, resulting in thousands of Illyrians killed, and more taken and enslaved. As time went on, though, Greeks and Thracians mingled with Illyrians, and the genes from these peoples also mingled and continue to flourish.

The Greeks named the island itself Pharos, which means "Lighthouse," after the Greek island from whence they came. And the ruins of some of their fortified towers and temples still exist throughout the island today. Starigrad Plain also features the oldest existing man-made land division structures in Europe: basically, rows of large white stones which served as markers for fences to be erected between individual properties.

In 229 BCE the Romans took control of the island when their Emperor sought revenge for Queen Teuta's bold killing of one of his emissaries whom he had sent to demand financial tributes to Rome. According to several historical accounts, the fellow had also insulted the fierce pirate queen, who responded by stealing his ship and sending his head back to Rome. (I guess that's what you get when you piss off a pirate queen.

I can't help but hope that somehow a drop of Queen Teuta's blood runs through my veins.)

This defiant action in turn enraged the Emperor who, already fed up with Teuta's pirating and plundering of Roman ships passing anywhere near Illyria, used the incident to declare war – known as the First Illyrian War – which resulted in the defeat of Queen Teuta's forces, after which she and her court and remaining forces fled to safety further up the coast. There the Queen established another base in what is now Albania, and (once she agreed not to pirate any more Roman ships) she was allowed to rule the area where she had settled.

Meanwhile, the Romans changed the place names in the region they now occupied – including Illyria itself, which became Illyrium, and the isle of Pharos became Phara.

When Slavs arrived in the sixth and seventh centuries, the Illyrian tribes that still inhabited the region were gradually assimilated or displaced by the Slavs. This process of assimilation and cultural exchange led to the formation of new ethnic groups and identities in the region. Over time, Slavic culture and language became dominant and the Illyrian tribes lost their distinctiveness. However, two major recent genetic studies show that the genes of many modern-day Southern Slavs in former Yugoslavia include the markers of Illyrian tribes.

Eventually the name of the island, Phara, was Slavicized to Hvar. A number of Roman and Venetian walls and mozaics are still to be seen in Starigrad in a couple of churches, the museum, even in a couple of stores, and in the basements of buildings, including our own Zaninović family dwelling.

Professor Zaninović told me many more interesting things about the family that I didn't know, including that when my great-great-grandfather Vincent Zaninović decided to leave Starigrad he was but one of several brothers, cousins, and an opera-singing uncle who decided to immigrate at the same time. They did not go straight to Australia; they first sailed to San Francisco where they shortened the name to Zan in an effort to once again fit in with the society around them.

In the old country the Zaninovićs had been shipbuilders and captains, and also vintners, growing grapes and making wine which they sold with many other local goods as they plied their ships up and down the

European coast and even as far as Africa. But when a grape blight spread across Europe, destroying harvests for several seasons, and the steamship was invented, which was faster than the tall ships that relied solely on wind to power them, the "Golden Age of Sail" ended. Since ship owners could not even sell their ships, many beautiful tall ships were simply left to rot along the coastline while their owners turned to other businesses or immigrated to other countries, in particular America and Australia, where the lure of the Gold Rush – like that siren call of mermaids to sailors in tales of old – was intoxicating and impossible to resist. The Zaninović men, centuries-old travellers – adventurers, explorers, sailors, merchants, and speculators – heeded that call and plied the waves yet again, this time as passengers on ocean liners to the New World.

After making a small fortune from the Gold Rush and successfully establishing themselves in San Fransisco, the family decided to split up, with some moving on to Portland, Oregon, where they established a successful broom factory they named Zan Brothers Brooms.

Later great-great-grandfather Vincent returned to Starigrad where he married Ursula Garbati (from another former sailing ship family) and they decided to immigrate with their five young children first to Melbourne, Australia, where they established the very first broom factory in that country. They called this one Zann Brooms. (Note they added an extra "n" to the name, thinking it more English that way, although they did experience bigotry in the early years, being called Wogs, a derogatory term for anyone with olive skin from Greece, Italy, Croatia, etc.

But eventually the Zanns moved to Sydney, where Vincent, along with his two now-grown sons Vincent Jr. and Marino (my great-grandfather), established a new broom factory, which they named the Excelsior Broom Factory, a name which resonates with me today because Stan Lee, the famed creator of Marvel Comics, often used Excelsior as his signature expression because it means "to constantly strive to go higher." The family had great success in business, thriving in their new home Down Under, including the sumptuous marriage of Marino Zaninović/Zann to Lucie Emelda Finigan, the granddaughter of one of Sydney's most colourful first mayors and aldermen: Michael McMahon.

Michael McMahon was an Irishman originally from Limerick, with successful businesses in sporting goods and combs and brushes. He was adamant that the burgeoning city of Sydney was in dire need of a new bridge to be built right across the harbour from his constituency of North Sydney to Circular Quay on the southern side of the harbour. This, he believed, would improve the lives, businesses, and commerce for his constituents and the entire city.

As is often the case (which I know all too well, having now had experience in politics myself), if you express a new idea and want to create positive change, there are always naysayers who are simply lacking vision, creativity, and guts. Mayor McMahon had all three in spades. And years later, after he was no longer in office, that bridge would be built. Sydney Harbour Bridge has become not only an integral transportation route but a beloved landmark for the city.

The area where great-great-great-grandfather Michael McMahon built his beautiful family home looking out over the north side of Sydney harbour is named McMahon's Point in his memory. And I can only imagine the excitement of the Zann Clan when one of their own, Marino Zann, from Starigrad, Hvar, married North Sydney mayor Michael McMahon's granddaughter. Both large Catholic families with successful businesses, it is clear from recently found family photos of large picnics, games of tennis, and summer vacations that the Zann-McMahon-Finigan families blended well with each other.

It was fascinating to hear for the first time about the roots of our Zaninović family from Professor Z on that train ride between Zagreb and Split, including the fact that one of my ancestors, Ante Zaninovic, was a member of the Austrian North Polar Expedition of 1873, which first announced the discovery of the archipelago Franz Josef Land. Mainly Croatians made up the crew for this almost fatal undertaking; Ante himself fell into a crevasse at one point and almost froze to death. In 1875 the Royal Geographical Society of London awarded Ante the Silver Cross for his bravery during this dangerous journey. The last living member of the expedition, he died on May 31, 1937, in Trieste, Italy, at the venerable age of eighty-eight. Having Ante as one of my ancestors goes some way to explaining my thirst for adventure.

But none of these stories answered my questions about why I was a performer. Where did the natural ability to act and sing come from? Although the musicality may have come simply from Mummy Marshall, who was a beautiful pianist and coloratura, I somehow felt sure that there must also be music or theatre handed down in my father's genes as well. By the time we got to Split, I had as many questions as answers and was determined to try to meet living relatives who could unveil more of the story.

Upon our train's arrival in Split, I bade Professor Zaninović farewell as he had a ferry to catch to Hvar Island. I needed to regroup, to store my suitcase safely at the station, and to find a Croatian tourist agency who could help me locate affordable lodging, as I'd heard that tourists were able to rent rooms in local homes very cheaply. Given my financial situation, that was exactly what was needed if I was to stay for any length of time. After Professor Z left for the ferry terminal, I parked my suitcase in the storage room at the station and asked where the nearest travel agency was before hightailing it to the waterfront, only to find the agency had closed thirty minutes earlier. Not knowing what to do next, I wandered down to the marina and watched the boats of all sizes coming and going from the pier.

At one point the captain of a mid-sized boat with a small group of tourists onboard was preparing to leave their berth when our eyes connected. He looked like a young Paul Newman, eyes as blue as the Adriatic with skin darkened to a burnished gold from a life spent upon the sea. I noticed the name of his boat: *Sudbina*.

As he saw me looking longingly at the boats leaving shore he waved me over with a grin, saying, "Hey! Goldilocks! Want to come?"

The sun was about to go down so I was hesitant, knowing that I really should be finding a place to sleep for the night.

But he said, "What are you waiting for? It's like life – you either get onboard for an adventure or the ship sails without you. Just jump!"

I realized that I was dying for the adventure and would take things as they came. Just as the ship was beginning to pull away, I took a leap of faith across the widening stretch of water onto the deck of the boat and into Bari's brawny arms.

"Good choice!" he grinned. "I could tell you were an adventurer! I'm Bari. Where you from?"

"Canada. I'm Lenore. What's the name for your boat mean?"

"*Sudbina*? Means destiny." There was that dazzling grin again. "You believe in destiny?"

"I think I'm beginning to," I replied.

And that was it. We were friends.

During the sunset tour of the harbour Bari let me sit up in the captain's cabin with him and even steer the boat some of the time. "You're a natural," he told me.

At one point he asked how long I'd be in Split and where I was staying. I told him the truth, that I didn't know, and that I would like to rent a room in someone's home if possible as I didn't have much money. I asked if he knew of any places.

He thought for a moment and then said "Well, you're welcome to sleep on the boat. There's a bed in the hold – I'm not using it. I wouldn't charge you if you'd like to help me out with the English-speaking tourists and invite them to come out for tours with us. Quid pro quo. How does that sound?"

Well, that sounded amazing to me. Not only would I have a place to stay – for free – but I'd get free tours of the islands as well. You can't beat that, I thought.

"Deal," I said.

And that was that. For the next couple of weeks, I had an amazing time getting to know Bari and the other local captains and sailors, café owners, and artisans selling their wares. And I managed to meet some local female travel agents who took me under their wing and offered to buy some of my outfits and jewellery to give me extra cash to live on.

I helped them and they helped me. Quid pro quo.

There's nothing like being on a ship on the Adriatic with its turquoise blue waters dotted with the rocky white coastlines of the Croatian archipelago. Bari and other captains all owned their own boats and their livelihood consisted of taking tourists island-hopping during the summer months to make enough money to keep them going through the slow winter months when the tourists disappeared.

During the time I spent on Bari's boat, we visited many islands, which was a fabulous way to see Croatia and get to know its people. One friend I made onshore in Split was an older man named Joseph, a devout socialist and lover of art and literature like Detective Inspector Ivan Čopčić, but with a difference: Joseph was also a devout Buddhist.

Joseph first noticed a book on Buddhism that I was reading in a little seaside café while sipping my daily cappuccino, and we got to talking. I said I was studying as much as I could on Buddhism to try to learn "how to be one with the moment" and stop feeling anxious about the future all the time. I'll never forget what he said.

"You know, most people walk through life asleep at the wheel. They don't know how to really *live*. The people who know how to *live* are few and far between. They're too scared to get out of their comfort zones and take any risks. But you," here he gestured towards me, "well, it's pretty clear to me that you are one of the few who really go out and *live*. Don't ever forget that. And don't ever let anyone squelch your joie de vivre! Because many will try. But don't let them throw water on your fire."

Then he set me on a Buddhist exercise. He said, "Go out to the sea's edge and just sit and look into a rock pool for an hour. Then come back and tell me what you've seen."

I thought this must be something like Marina's exercise, so I was expecting to see colours and visions, but no such luck. All I saw were a few little hermit crabs scurrying around, jostling each other and swapping shells, and seaweed billowing with the tiny tidal waves. Nothing more.

After an hour I went dutifully back and told him this was all I'd seen. Nothing else. Nothing interesting happening. Mainly just stillness in that rock pool.

"Ah! Wonderful!" he exclaimed. "So you saw nothing! Yet you stayed in place, sitting, and simply observed. That's good. That's Buddhism. Just stay in the moment for as long as you can. Forget the past and don't worry about the future. Focus on your breath, on the sensation of breathing. The cool air flows in. The warmer air flows out. Or think of it as coloured light or smoke: the white clear light of enlightenment flows in and the dark air full of distractions flows out. Breathe in. Breathe out.

"Ponder 'Who is it that is breathing?' Just observe. Keep it up. Do this every day and someday you will find peace of mind. That's what is known as mindfulness. And maybe sometime in this life, or the next, you will even become enlightened, like the Buddha. Anyone can be a Buddha,

you know. All the word Buddha means is 'one who is enlightened.' …
Now this reminds me of a story …"

Then Joseph proceeded to tell me the following tale:

"Once there was a bright little fish who was very curious. A little confused, but curious just the same, which is a good thing. Now one day this little fish went to the Queen Fish and said, 'I've heard a bunch of fish talking about this thing called 'the sea' but I've never seen it myself. What is it? And how do I know if it really exists?'

"The Queen Fish smiled and put her fin around the little fish, explaining gently, 'We were born in the sea, and we will die in the sea. The sea is within you and without you; you are a part of the sea and the sea is a part of you. It is your very being.'"

Then Joseph gave me a little book of Buddhist koans, saying, "The answers to all your questions, Little Fish, lie within. Take your time and read carefully between the lines."

Little did I know then just how important that book of koans would become in a tight situation. "Breathe in – breathe out." How the hell do you simply focus on that? I thought. But I started practising.

Sure enough, it helped begin to calm my racing thoughts and constantly busy mind. True serenity and self-acceptance were still a long way off. But I was taking the first steps along the path to finding peace of mind.

CHAPTER 16

AN ACTOR'S GUIDE TO
THE UNIVERSE (PART 3)

Sometime after Joseph's lesson in Buddhism, Bari was taking a boatload of tourists to Jelsa, a town on the island of Hvar. They would be staying overnight, he said, but he would be sailing back to Split and returning for them the next day. I decided to stay overnight as well. We had not yet travelled to Starigrad, which Bari said was scheduled for the following week. But I was itching to see Hvar and begin to familiarize myself with this island I'd heard so much about.

We arrived in full sunshine with tourists all milling about the harbour interacting with local artisans selling their wares. I quickly made friends with a group of artists who were selling their paintings of local vistas and sketching and painting portraits. We made a deal for me to speak to prospective portrait clients in English, French, or Spanish and in turn the artists would share their wine, bread, cheese, salami, and olives with me and arrange a place for me to sleep that evening.

Quid pro quo. Who needs anything more? I thought.

So after a beautiful afternoon hanging out with the artists, followed by an evening of song with more wine and guitars, it was arranged that I would share a room and a bed with a young woman who worked at a nearby hotel. Although she couldn't speak a word of English, she was friendly, and the artists explained that I only needed a place to crash for the night.

Before heading to bed, I washed my blue jean cut-off shorts and T-shirt in her bathroom sink and hung them on a cherry tree branch outside the window. We settled in for the night and I was dead to the world as soon as my head hit the pillow.

Suddenly I was woken with a start by a loud banging on the door. My hostess also woke up and after a couple of minutes, we heard angry men's voices, demanding that she come to the door and open up.

The girl looked stricken, terrified, and in Croatian seemed to be telling me to hide under the bed. I had no idea what was happening, who these men were, or why they were here. But I knew one thing: I did not want to be found naked under a bed in the middle of the night in Yugoslavia. So I wrapped the top bedsheet around me and went to the bathroom, where I hid, closing the door behind me.

Shortly, I heard the girl open the front door and heard the same loud men angrily demanding something from her, yelling, and I heard her tearful responses, but couldn't understand what they were saying. This dialogue and dynamic continued for some time – the deep, angry men's voices and the girl's softer, timid responses back and forth and punctuated with sobbing. Finally, there was silence.

I strained my ears to hear something, anything, but it was as if the men had suddenly disappeared, and I wondered if perhaps the girl had appeased them, and they'd gone away. It soon became apparent that was not the case as quietly, slowly but surely, the bathroom door began to swing open, and a hand appeared on the doorknob – a huge, beefy, male hand.

I held my breath and for a moment I thought my heart was going to stop beating. I looked up in what seemed like a slow-motion camera shot to discover a big beefy face to match the hand, and finally the man stepped into the room, wearing a dark uniform with a dark, scowling expression to match. He said something in Croatian and gestured for me to come out of the bathroom.

"Zašto? Koji je razlog?" I replied. ("Why? For what reason?")

"Militzia!" came his response.

"Dokaži mi to!" ("Prove it!")

Then he opened his topcoat and showed me his badge, telling me to leave. Another officer was waiting in the door of the main room, and they made it clear I was to leave with them. I managed to make them understand I wanted to get dressed first, in private. So with the girl still shaking and sobbing, I apologized to her for the trouble I seemed to have caused and got my still-soaking clothes off the branch and pulled them on, glancing at my watch. It was 2 a.m.

Once I was dressed, the two men started banging on and yelling at another door nearby. They roughed up the young man who appeared before pushing him towards me. Then the two of us were being prodded up a dark path through a pine wood with no idea where we were headed, why, or what lay in store. It was about this time that I realized this could end very badly for me.

I had my passport with me and a small carry bag with a single change of clothes and a few books. A bit of money. That was it. It crossed my mind that it would be easy to make me "disappear." I had heard and read that this sometimes happened to young women tourists who ended up in the wrong place at the wrong time. These men had semi-automatic weapons. Were they taking us to some place where they would use them? I had no idea.

In any case, since I'd been practising my Buddhist meditations daily by now, I was developing a faith that the Universe would take care of me, that everything happened for a reason, and that each and every event or "chance" meeting were not accidents – that they were meant to be – and that I should look at everything that happened as a spiritual lesson from which to learn.

That's easier said than done while you're being herded through a pine forest in the dark in a foreign country. However, eventually I could make out a large building ahead of us. It turned out to be a hotel and when the militzia guys prodded us towards it, I was relieved that we were not to be polished off in the forest.

They made us sit down in the foyer as they seemed to begin waiting for something – or somebody. Still in my wet clothes my body began to shiver and after about a half an hour (which felt like eons) another man showed up, clearly the Commandant, dressed as he was to the hilt in uniform and from the deferential behaviour of his foot soldiers.

After speaking amongst each other and glancing over at the two of us, the Commandant took the young man aside and berated him, barking out questions. The poor kid stammered a lot and managed to bleat out some responses that eventually seemed to appease the Chief, who finally dismissed him, and he hightailed it out of there as fast as his legs could carry him, without looking back. I never did find out what it was he'd done to run afoul of the militzia.

But his departure left me alone – and the Commandant finally turned his attention to me. As he turned his face in my direction, it suddenly dawned on me that I had seen this man before. I recognized him from the previous afternoon when I was sitting with the artists in the harbour. He had been among the throngs of people, but in plain clothes, watching me as I was negotiating with the tourists on behalf of the artists. Suddenly an unpleasant thought came to me about *why* I was here. Perhaps this guy had sent his men to track me down, had questioned the artists to find out who I was and where I was staying, and then sent his foot soldiers to drag me out and bring me to him. Later on, I found out that this was indeed exactly what had occurred. My instincts were spot on.

First, he asked me why I was not staying in the hotel as a tourist and instead staying overnight in the room of a hotel employee. This, he said, was illegal, as all foreigners to Yugoslavia needed to be accounted for, and in order to do that they had to leave their passports at their hotel reception desks. I told him I'd been robbed in Zagreb and was searching for my roots and that I was only staying for the night in Jelsa and planned to head back to Split in the morning. He asked me where my luggage was. And I told him the truth: stored at the bus station in Split.

Then he said, "Okay, well, I'm going to have to take you in to the police station."

Great, I thought. But what could I do?

Then he said something to the other officers, and they laughed. I did not like the sound of it. But there was nothing I could do other than go with them to their police cars and the Commandant drove me to the station with the others following in a second police car.

Once we arrived at the station, I was told to sit on a stool that was in the corner of the room. Then the three officers sat at a wooden table playing cards. They kept looking over at me and laughing as they played, and I started to wonder if they were maybe playing for *me*. I had no way of knowing what was really going on. After about an hour of this, feeling nervous about what my instincts told me was to come, I decided to take a book out of my bag and pretend to read nonchalantly.

But as I grabbed the first book that came to hand, I saw it was the little book of Buddhist koans that my Buddhist friend, Joseph, had given me. And that was when I "knew" instinctively that this entire experience was yet another spiritual lesson from which I was meant to learn something. I closed my eyes and asked the Universe to tell me how to deal with whatever was about to happen. Then, eyes still closed, I opened the book and let my forefinger point to a spot on the page. Okay, Universe, I thought, how do I get out of *this* one? Opening my eyes, I saw my finger had come to rest on a koan. I was ready for the Universe's advice. And this is what it said:

"The Master said to the student: 'All right. Your lesson is over for today. You may leave now – but not through the door.' Bewildered, the student looked around the room, then asked: 'What, Master? Should I leave through the window then?' The Master replied, 'No. Just leave.'"

And with that I had my answer. I thanked the Universe, closed the book, and put it back in my bag. I knew what I had to do. Whatever happened to my body would not matter. *I myself* would not be there. What this realization did for me at that time was to make me feel completely calm. My nervousness was gone. And I was ready. For whatever happened.

Shortly after this the Commandant seemed to call an end to the card game and dismissed the two officers. And just as I'd thought he would, he turned and came directly to me, and began to run his hand through my hair, touching my face.

"You are very beautiful," he said.

In my head I was saying, Oh yeah, sure, buddy, here we go.

Then suddenly, unbidden, a name floated into my consciousness, like a thought bubble appearing over my head, and I realized that while the Commandant had been playing cards and laughing at my expense all night, I now had one card of my own to play.

"Ivan Čopčić," I said.

"What ... What did you say?" the Commandant stammered, suddenly looking less confident than he had a moment before. And the hand that had been slowly but surely moving down my throat towards my breast paused.

"Ivan Čopčić," I repeated, slowly and deliberately, gazing solemnly deep into his eyes, with the best poker face I could muster. "Remember I told you I was robbed in Zagreb? Well, Detective Inspector Čopčić is handling my case, and he told me explicitly that I am under his personal protection for the rest of my stay in Yugoslavia and that if I get into any more trouble, I am to call him immediately. So, since you've brought me here to your police station, I guess I'm in trouble again, so I think we should call him. Right away. Don't you?"

The change that came over the Commandant was immediate – and priceless. Whatever soft side I had come to know of the detective inspector in Zagreb was clearly not one that this Commandant knew.

It was as if a secret release valve had been pressed on a hidden door, as the hand that was poised between my breasts was suddenly removed, as was the arm around my waist.

All of the bravado and cocksureness that the Commandant had possessed all evening as he swaggered about and played his game of cards seemed to disappear in a puff of smoke. All that remained was a disgruntled officer who had been beaten at his own game, by my ace in the hole.

CHAPTER 17

AN ACTOR'S GUIDE TO THE UNIVERSE (PART 4)

The week after our trip to Jelsa, Bari told me we were finally headed to Starigrad and that we'd be returning to Split at midnight. The sunset that night was spectacular. When we came into Starigrad Harbour the sky was a velvet purple spangled with stars. The warm air was scented with a magic combination of pine, rosemary, and lavender, which grew in profusion all over the island. In a word, Starigrad was heavenly.

As the tourists went off to explore the old town and visit restaurants and bars, Bari kindly took me out to dinner at his favourite café where the locals all greeted him with hugs and high-fives. He introduced me as "a famous actress from Canada" who was searching for her family roots, which excited his friends and got them talking amongst themselves regarding which Zaninović branch might be mine – they said there were many on the island with that family name.

After dinner Bari suggested we visit a bar in the main plaza he said was frequented by folks in the arts, and it was here that I heard klapa for the first time. Klapa is an oral, multipart singing tradition of the southern Croatian regions of Dalmatia. Traditionally sung by men, its main features are made up of a capella homophonic singing. The leader of each singing group is the first tenor, followed by several tenor, baritone, and bass voices. It was beautiful and hearing the harmonies brought tears to my eyes. When the men were leaving to go sing at another café, they surrounded me singing, "Laku Noch" to me, meaning "Good night" and wished me well on my quest.

Another friend of Bari's showed up at the bar a little later, and after more hugs and high-fives, Bari introduced me to Stevo, and the two friends excitedly exchanged a torrent of words. Bari turned to me and explained his friend was a journalist who wrote for many publications, including Yugoslavia's national newspaper. Stevo was so interested in my quest to find my roots that he wanted to write a story about me for the national newspaper.

Then Stevo took over, in English, saying he felt the public would be very interested in an actress from Canada coming all the way to search for her Croatian roots. By publishing the story, it might even help flush out members of my family who might remember the family who had immigrated to Australia. I immediately agreed and we arranged to meet for coffee in Split in a couple of days to do the interview. Stevo said he would also send a staff photographer to take my picture for the article, and we agreed that I'd meet the photographer at a café near the harbour the following afternoon.

Upon returning to Split I realized I hadn't showered in a while, having been swimming in the pristine ocean water several times a day for the past couple of weeks. So I asked a young man, Luka, who often came to help Bari clean the boat, if he knew where there were any public showers. Luka said he didn't know of any, but that his cousin had an apartment not far away where he lived with his mother and sister. He offered to ask his cousin if I could take a shower there and the next morning told me his cousin was happy to pick me up in his car and bring me to his family's apartment to shower and dress, and then to the café for my photo session. The following day, his cousin arrived on time by car, and drove me to the apartment where I met his mother and his sister. None of them spoke English, but they showed me where the shower was in their small bathroom and also a bedroom where I could change.

As I began to shower, I revelled in hot, soapy, water, washing my hair and enjoying the feeling of getting clean. But at one point as I cleared the soap out of one eye, I noticed with a start that the young man was now standing in the doorway. He was fully clothed and wearing boots, and as he gazed at me, his eyes travelled up and down my body from my feet to my breasts, while he applauded slowly.

I was dumbfounded. I just didn't know what to do. I had never been in a situation like this before, and since I had a great deal of trust in people, I could not believe this was even happening. Without going into gory details, he raped me in the shower. I am not a violent person, but at the time all I could think about were the men in my life who, if this were happening in Canada, I could tell, would want to come back with baseball bats and beat the hell out of him. But such was not the case.

After this ordeal he left me to finish getting ready. So, in shock, I showered extra long to make myself "clean" again, telling myself, "It's only your body. It's not you. This happened to your body – it didn't happen to *you*. So you can just put it out of your mind and pretend it never happened."

And suddenly my professionalism took over: I had a photo session to get to and by God I was going to make it and look my best! So I did my makeup and hair and got dressed. I was dreading having to even look at that creep again but I had no idea where I was and I had an appointment I needed to keep. So I let the guy drive me to the plaza in the centre of town where the photographer was waiting.

Although no words had been spoken between us on the drive, as soon as I was safely out of the car, I slammed the door and (although he couldn't speak English) told him in no uncertain terms what an absolute arsehole he was. He peeled off and I never saw him again.

I immediately turned my attention to the job at hand, walking briskly to the café and greeting the journalist, Stevo, and his photographer. We ordered cappuccinos and got to work. And I said nothing about what had just occurred. For one thing I was still in shock and had simply gone into "performance" mode, and for another, I did not want the story to be about anything negative that would upset Yugoslavians reading it. I wanted them to feel *good* about their country and the fact that someone had come all this way after so many years to discover their country for herself.

But just as my picture was being taken, I remember thinking, "Nobody who sees this photo will have any idea of what just happened to me within the past hour. But when I look into my eyes in the photo, no matter how far in the future, *I* will know." And then I "hit my mark" and smiled for the camera.

The article turned out to be well-written and served its purpose, as Stevo told me later that it garnered a lot of attention around the country, with the newspaper receiving messages from relatives who remembered my family. In particular, I heard from one cousin, Lana Listés, who worked in the TV industry in Belgrade, and came all the way to Split to take me to meet her two aunties, both in their nineties, who remembered receiving care packages from Australia during the war years and showed me the publicity shot of a great-great-great-uncle Nikolai Zaninovic, who became a famous opera singer in Oregon. They also showed me a very old album of a singing group, The Zaninovic Sisters, who had recorded Croatian folk songs many years ago. Now, finally, I was seeing *proof* that I was not an anomaly, that there were other creatives and professional performers in my Zann family tree.

Some of you may be wondering why I did not report the rape to the police. The fact of the matter is I did not speak a word about it to anyone, not even Bari, who had been so kind and helpful to me. Like so many women who are victims of rape, no matter what the situation may be – whether perpetrated by a stranger or by someone they know – I felt *ashamed.* I believed that if I told anyone what had happened, including Bari, or the police, or even my family, they would say I had brought it on myself. And, truth be told, deep down I wondered if that was true. And it made me hate and despise myself.

I decided to bury the whole thing – to sweep it under the rug, so to speak. It never even occurred to me to talk to a counsellor or seek therapy. I thought I was tough enough to handle it by myself. So I kept the secret for years – until now.

But here's the thing about sweeping traumatic events under the rug: over the years they build up. And one day, when you try to sweep yet another traumatic or painful experience under the rug, you suddenly find a bunch of angry, terrified, grieving eyes staring back at you and you realize there's no more room left to hide. But at twenty-six I was just dancing as fast as I could, doing anything and everything to relieve the pain and the shame – to forget it ever happened.

Not surprisingly, my drinking increased and if there were any kind of drugs offered I'd do them too, without a second thought. I would *do* anything, *try* anything to feel numb – to feel … *nothing*. I just wanted to obliterate any memory of what had happened. And, better yet, to obliterate the girl whose fault it was that it happened at all.

So my (unsolicited) advice to anyone who has had a similar experience but who may be suffering in silence: Don't believe it's your fault. It's not. It's squarely the fault of the person who is the rapist. Stop blaming yourself, and please get professional counselling as soon as possible to deal with the trauma. Or it will come back to bite you. At the very least tell a trusted friend and talk it through. It will save you years of pain. And while numbing ourselves with substances or other compulsive behaviours and addictions might seem to be an easy way out, they're not. They will only compound the problem.

Meanwhile, however, back in 1986, after the buzz from finally meeting relatives descended from family members who stayed in or returned to the old country, when I had a moment to slow down, I realized I was still in shock from the rape. I had been running on adrenaline and alcohol as a coping mechanism, but now that the "show was over," I felt on the verge of collapse and needed some quiet time alone to recover. I also needed to sell some more clothes to pay for things, so I went to the bus depot to retrieve some items from my suitcase. After folding a few outfits, shoes, and purses into my backpack, I slipped into the women's washroom to take refuge in a toilet stall where I finally allowed myself to feel my emotions and cried my eyes out.

After about twenty minutes of this I wandered out, dazed, back through the byzantine twists and turns of the streets at the heart of the medieval palace city of Split. Historically known as Spalato (from the Venetian), this ancient metropolis is Croatia's second-largest city after Zagreb. Like Starigrad, Split was founded by the Greeks as the colony of Aspálathos. However, when a Dalmatian named Diocletian was proclaimed Emperor of Rome, he decided to build his palace there, which automatically made this port city much more prominent, attracting citizens, trade, and wealth.

Over the years Split lost its importance but in the summer of 1986 it was full of colour, noise, music, shops, and outdoor restaurants with numerous lines of washing strung up high above the multitude of tiny apartments that had sprung up within the very walls of what was once the palace. It was into this cacophony of sights and sounds that I felt myself being pulled, almost like a windup toy on an invisible string. I had no idea where I was going, and since Bari had gone out of town for a couple of weeks, no idea where I would be able to lay my head that night. Yet I somehow felt I was where I was supposed to be. I wasn't thinking with my head anymore. Instead, I was being guided by a sense emanating from deep inside – from my body. As Fritz Perls once said, "Lose your mind and come to your senses."

When my body finally came to a halt, I looked up to see that I was standing in front of a large, stately yellow building. I had no idea what type of building it was, although it felt like a church. I found myself walking up the stairs to the huge brass-bound oak doors and using the large metal door knocker to knock.

To my surprise the huge door suddenly swung open, revealing a wizened little old man. He looked as surprised to see me as I did him and as he looked at me quizzically, he asked in Croatian what I wanted. I replied in my halting new/old language that I was wondering if the building was a church, or a museum. He shook his head saying, "Ne. Ovo je kazalište." ("No. This is a theatre.")

My heart skipped a beat, and my eyes must have shown my delight as I replied, excitedly, "Ah. Okay. Ja sam iz Kanade and Ja sam glumica en kazalište!" ("Ah. Okay. I am from Canada, and I am an actress in the theatre!")

"Ahhhh, predivno!" came the response from the little man. "Ući! Ući! Odvest ću te u obilazak! Dobrodošli ste ovdje. Ovo je tvoj dom!" ("Ahhh, wonderful! Come in! Come in! I will give you a tour. You are welcome here. This is your home!")

And with that, he ushered me inside, taking my arm, and guided me through dark corridors and back ways, up a staircase and through a tunnel into what felt like a wide-open space but since it was pitch black I couldn't see a thing and simply went on trust and my gut feeling that this little man meant no harm, was really on my side, and that we were members of the same "tribe."

At this point he told me to stand still and not to move, that he'd be back in a moment. I stood stock still until ... Suddenly there was light! The whole place lit up and I saw that I was standing centre stage in the most beautiful old theatre one could imagine – with crystal candelabras, and hand-painted cherubs, Grecian nymphs, and satyrs frolicking along the walls and ceiling in a rural country setting. And the red velvet seats and damask curtains throughout tinted with gold were a sublime touch.

Oh, how the audiences must enjoy coming here, I thought. And suddenly, as tears sprang unbidden to my eyes and fell down my cheeks for the second time that day, I realized something profound: it didn't matter what country I was in, or what language was being spoken – once onstage I knew exactly who I was and where I belonged. Now I saw clearly that the theatre felt like a church to me.

As I stood centre stage, bathed in light, looking out over the vast empty theatre, my mind began flashing through all of the roles I had performed in the past twenty years, and suddenly it seemed as if the seats were full. I pictured audiences throughout the ages as I realized that the theatre is indeed a sacred space – an altar where visions are created and shared, where priestesses like the Oracle of Delphi once recited incantations and prayers to the Gods ... And, before that, where shamans led community members in dance and song, sharing stories about everything from a successful hunt to births and deaths, to the creation of the Universe and everything in it.

I saw that we actors weave our spells to make an audience forget their cares and woes for a time, lifting their minds and spirits with the magical rhythm and repetition of words. Words that, with the right tone and intention, become spells. Using the entwined energies of actor and audience, growing and pulsating – ecstatic, like lovers in a warm summer rain – we drive our audience on through despair and hopelessness and grief to relief, acceptance, and joy, lifting them to a climax and then ... catharsis, before leading them back firmly, inexorably, to inhabit their own bodies once more, until, surprised, they find themselves back in the theatre, and realize that they have been on a journey, and that they are not alone.

We have so much more in common with others than we think. We all feel similar emotions, and the theatre is the place where we are shown the mirror to remind us of our shared humanity. Audiences can feel the energy connecting them not only to the performers onstage but to their fellow audience members. It's the same feeling as when a crowd oohs and aahs together watching fireworks or a sports game, or some daring, death-defying feat. Everything that happens in our lives, and in the countless generations of our ancestors' lives, has led to this place and time. This very moment. I smiled at the realization that my search for family and belonging was being fulfilled right here and now. Sometimes the Universe provides us with what we truly need in the most ingenious and unexpected ways.

I was finally home.

CHAPTER 18

CALIFORNIA DREAMIN':
THE RAVEN AND THE GOPHER

After my "year of living dangerously" in Europe, with all of its adventures – and misadventures – I was more than ready to return to North America. No sooner had I arrived in Toronto than I was cast in another horror film – this one called *Pretty Kill* – and during filming I became friends with L.A. actor Season Hubley, who introduced me to her boyfriend Fisher Stevens and his pal Matt Dillon (*The Outsiders, There's Something About Mary*). Season arranged for the four of us to go out together for a date one night, which was fun. Matt was sweet, kind of shy, and nothing came of it, but a few years later when I appeared in a play in New York he waited to say hello after the performance.

After doing more TV in Toronto in the fall of '86, I flew back to Los Angeles to visit my friend Dawna Shuman, a good friend of my agent, Norah Taylor, having done a stint for a time working with her at Bill Boyle's talent agency in Toronto. But Dawna was an actress and writer herself, having left her husband and safe but boring life in Kingston, Ontario, with nothing but a backpack and dreams of a more fulfilling life somewhere along the Boulevard of Dreams. She now had a cozy, magical studio apartment on Cheremoya Avenue in Hollywood in a quaint complex that was like a magnet for Canadian actors coming to L.A. Nestled among the trees in Beachwood Canyon, it was a mecca for young actors, including Robert Downey Jr. and Sarah Jessica Parker.

During this visit to L.A., I was also invited to visit Mexico for the first time. I had recently met an older woman, a healer who made her own natural products and believed in the healing energy and natural medicine of Mother Nature. She wore only white clothing, and was renting a little cottage right on the sea in Baja for a week. She invited me to come and stay with her.

I wanted to do a complete cleanse so she guided me as I fasted for a week, at first giving me fresh juice twice a day before tapering off to only water. As the week went on, I felt lighter and lighter, both in body and mind, and at the end of the week she told me she knew of a Yaqui medicine man who lived not far away, whom she felt had "a spiritual lesson" to share with me. So one afternoon we drove a long way down a narrow dirt track 'til we came to a small, brown mud hut in the middle of a field where he lived alone with his pet raven. I don't remember the medicine man's name, but I'll never forget the bird, which he called El Negro.

As soon as we drove into the yard, he appeared in the doorway of the hut – a short, wiry, middle-aged man, with leathered brown skin and shiny jet-black eyes that equalled his pet's in darkness, intensity, and unfathomability.

I thanked him in Spanish for allowing us to visit and told him that my name, Lenore, comes from a poem called "The Raven" by Edgar Allan Poe. He nodded and let out a toothless but hearty laugh as his pitch-black eyes lit up with glee.

"Vamos, vamos!" ("Come, come!") he told me, as he brought El Negro out and gestured for me to follow them across the muddy field. I did as I was bidden, while my friend remained behind in her van, preferring the AC to the late afternoon heat. Besides, she said, the lesson was for me, not her.

El Negro was beginning to get extremely excited, hopping up and down and doing a little anticipatory dance. We soon arrived at a spot in the middle of the field where I noticed an old, rusty chain coming out of the ground. How odd, I thought.

My companion then began hauling on the chain. What in the world …? But before I could finish that thought, El Negro began jumping up and down again, barely able to contain his excitement. And eventually I saw why. At the end of the chain was a very small cage that had been buried deep in the earth. And it was not empty. I could just make out the form of a small, furry, rather plump, cute, absolutely terrified gopher.

As soon as the cage was placed on the ground El Negro ferociously went to town, using his sharp beak to savagely peck at the poor little creature through the bars.

There was no escape.

In my state of light-headedness due to fasting, mixed with the desert heat and growing horror, a sense of heightened awareness came over me and I began to feel like I was about to levitate right out of my body. The medicine man just grinned at my discomfort.

Then he shrugged, smiling wide, and said in Spanish, almost apologetically, "Man's life is short. Our energy here on Earth – our life force – is limited. We can either be the raven or the gopher. Which do you choose?"

And at that moment an innate "knowing" arose inside me, the firm and unwavering knowledge that, although I had no desire to be like El Negro (who, I realized, simply needed to eat, and the gopher was his dinner), there was absolutely *no way* I ever wanted to find myself stuck in the position of that poor, fat little gopher – stuck in a cage with no escape, no alternate choices available. And at this moment I saw that time was a-ticking, and that when it came to creating a plan for the life I had remaining, I needed to get my shit together ... and fast.

I had no desire to watch the demise of the gopher, nor the triumph of the hungry raven. The ending of that story had begun as soon as the gopher stepped into the trap. I thanked the medicine man and walked briskly back to the van where I promptly threw up. Then off we drove, back to L.A.

Christmas was coming, which meant I would soon be heading home to Nova Scotia to see my family. My friend Courtney Gains (who, at eighteen, had played Malachi in the cult film classic *Children of the Corn* and shared my interest in spiritual matters) invited me to spend a few days in Big Sur with him before I left for the East Coast.

Courtney was excited to introduce me to Big Sur for my first time, as he knew me well and was sure I would fall in love with the place, with its breathtaking vistas, and the raw power and energy the Pacific Ocean creates as it continually pounds the tall, craggy cliffs. He also wanted to introduce me his friend Jim, who lived in Big Sur and had studied shamanism with Michael Harner, the author of *The Way of the Shaman*.

Courtney was right. I fell in love with Big Sur. I've been back many times over the years. In particular, I'm grateful to Courtney for introducing me to the Eselen Institute, a magical place where I go on retreat whenever I need a spiritual renewal or rejuvenation of some kind.

On Christmas Day, 1986, Courtney's friend offered us magic mushrooms before taking us on an absolutely amazing spiritual journey through the redwood forest of his property in Big Sur: through vibrant woods full of birdsong, up a mountain and down into a deep, green canyon where a stream gurgled and sang. And as our guide led us onwards, he remained always just out of sight, leading us purely by sound by shaking little silvery, tinkling bells whose crystal tones reverberated in the forest and glens, sounding like Tinkerbell's pixie dust, or the peeling laughter of fairies calling us to join them.

Courtney and I both had profound experiences. I had been worrying about my grandmother for the past couple of years as she was now in her eighties, and I was fearful about her death and of losing her. So this thought came to mind at one point as I slid down a soft, deep dark bank of earth. As I slid down the bank, the dark earth felt warm, and I smelled the pungent black, moist soil. I heard a woman's voice in my head reassuring me that "the Earth is our Mother. She loves all her children, and it's okay to return home to her womb when our time comes to leave this material plane of existence."

Wow. Just *wow*. What a powerful message. I lay in the warm dark soil for a while, comfortable with this thought and the feeling of being one with the Earth. Suddenly, for the first time, I was not afraid of death, or of being laid in the ground when my time here is done.

The tinkling of the bells broke my reverie. I got up and followed, finding Courtney in a similar state of bliss. And by the time we crested the top of the final hill it was sunset, the Golden Hour, and Big Sur was spread out before us in all her glory, golden and green and *alive*. Butterflies were floating with wings aglow, and birds were flying from tree to tree calling out to each other, getting ready to settle down in their canopies for the night.

Courtney and I just stood there, mouths agape, at the wondrous glory of it all. Then, just as the sun dipped below the horizon, I saw something that I'd never seen before, and can only be described as the Earth *breathing*. It was as if she was letting out a long, peaceful sigh of contentment in the form of a mist as the air slightly cooled above her warm, damp, black body. And it created a pearly dew that shimmered on the greenery surrounding us.

"Do you see that, Courtney?" I whispered. "The Earth is breathing!"

He nodded, speechless.

A truly "Aha!" moment. After the raven and the gopher experience in Mexico, followed by this magical trip to Big Sur, I was ready to get back to Canada, see my family in Nova Scotia, and resume my career. But one more "Aha!" moment lay in store before the City of Angels would let me go home.

CHAPTER 19

THE WAY OF THE SHAMAN, SHAPE-SHIFTING, AND THE GOOD RED ROAD

The first time I'd been introduced to the concept of shamanism was at the age of twelve, by my father, when he gave me Carlos Castaneda's *The Teachings of Don Juan: A Yaqui Way of Knowledge*. He also gave me my first books on Buddhism, and poetry and essays by freethinkers like Allen Ginsberg and Alan Watts, who spoke of harmony and the importance of social ethics to lead to spiritual realization within the inner self. The concepts expressed by these authors simply blew my mind. So I asked Dad if reincarnation could be real, and if shamans, sorcerers, and Indigenous medicine men and women actually exist. Dad's response was, "Anything is possible."

Those simple three words gave me the green light to explore all kinds of spirituality and from that moment on I became a seeker of knowledge, reading as many books as I could find, and saying yes to any and all opportunities to have mystical experiences (with or without the help of drugs), as well as travelling far and wide to learn about the spirituality of other cultures. Like my father, I remain open to the possibility that there is more to "reality" than what we perceive only with our eyes.

So, like many in their early twenties, when I first came to California I was ready for anything. Upon receiving an invitation to meet Hyemeyohsts Storm, an Indigenous shaman who apparently possessed the ability to "see" one's medicine animal totem – not to mention an author whose first book, *Seven Arrows*, launched the first Native American division of a major publishing house in the United States – I was not about to turn it down.

I was taken to meet Storm at his home in Ojai, not far from L.A., and had been advised to take a small pouch of tobacco to give him upon my arrival, since traditional tobacco is considered a sacred plant by Indigenous cultures. As such, it is used as an offering to the Creator or to another person, place, or being. A gift of traditional tobacco is a sign of respect and may be offered when asking for help, guidance, or protection, and, when it is burned, can carry prayers to the spirit world.

My friend Dawna Shuman and my Canadian agent, Norah Taylor, accompanied me. Norah and I had flown in to L.A. to stay with Dawna in Hollywood once again, and as it turned out, Norah's current boyfriend, Bob, was studying shamanism with author Lynn Andrews, who also wrote many books about her own shamanic experiences and knew Hyemeyohsts. So Bob had agreed to introduce me to him.

Once we arrived in Ojai we were greeted at the door of a small single-storied home by a handsome, young Indigenous man with long black hair wearing a red headband sitting cross-legged outside the door. His eyes were closed, and he was blowing smoke rings from a clove cigarette. When I approached, he opened his eyes and looked up, then asked me my name, and when I told him a smile lit up his face as he said, "That figures. I'm Raven."

He told us to go in and once inside we saw there were a dozen other people sitting in a circle in the small living room. Bob made introductions and I gave my small pouch of tobacco to Storm, who was a large man with a huge head of long, shaggy, silver-grey hair, with eyes that appeared milky due to cataracts. He was wearing a loose-fitting dashiki and blue jeans with a turquoise belt buckle and a number of silver and turquoise rings on his hands. He accepted my offering graciously and said, "So. I hear you've got some questions for me."

I blushed as everyone suddenly turned in my direction, but I did have questions so I first asked, "I've read that some people can shape-shift to become other animals and that it's also possible to travel lucidly while dreaming. Does that mean someone physically travels elsewhere, or are they only using their imagination?"

Storm listened to my question intently, then laughed as he looked around at his companions and then back at me, saying, "Let's put it this way: you can go to the moon. But you can't bring back any rocks."

I let this sink in. And then I asked, "If someone wants to follow a truly spiritual path, how is it possible to have regular earthly goals of making a lot of money, or becoming famous, or all the things that society tells us we should desire? I mean, everyone keeps telling me that as an actress I can be a 'star' and that I should spend every waking moment trying to accomplish becoming rich and famous, but in the grand scheme of things that means nothing to me. So why would I even keep trying to be 'successful' at anything? What's it matter?"

At that, he paused, saying, "It's definitely possible to do both, but one doesn't have to take on the Hollywood attitude of focusing solely on wealth or fame. It's all about what brings you joy and embracing one's skills. It also depends on one's motivation. For instance, I am an artist and writer by trade, a spiritual chronicler. I make money from sharing my art and have reached a certain degree of fame. And yet I follow the Way of the Medicine Wheels and the Good Red Road and try to inspire others to do the same.

"This fellow over here to my right, Heyoka, now he is a jeweller who creates spiritual altars made of fine metals and precious jewels for celebrities like the Beatles, for instance. He makes a lot of money from this. And yet he is a spiritual seeker following the Way of the Medicine Wheels and the Good Red Road.

"And this woman here, my friend Cheyenne, she is a beautiful artist who inspires others with her vibrant paintings ... So you see, we all have skills which we share with our fellow men and women. We don't do it to get rich; we do it to enrich others. And we all have private spiritual lives which we share with a chosen few, as we walk the Good Red Road."

This was the first time I had heard of the Good Red Road and Storm explained that it signifies a commitment to living life in the best way possible – with an intrinsic respect for others, oneself, and creation; having emotional, spiritual, mental, and physical well-being; having a plan in place to maintain that balance; and practising what you consider as your strength – the strength that comes from core values and beliefs. It also usually means abstaining from alcohol and drugs.

Then Storm proceeded to talk about what he called the Way of the Medicine Wheels, which he explained is "a Native American spiritual philosophy and earth science that reaches far back into antiquity and constantly renews our understanding of the intelligence of our Mother Earth, and Creation, teaching us that without healing of the self, there can be no lasting healing in the world."

I had one final burning question for him, "Storm, can you tell me what my true life's purpose is?"

Storm took my hand and gazed deep into my soul.

"Your true purpose, little sister, is this: You are the bridge between the worlds. You are full of light, and you will attract many, bringing people together for a common purpose wherever you go and whatever you do. There will always be some who are jealous, embittered, and vengeful, who can't stand the fact that you shine so brightly. They will try to halt your progress, make you doubt yourself, and extinguish your light. But just remember this: nobody can dim your light unless you let them. Don't let them."

Then Storm told me he wanted to give medicine to help me on my journey. He took out a small leather medicine pouch and began to fill it with special things, including some sweetgrass, sage, and a songbird's wing. Then he prayed over the bag and passed it around the circle, and the others prayed over it as well, passing it on until it came to me.

"Put it under your pillow tonight. I will come to you in your dreams to teach you about your medicine animal. Now go. You will see me again."

I thanked him and Storm nodded, then began chanting and the others soon joined in, lifting their voices in song, as one. We could hear them as we drove off into the night.

As we left, Norah began saying that she thought the whole thing was bogus and that Storm was a fake. Bob, who was driving, remained silent. Then, a moment later he said, "Hey … What's that ahead on the road?"

I was sitting in the back seat on the right-hand side, behind Norah. I leaned forward to try to see what Bob was referring to and at first all I could make out was the dark shape of something that seemed to be taking up a great deal of space in the middle of the highway. There were no streetlights, and when the almost full moon suddenly appeared from behind a cloud, while it shed a silvery light on the object, we could still not make out what was blocking our path. Not wanting to hit it (whatever it was), Bob slowed the car down until we came to a complete stop.

And there, in the headlights, we saw what appeared to be a large wolf hunkered down on the pavement. It was not a dog. It was much bigger than that. Its fur was silvery-grey, and it seemed completely nonplussed by our car, or indeed, us. We, on the other hand, were speechless.

The creature finally got up nonchalantly, watching us all the while. And as it slowly ambled over to the right side of the road, Bob gradually started to drive forward once more. Instead of staying put, however, the wolf began to lope alongside the car. And as Bob picked up speed, so did the wolf. It kept pace with the car and began jumping at Norah's window, snarling ferociously at her through the glass. Norah drew back in fear, but for some reason I felt very calm, as something told me the wolf was not there for me.

I can understand if you do not believe me – I would not have believed it myself unless I was there. But luckily there were three others in the car with me as witnesses, who all swore later that they had seen the same thing I did.

Eventually, the wolf fell back and stopped chasing us. But as I looked behind, through the back window, I saw it just standing there in the middle of the road, lit perfectly by the silvery moon, watching our car disappear.

And then ... I saw several other dark shapes join it on the road.

Then we were gone.

Until now the car been completely silent. But now we erupted: "Did you see that?" "What was that?" "Did that really happen?" But Bob remained silent, simply driving. He waited until there was a lull in our conversation, but when he finally spoke, it was a question.

"Well. That was very interesting. Do y'all wanna guess what Storm's medicine animal is?"

"Wolf."

That night I placed the medicine bag under my pillow and silently asked the Universe to let me know my medicine animal. I had a vivid dream in which Hyemeyohsts Storm, Heyoka, and Raven were all with me walking along a high cliff overlooking a valley. They were pointing out nests and small birds that looked to me like hawks, and they were explaining how the birds liked to nest high up so that they could see the larger picture, keeping an eye out for danger and protecting their nests.

I awoke in Dawna's beautiful apartment with the vision still strong in my mind. As I'd been advised by Storm, I didn't share it with anyone. But it made me wonder what type of birds they were, and whether I'd really ever see Storm again.

A couple of weeks passed and the day before I was due to fly back to Canada my L.A. agents from the William Morris Agency invited me out for lunch. They asked where I'd like to go and I told them, "Well, I love Mexican, so you choose your favourite." We drove to El Coyote, and had just been seated at a table when I looked up from the menu to see Storm, his son Rock, and a retinue of friends walking into the restaurant where they were ushered in to sit around a large table.

After a few moments I excused myself from my two agents, crossing over to Storm's table. I apologized for interrupting and reintroduced myself. Storm immediately responded with a chuckle, "So. You know what your medicine animal is now?"

I said I wasn't entirely sure.

He said, "But I came to you in your dreams and gave you the teaching. Don't you remember?

"Well, yes, I did have a dream," I said. "But I'm not exactly sure what it meant."

Then Storm looked up at me with his opalescent eyes, and said, "You're a sparrow hawk, little sister. Learn their ways. This will help you grow into the powerful woman you will become. But make no mistake, you have much to learn and you will not remain as you are now. For, like me, you are a shape-shifter. You will take many forms during your time here on Earth, and long after. But you must follow the Good Red Road and the Way of the Medicine Wheels. In order to gain the knowledge you seek, you have to sacrifice the things that are destroying you. You will inspire others to do the same, for you are destined to help many who are hurting in this world. Sparrow Hawk will eventually become Golden Eagle. This is a special gift. Use it wisely. Now go. Have a safe trip back home and pass on your gifts to our brothers and sisters in the

Eastern Nation of the Mi'kmaw, the People of the Dawn." He dismissed me with a hand wave.

I returned to the table to "do lunch" with my Hollywood agents, not bothering to tell them what had just transpired, as I didn't think they'd understand. How many people would? Instead, our conversation revolved around the fact that the William Morris Agency believed I could make millions of dollars if I wanted to focus on that as my main goal in Hollywood. And they were prepared to help me do that. Now, I suppose that proposal would sound like music to most people's ears. But it reminded me of the businessmen who had flown me to New York years ago to meet at the Waldorf Astoria, who were interested in making a twenty-year-old famous by focusing on only one aspect of her abilities. That just seemed boring to me. I knew then that it would stifle my creativity and eventually my joy.

And having just turned twenty-seven, after everything I'd experienced in the past year, I knew myself well enough to realize that simply getting rich was not the answer to happiness and fulfillment. I needed something more. But what, I did not yet know.

I kept thinking of the raven and the gopher. And it suddenly came to me that when I had been in that shower in Split, naked and vulnerable, I was the gopher in that situation, at the mercy of the hungry raven who wanted to rip open the gopher's soft flesh and satiate its appetite. And I resolved never to leave myself open in such a way again. I also wanted to contribute something truly worthwhile to the world before succumbing to the raven's ravenous beak which, let's face it, finally comes for us all. I had a lot to think about. It was time for the sparrow hawk to go home to nest, rest, recuperate, and come up with a plan for the next chapter of my life.

CHAPTER 20

RITA MACNEIL, PRISCILLA PRESLEY, AND A ROCK 'N' ROLL WEDDING

In January of 1987 I returned home to Nova Scotia to spend some time with the family. I had no idea when my next job may be, or what it might entail, so I was pleasantly surprised to receive a phone call from an old friend, Ron Wheatley, offering me a job performing in a musical in Halifax in the new year. I accepted his offer. The show was called *Sleeping Arrangements*, by Andrew MacBean, and we began rehearsals almost immediately.

As usual when performing in Halifax, I took a room at the Lord Nelson Hotel and it was here that I met Canadian singing sensation Rita MacNeil, who hailed from the island of Cape Breton, located at the eastern end of Nova Scotia and joined to the peninsula by a causeway. Cape Bretoners are proud of their island and their Gaelic heritage, and many talented musicians call Cape Breton home. But Rita MacNeil put it squarely on the map with her haunting songs and soaring voice, bringing the home she loved to international attention.

I had seen a poster at the hotel advertising that Rita would be performing at the local bar adjoining the hotel and ever since my dad had first introduced me to her music, I'd become a fan. I therefore decided I could not miss the opportunity of hearing her perform live.

During an intermission between sets Rita and I were introduced by her drummer, John Alphonse, who had played for shows I'd done previously in Halifax. Rita and I hit it off immediately, as it turned out she had seen me perform in movies and TV and loved my work. And thus began another "mutual admiration society" that was to last until her death in 2013.

Not only did I love Rita's voice, but her songs had given me comfort while I was away from home, feeling homesick for my family and Nova Scotia. So I had played her cassette tapes incessantly while stuck in bumper-to-bumper traffic in L.A., or for anyone who would listen.

Not only did Rita and I feel an immediate bond upon our introduction, but the same happened between me and Ralph Dillon (her band director, keyboardist, and album producer) as well. The only way I can describe our first meeting – again thanks to our introduction by John Alphonse at that first gig – would be to say that it was electric and serendipitous.

Soon after our first introduction at Rita's gig, Ralph came to see me perform in my show *Sleeping Arrangements* and invited me back to his apartment on Hollis Street, in the top floor of an historic old Halifax tavern called Ginger's Tavern and Brewery.

I went there that night and never left. What can I say? It was kismet. We were both smitten. I gave my notice at the Lord Nelson and moved into Ginger's with Ralph. It was as if our "sleeping arrangements" had been decided for us.

To be honest, after everything that had happened to me in Croatia, I longed to have a long-term, serious relationship – maybe even marriage – in order to feel safe and secure. A relationship with Ralph, who was nine years older than I and seemed to be balanced, provided the feeling of safety and belonging I truly needed at the time. Being in Halifax meant I was close to many old friends, as well as an hour away from my family and friends in Truro.

Ron Wheatley and I decided to do a second show, an original one-woman musical about Mae West, called *Getting Into Mae,* written and composed by musician Barry Stagg, who had also once written a musical with my dad called *Strike!* which our local CEC high school had performed. So I was happily busy, performing at night and rehearsing by day, and soon was also offered a role in *Something About Love,* a feature film by Stefan Wodoslawsky that was shooting in Cape Breton. I enjoyed shooting on location, playing Stefan's sister, the daughter of Jan Rubeš, whose character had Alzheimer's, with my husband played by comedian

Ron James. It's a beautiful film, one of the first done about the tragedy of Alzheimer's disease.

At the time, my dad, now retired from his job as a professor, was enjoying doing work as an extra in films and TV shot in Nova Scotia, so I got him a job for a couple of days on our film. We loved this time together on set. Dad was excited to be on a film with his daughter playing a leading role, and I was excited to have my dad enter my film world.

I'll never forget the day Dad was on set as an extra during the funeral scene for my film father. My character is leaving the churchyard after her father's funeral, being driven in a black limo, and I was to turn and look back at the graveyard. Well, there was my *real* dad standing at the gravesite with a couple of other extras, yucking it up, and it took all I had to hide the warmth and laughter that bubbled up inside as my black limousine drove away from the funeral. I made a decision then that when the time came that my father would actually die, I would remember this image of him. Sadly, that day finally did arrive, and I can still see my dad in my mind's eye, laughing and carrying on above his own grave.

Upon returning to Halifax after the shoot, Ralph and I began to make music with friends. Like Rita MacNeil, Ralph was a proud Cape Bretoner, as was Leon Dubinsky, whose beautiful song "We Rise Again" has been performed by choirs around the world and famously by fellow Cape Bretoners the Rankins. In pre-Rita days, Leon and Ralph had performed together in the popular Cape Breton band Buddy and the Boys. Leon and his wife Beth were also living at Ginger's and they became good friends of mine. Ralph and I, along with John Alphonse and Ralph's good friends Marilyn Richardson and David Weir, formed a band we called The Carnations, and we performed some gigs around Halifax. It was a total blast.

During the run of *Getting Into Mae*, a director, Walter Learning, came to see the show and asked me afterwards if I'd be interested in going back to the Charlottetown Festival the following summer to play Priscilla Presley in the musical *Are You Lonesome Tonight?* as well as a lead in a new Cliff Jones musical, *Babies*. I agreed immediately since it meant I'd still be working in the region close to both Ralph and my family.

Soon after that, Ralph and I decided to be married on July 26, 1987, and Walter Learning was kind enough to give me ten days off to get married and have a honeymoon in the middle of the summer season. We were married in the First United Church in Truro. My dad proudly walked me down the aisle. The bride and retinue (sister Tamara, school friends Cheryll Sickles and Corrine Cox) wore white and pink and the boys (Ralph, David Weir, David MacQueen, Steve MacDonald, and best man Max MacDonald, who had been lead singer of Buddy and the Boys and co-founder of the Celtic Colours Music Festival in Cape Breton, and the ring bearer, Max's young son Rory MacDonald) wore white suits with pink carnations and pink high-top sneakers.

Rita MacNeil and Frank MacKay both sang in the church, and actor Walter Borden (Order of Nova Scotia and Governor General award recipient) recited a poem written for the occasion. Friends came from near and far, including colleagues from the Charlottetown Festival, and my wonderful friends Dawna Shuman and Courtney Gains came from L.A.

And at the wedding dinner, instead of the Father of the Bride giving a speech, Dad (ever mindful of politics) took the opportunity to give New Democratic Party Leader Alexa McDonough the chance to "give the bride away" with a speech, knowing Truro was considered "the hub" not only of Nova Scotia but of the Conservative Party as well, since it had spawned two Conservative premiers, Robert Stanfield and G.I. Smith. What an opportunity for Alexa with a captive audience of more than three hundred people. Dad was so proud of himself! And since most of our guests were progressive, artistic, and left-wingers anyway, her speech was received enthusiastically.

After dinner what was there to do but hold a great rock 'n' roll party, which went on until the wee hours with Buddy and the Boys playing a reunion concert, Sam Moon stepping up to sing with the band, and Frank MacKay and I performing a duet of "Somewhere Out There." We danced all night.

Later the next day Ralph and I were flown by a family friend in a tiny four-seater plane (with a "Just Married" sign trailing from the tail) from a small airfield in Debert to Les Îles-de-la-Madeleine just north of Prince Edward Island. Before landing, the pilot flew us over the whole island.

The Magdalene Islands are a small archipelago in the Gulf of Saint Lawrence. While they are part of the Province of Quebec, the islands are closer to the Maritime provinces. A picturesque, romantic place, with long, sweeping white sand beaches and where French is spoken, they constitute a part of the Epegwitg aq Pigtug district of traditional Mi'kma'ki, the country of the Mi'kmaw Nation, who call the islands Menagoesenog, meaning "islands battered by the surf."

After a romantic week in the sun-drenched archipelagos, we travelled to Dunvegan, Cape Breton, where our best man, Max MacDonald, and Cape Breton rock legend Matt Minglewood had set up our honeymoon tent, with several plastic pink flamingoes gambolling around it, at MacLeod's Campground. Many of Ralph's friends were there already. Camped out under the stars with a campfire each night, around which we all gathered to play guitars and sing, with rum and Cokes flowing, what a time we had! I fell in love with Cape Breton and its people that week and for many years we went back to Dunvegan as the highlight of each summer.

After our honeymoon, I returned to Prince Edward Island to complete the Charlottetown Festival season, and the following fall and winter I travelled with Ralph and Rita MacNeil as they toured across Canada and around the world. Rita was on fire in those days. Her album *Flying On Your Own*, which Ralph had produced, had gone platinum, so Rita was in great demand, with her popularity growing by the year.

Over the next two years, I travelled with the band to Ireland, Scotland, and England, where Rita sold out the Royal Albert Hall in London. And in 1988, we travelled to Australia where we celebrated Ralph's fortieth birthday and met up in Sydney with my Aussie family and best friend from our Ermington Public Elementary School days, Vivian Burns, with whom who I'd stayed in touch for twenty years. Once we got together it was easy to see why we had been such good mates from the first day in Primary, when I was five and Viv was just four. Good friendships like ours never change.

Upon our return from Australia, Rita and the band also toured across Canada several times, and I accompanied them on a few of these tours. I'll never forget one time in Nelson, British Columbia, when our tour bus sank into a sinkhole. It was crazy. And, of course, with Rita's famous "plus size," you can imagine some of the jokes the band – and Rita herself – came up with for that event.

I remember her story about what inspired her to write her biggest hit, "Flying on Your Own," which she said was about her fear of throwing the quarter (back when it was only a quarter) for the toll in the bucket at the Macdonald Bridge whenever she had to drive to Halifax from Cape Breton. She said she was so scared to do it by herself that she always made sure someone drove her to Halifax so she wouldn't have to throw the money in the bucket.

She always told the story onstage about that before she sang the song. She'd preface it with "You know there are some challenges in life that people find really hard to do – and some things that a person might think nothing of doing, but it would terrify another person. This song is about overcoming one's fears and getting the courage up to do something that scares you, but finally getting the courage to do it anyway." And then she'd say that because of her size she was always terrified she'd miss the bucket and would have to get out of the car and pick up the quarter and people would laugh. But she said she finally got her courage up one day to cross over the bridge by herself and throw the money in the bucket. And when she did that she felt so free – flying over the bridge – she was flying on her own.

Another event I'll never forget took place at the East Coast Music Awards in Sydney, Cape Breton, when a few of us stayed up late partying with Rita one night after a concert and someone – I don't remember who – brought out some acid which we all ended up taking. It was Rita's first time. As band director, Ralph had (wisely) already gone to bed. But Rita was up for a party that night, so a bunch of us stayed up with her, playing guitars and singing until dawn, and even went for an early breakfast at a local diner. When our food came, Rita swore that the eggs on her plate were moving. We told her, "No, Rita, you just have a bit of a buzz on!" She had a good laugh at that.

Touring with Rita and her friend Noreen and the band (Ralph Dillon, Scott Macmillan, John Alphonse, Dave Burton, Al Bennet, Clarence Deveau, Al Macumber, Lisa MacDougall, Bruce Dixon, and Billy McCauley) was exciting and just so much fun for all of us. I'll never forget the camaraderie, the laughs, the crazy adventures, Rita's wonderful fans all around the world, and, of course, Rita MacNeil herself, and her music. While Rita is sadly gone, her energy and spirit live on in her many albums.

CHAPTER 21

UNIDENTIFIED HUMAN REMAINS AND THE TRUE NATURE OF LOVE

In 1990 Ralph and I moved to Toronto, since I had been booking a number of lead roles in film and TV shows that were all shot in Toronto, and my agent at the time, Nancy LeFeaver, suggested it would be beneficial if I moved to the city. I talked about it with Ralph, who was not particularly interested in moving because his gig with Rita meant he didn't need to look for other work. But I did. And there was only so much an actor could do to survive in Nova Scotia. A serendipitous encounter with Ivan Fecan, the head of the Canadian Broadcasting Corporation, at the premiere of Quebec director Denys Arcand's iconic film *Jesus of Montreal* at the Toronto International Film Festival sealed the deal for the move to Toronto.

I had just crashed the party for the film's premiere with another East-coast rebel, award-winning documentary filmmaker John Hopkins (Square Deal Productions), and a couple of Indigenous friends from Six Nations who, like us, had no tickets to the party. However, since we were all dressed up to the nines, hell, we looked like we were in the movie! And John and I were old hands by now at crashing film festival parties. We had learned long ago that, if you don't have a ticket, you just walk in like you own the joint. So the four of us strutted in to this big church where the party was being held, and the doormen welcomed us with open arms.

No sooner had we arrived and found a table than we ran into Ivan Fecan. Ivan and I had met several years before, in 1984, on a bus from Halifax to Truro where *The King of Friday Night* (the screen version of John Gray's musical *Rock and Roll*) was being shot. At the time, I had no idea who Ivan was. But we happened to sit together on the bus and got along famously. I had just arrived home from my trip to the U.S.S.R. with Mummy Marshall, and, since some of Ivan's family roots were Russian, he was interested to hear about my firsthand experience in the country that was still, at that time, behind the Iron Curtain. We discussed the importance of cultural exchanges between nations and had a great discussion about politics in general. It was only once we arrived in Truro that I learned Ivan was producing the show.

I kept an eye on Ivan's career after that and was excited for him when, at the age of thirty-one, he was offered a job in the United States with NBC, serving as their Vice-President of Creative Development for two years, before returning to Canada in 1987 as Director of Television Programming for CBC. Some of the shows Fecan ushered in during his tenure at CBC include *Degrassi High, Road to Avonlea, The Kids in the Hall, Royal Canadian Air Farce*, and *This Hour Has 22 Minutes*, as well as several shows in which I performed.

At the time I ran into him at the *Jesus of Montreal* party, one of my films, *Love and Hate: A Marriage Made in Hell* (now on Turner Classic Movies), had just aired on CBC to great fanfare: rave reviews and huge ratings. Written by Suzette Couture and Maggie Siggins, and directed by Francis Mankiewicz, this two-part miniseries is a true story about narcissistic Conservative politician Colin Thatcher, whose bitter divorce from his wife JoAnn ended up with the court ruling in JoAnn's favour. Thatcher hired a hit man to kill her and, thinking he was above the law, famously bragged, "Why should I pay her alimony when a bullet only costs a dollar?" He also famously told his co-conspirator how to deal with police questions: "Deny, deny, deny."

Kenneth Welsh portrays Colin Thatcher and Kate Nelligan his long-suffering wife, while I play his American girlfriend who, after being brutalized by Thatcher, ends up turning him in to the police and serves as a witness for the prosecution in court. Kenny Welsh was a delight to work with and rightfully won an ACTRA award for his chilling performance as Colin Thatcher.

At the *Jesus of Montreal* party, Ivan Fecan was beaming as he told the folks at my table that he had viewed the show several times throughout its editing process and was absolutely thrilled with the final result. In one of the rare instances of my life, I was tongue-tied, firstly as I was still coming to terms with the fact that we'd managed to pull off our entry at all, secondly because I was not expecting to run into Ivan right away, and thirdly because I was gobsmacked that he was so taken with *Love and Hate* and my performance. However (as usual), John Hopkins was having no trouble talking for both of us. And when he suddenly leaned towards Ivan and said, "Hey, Ivan, I'm curious. Lenore Zann is one of Canada's best actresses. How come she doesn't have her own series on CBC yet?" I was mortified! But I'll never forget what happened next. Ivan just looked at John. Then he looked at me and said, without missing a beat, "Because she hasn't asked for it." And then he added, "I love your work, Lenore. So, if you're interested in following up on this, give my office a call next week and we'll set up a meeting to discuss it." And that was how Ralph and I ended up moving to Toronto.

CBC put me on a retainer for $30,000, which was to cover the costs for our move from Halifax to Toronto and gave CBC the first rights to use me in various CBC productions. This led to another great role in the CBC miniseries *Gross Misconduct: The Life of Brian Spencer* by Paul Gross, directed by Atom Egoyan.

Another true story, this time looking at the darker side of professional sports, *Gross Misconduct* tells the story of the troubled life of Brian "Spinner" Spencer. A boy from a small rural town with dreams of becoming a hockey star, Spinner gained fame early due to his aggressive skating style and a promising career with the Toronto Maple Leafs but struggled to deal with his temper (and alcohol and drug use) on and off the ice, which precipitated a trade to the Pittsburgh Penguins. Spinner trashed the team's name during his first television interview: "*Penguins*? A bunch of stupid little birds? What kind of name is that for a hockey team?" He was abruptly (and unsurprisingly) fired. So he took off to Florida.

And that's where I came in. I happily played his "white trailer-trash" girlfriend, Diane, who helps him go down the tubes – and the series ends with his untimely murder. I loved working with director Atom Egoyan on this project. An actor's director and a real artist, Atom believes in his actors and gives them the license to take risks and try things out in a safe and supportive environment. What a gift!

Later, I was offered a recurring role in the final season of CBC's long-running series *Street Legal.* Nina is a wealthy designer who is married but having an affair with a younger man, a lawyer, Rob Diamond, played by Albert Schultz. While I did pitch some ideas to the CBC drama department for a series of my own, that unfortunately didn't pan out. Regardless, I enjoyed the roles I played and all three of these shows have cast lists that are a veritable Who's Who of Canadian actors. I'm still proud to have participated in these productions and will always be grateful to Ivan Fecan for believing in me.

During this time Ralph was also working for CBC, as a musician in Rita's backup band in a popular weekly variety show, *Rita MacNeil and Friends,* produced by Ivan Fecan's wife, Sandra Faire. So despite Ralph's earlier reluctance, our move to Toronto had proven to be a wise choice since the show was shot each week in Toronto's downtown CBC studio. Unfortunately, while my acting career was now flourishing, Ralph was becoming dissatisfied with his role in Rita's band. As Rita's fame and popularity grew, he felt he was being pushed out of the picture. For one thing, his responsibilities were being diminished. He had begun as the producer of her albums and her band leader only to be replaced by Toronto album producer Declan O'Dougherty. And when Rita went on the road, while Ralph was still a member of her touring band, he was no longer band director. This was soul-crushing for Ralph. Privately he felt very bitter about it, after working with Rita for so many years and helping her get to the top. I tried to convince him to go out and hear other bands in Toronto and find new artists to produce. But he steadfastly refused, spending more and more time alone in his small studio in our home in Toronto's east end. He was not a happy camper during this time. He resented Rita. And he resented me.

While this was going on, though, I was busy with my own career and when I was offered a cool role in a new Canadian play I took it. When I first read Brad Fraser's edgy play *Unidentified Human Remains and the*

True Nature of Love, a voice inside me said, "This play is going to take you to New York." And it did.

I met director Jim Milan and Mackenzie Gray, of Crow's Theatre Company, at an opening night party for a show at Theatre Passe Muraille in Toronto's west end. I was wearing some saucy little number, ordering a drink at the bar upstairs. A handsome, rather rakish guy at the other end of the bar was also waiting for a drink. He looked over at me and called out, "Has anyone ever told you you look a lot like Lenore Zann?"

I laughed and replied, "Yeah, I get that all the time!"

At which point Mackenzie Gray said, "Oh my God! You *are* Lenore Zann, aren't you? ... I don't suppose you would be open to doing a play for a small theatre company for hardly any money?"

To which I replied, "Well, it would depend on the play. I'd be happy to do it if I like the role and the script."

In a nutshell, the play is set in Edmonton, Alberta, where Brad Fraser is from, and where I had portrayed Marilyn Monroe a decade previously. The drama-comedy follows the lives of several sexually frustrated thirty-somethings who are looking for love in all the wrong places. And, meanwhile, a serial killer is terrorizing the city. I was hooked. And that's how my two-year stint doing a live play began.

After I had finished reading the script, I called Mackenzie to say I would be happy to play Candy and asked who they were considering for the male lead. Mackenzie said their number one choice was Brent Carver. Now, I knew Brent and, as it turned out, had plans to see him in Halifax shortly at the Neptune Theatre where he was performing. So I told Mackenzie and Jim I'd be happy to talk to Brent in Halifax and try to convince him to do their show with me – and for the same pay, so that Crow's Theatre could afford us. And that's what transpired.

In 1990 we were raring to go with an absolutely electric cast, and on opening night at the Poor Alex Theatre the energy was so high it was as if we all had been shot out of a cannon. And it never stopped until the very last line, which evoked a stunned silence from the audience every night followed by thunderous applause. The chemistry of that cast was exhilarating and we felt like rock stars every time we came out for the curtain call. The show became an immediate runaway hit for Crow's Theatre and its incredible artistic director Jim Milan and producers

Mackenzie Gray and Nancy MacLeod, with lineups around the block for the whole run.

The exceptional cast in that 1990 Crow's Theatre production in Toronto was as follows:

Brent Carver (David)
Lenore Zann (Candy)
Daniel Kash (Bernie)
Kristina Nicholl (Benita)
Duncan Olleranshaw (Kane)
Arlene Mazzerole (Jerri)
Joe-Norman Shaw (Robert)

Human Remains was controversial for its violence, nudity, frank dialogue, and sexual explicitness. Nevertheless, it received critical acclaim and was named one of the ten best plays of the year by *Time*.

We decided to keep the play running in order to try to get American producers to come see it and take it to New York. In order to do that, it entailed moving the production to another venue, Theatre Passe Muraille, where I had originally met Mackenzie. Brent and some of the other actors decided to move on to other shows at that time too, so we had to keep rehearsing the play in order to replace them. This included the character of Robert, with whom I had a couple of nude love scenes. This meant that I had to work with several different "Roberts" and by the time the Toronto run of the play was over, I'd become immune to both the nudity and the love scenes, although one of the hazards of the job was to try to keep the sex "simulated," which can be hard (pun intended) when two people are naked under a sheet. On the other hand, I stayed with the show throughout the run because I thoroughly enjoyed being back "on the boards" doing live theatre, and I still had a small voice inside telling me that this show would somehow get me to New York.

At some point after running the play for several months, we heard the news we'd been hoping for: after reading the great reviews about our show in the trade papers, American producers had quietly flown into town from New York to see our production. The bad news was that they had made a deal with Brad Fraser's literary agent to produce it in the U.S. themselves. Needless to say, this was a throughly disappointing turn of events for Crow's Theatre and for our dedicated cast, as we had put so much of our effort, goodwill, hope – and our own money – into keeping the show running long enough for American producers to see it. We didn't begrudge Brad Fraser's opportunity to get his play produced in the States. We just wished they'd taken our production instead.

Now, our dreams dashed, we let the show come to its natural conclusion. But as a company we had accomplished something no other independent theatre in Toronto had ever done: no shows except big musicals had ever done open-ended runs before. Crow's Theatre had proved it possible. Now other companies could follow suit. The little engine that could had done it again.

CHAPTER 22

ON WITH THE SHOW: THE POWER OF RADICAL FORGIVENESS

A few weeks after *Unidentified Human Remains and the True Nature of Love* closed at Theatre Passe Muraille, I had gone out for brunch to my favourite haunt on Toronto's Danforth Avenue, The Only Café, when a young waiter came over to take my order. He seemed a little nervous but at the same time excited when he said, "Oh, Ms. Zann, I just have to say, I saw you in *Unidentified Human Remains* recently at Passe Muraille, and you were fantastic! I just loved the show! And I'm going to be working on it in the States!"

My heart lurched. I thanked him for the compliment, asked for his name (James), and what he meant by "working on it." James replied that he'd recently been hired as assistant to the director of the upcoming American production, which he said would be produced in Chicago and later hopefully move to New York. I asked who the director was and he told me Derek Goldby, whom I had never met, but his reputation preceded him.

Australian-born like me, Derek Goldby was an *enfant terrible* of the theatre and had directed productions at the Stratford Festival (Canada's prestigious classical theatre) as well as other major theatres across the country. His biggest success, however, had been on Broadway. He had directed *Rosencrantz and Guildenstern are Dead*, which was nominated for eight Tony Awards and received four, including Best Play. Goldby went on to direct several other productions on Broadway, including *Loot* by Joe Orton.

I immediately asked James if the Chicago production was cast. "No," he replied. "They'll be holding auditions in New York."

So I asked, "Do you think it would be possible for me to audition for my role as Candy?"

To which James replied innocently, "Would you want to?"

"Yes! Absolutely!" I nearly shouted.

Before my eggs Benedict had even been relegated to a recent memory, I had the phone number for Derek Goldby's agent in my hot little hand. I thanked James for the information and, make no mistake, I ran all the way home to phone my agent Nancy LeFeaver, who made the call to Mr. Goldby's agent. It did not take her long to call me back to say that I could audition in New York a couple of weeks later. But I'd have to fly myself down. No problem! I was so excited, I couldn't wait to tell my husband about this marvellous opportunity. But, apart from my agent, he was the only one who knew.

When I stepped onto the plane to New York, the first person I saw already seated was Brent Carver. He told me the American producers were flying him down to audition for the lead role of David, which he'd played so incredibly in our first Crow's Theatre production at the Poor Alex (for which he had also won a Toronto Theatre Award for Best Performance).

Wow, I thought. They must be really interested in Brent if they're paying for his flight. They didn't offer to fly me in. This thought made me more nervous than I was already. But on with the show!

I had booked a hotel within walking distance of the studio where *Human Remains* auditions would be held. I had arrived early, with lots of time before my audition at 4:00 that afternoon. However, to make sure I knew where to go, I took a taxi from the airport directly to the studio.

I got into the elevator, which was crammed full of other young hopefuls, to the floor where auditions were being held, and the elevator doors opened onto a scene straight from *A Chorus Line.*

The hallway was chock full of actors, dancers, and singers all preparing at the same time for different auditions for multiple productions. This is New York! "Start spreading the news ..."

Once I found the right room where the *Human Remains* auditions had already begun, a stage manager came out of the room to call for the next actor, so I politely asked if he could confirm my audition slot. When I told him my name, he said, "Oh! You're early. Stay here please, the director wants to speak to you." What in the name of God could he want? I thought, instantly even more nervous.

The next thing I knew, out came an older man who looked rather like a mad professor, wearing a rumpled suit jacket and jeans, with spiky hair and glasses, whom I assumed was Derek Goldby.

"Right! Good! You're early! Look, you know this play inside out – better than anyone – so would you mind coming in and being our reader for the rest of the day?"

My heart sank. I said, "But ... Mr. Goldby, I haven't even been to my hotel yet. I need to change and get ready for my own audition."

He gave me a befuddled look. "What? What audition? What on earth do you mean?"

Now I was worried. There seemed to have been a mix-up of some sort. I thought, Maybe it's because I'm Canadian. Maybe they won't let me audition after all.

I tried not to let my fears show as I said, trying to sound calm, "Well, Mr. Goldby, I was told I could audition for Candy, the role I played in Toronto. My time slot is four this afternoon."

Now Mr. Goldby said, "Oh no, no, no. You don't have an audition slot. You don't have to audition. We saw you in the play. You're brilliant! It's just that one of the producers didn't get to see the show in Toronto so we wanted him to meet you. You already got the part!"

Well. You could have knocked me over with a feather. I was so excited I could barely believe my good fortune.

However, back in Toronto, my husband, Ralph, was not happy. When I called him immediately to share the good news, Ralph responded, "You could have asked me first."

I was flabbergasted. I thought he'd be happy for me. Why on earth would I have flown to New York if I wasn't going to accept the role if I was lucky enough to be cast in the American production? Needless to say, this was the beginning of the end of my marriage to Ralph.

We did the run in Chicago, but Brent Carver was not cast in the lead male role of David. A New York-based actor, Scott Renderer, was chosen instead. I was the only Canadian actor cast in the American production. Rehearsals began in Chicago in early January of 1991. The production was received well, so we ran for several months, and later that year we received word we would be moving to New York, to the Orpheum Theatre, off Broadway. It was a dream come true.

And that's how my instincts were proven correct that *Unidentified Human Remains and the True Nature of Love* – the little play that could – would eventually get me to New York.

The New York cast included actor-writer-director Clark Gregg as Bernie (with Gregg best known for playing Shield agent Phil Coulson in films and television series set in the Marvel Cinematic Universe). When Clark left the show to perform in another play, I was happy to suggest Canadian actor Daniel Cash to replace him as Daniel had been our original Bernie in the Poor Alex production in Toronto.

Throughout the production I thoroughly enjoyed working with one of my favourite actors, Sam Rockwell, who played my boyfriend Robert, with whom I had several intense onstage love scenes. And, as directed by Derek Goldby, both of us appeared completely nude, without even a sheet between us and the audience. Sam was a dedicated and serious actor and I loved working with him. I had no doubt that he would go far, so it did not surprise me when he earned two Screen Actors Guild awards, a Golden Globe, and an Academy Award as Best Supporting Actor for his portrayal of troubled police deputy Jason Dixon in Martin McDonagh's moving crime drama *Three Billboards Outside Ebbing, Missouri*. Sam continues to take on very interesting roles to which he brings his wonderful zany personality and multilayered nuances. Since working together in the play in 1991 I've had the pleasure of seeing Sam perform in a couple of plays in New York as well, and he is always generous with his time to reconnect after the shows.

All in all, I ended up performing in Brad Fraser's *Unidentified Human Remains and the True Nature of Love* in basically back-to-back productions for two years from that first hit show in Toronto and subsequent second run, to the run in Chicago and ultimately New York. I enjoyed performing in each and every production and I am grateful to have shared the stage and dressing rooms with so many amazing cast members. But I must admit that my truly favourite acting partner of all time was our Canadian legend Brent Carver – that mysterious, ephemeral, mercurial, powerful sprite who went on to win a Tony Award for his breathtaking performance starring opposite Chita Rivera in *Kiss of the Spider Woman* on Broadway.

In January 2024, Chita Rivera passed away. She joins our beloved Brent, who we tragically lost in 2020 during the Covid-19 pandemic. Many of us were suffering from depression and anxiety to a greater or lesser extent. Sadly, Brent's mental health failed him during this time.

It was a terrible time when professional performers were unable to do the work they loved. I can understand how difficult it was for this great lion of the theatre to feel stuck in a cage, unable to perform onstage where he felt most at home and could truly be himself. He must have felt so very desperate and lonely, unable to see that light at the end of the tunnel. And I can only say, "There but for the grace of God go I." I'm sure some who are reading this can also relate. If you do, my message is simple: Don't give up.

Throughout all of the iterations of *Human Remains*, my favourite theatre director was Jim Milan, who really gave us room to explore our characters and grow with each new version of the play. Performing the same play nightly has its pluses, but when you do live theatre, your entire life really must revolve around the fact that you have a show to do at the end of the day. So when most people are going home after work, your job is only just beginning. I'm sure that's why I'm a night owl; once the sun goes down, my energy is just revving up. New York suited me that way as "the city that never sleeps." I gave my all to the show and was rewarded by getting a great talent agent, Bill Butler, from the William Morris Agency, who offered to represent me after attending a performance.

Doing live theatre is wonderful too because you meet so many other incredible actors who come to see your show and, when you're not performing, you reciprocate by seeing their shows as well. It's like we belong to a huge theatre family – a place of "found kinship," which is so comforting as many actors felt like outsiders growing up and just wanting to "belong."

It was in this way that I met another of my favourite actors, Giancarlo Esposito, who was performing with the Atlantic Theatre Company in the play that Clark Gregg left our show to do. I had already seen Giancarlo in several films by one of my all-time favourite filmmakers, Spike Lee: *School Daze* (1988), *Do the Right Thing* (1989), and *Mo' Better Blues* (1990). But he is now likely best known for playing Gus Fring in the AMC crime drama series *Breaking Bad*, from 2009 to 2011, as well as in its prequel series *Better Call Saul*, from 2017 to 2022. For this role, he won the Critics' Choice Television Award for Best Supporting Actor in a Drama Series (2012) and earned three Primetime Emmy Award nominations for Outstanding Supporting Actor in a Drama Series. Giancarlo has done many other great roles as well, including in *The Mandalorian* (Disney+) and most recently portraying Sidewinder, the leader of the villainous Serpent Society in the new Marvel film, *Captain America: Brave New World*.

Giancarlo and I hit it off immediately and would often get together between shows on the weekends to talk and walk through Central Park to discuss theatre, politics, our own lives, hopes and dreams, and the events that had made us who we were. Giancarlo was gracious, curious, and open-hearted and we admitted to each other that above all else we were on spiritual missions to find peace of mind and serenity.

Neither of us were drinking either, which was great since it was while performing in *Human Remains* that I finally began to admit that I had a problem with alcohol; before that I was in denial. Since the age of sixteen when I first began performing in professional shows, I had become so used to "life in the theatre" – of going out after shows every night to eat and drink with my play colleagues or friends who had come to see the show – I didn't know any other life. But during that last year of *Human Remains* in New York I was trying a new way of living. And it wasn't easy.

So meeting Giancarlo and trusting each other enough to share our stories of past traumas and spiritual things was good for both of us. While clearly attracted to each other, we were both in relationships at the time, so we enjoyed a platonic friendship that was very supportive, healing, and full of light and laughter – and also some tears.

It was while lying in the grass in the large public meadow at the heart of Central Park, watching big puffy white clouds drift idly across the sky, that we shared some of our trauma stories and Giancarlo shared that he had gone through tough times with a father who was bullying and abusive, so he was actively healing from generational trauma.

Sadly, he would also go through tough times in the years to come and has publicly admitted in recent years to suffering from depression and becoming so desperate at one point both emotionally and financially (during a period when acting work had dried up) that he even considered suicide before landing his life-changing role in *Breaking Bad*. He now calls this turning point a "godsend" and the "light at the end of the tunnel."

I can relate.

I've seen Giancarlo a couple of times recently and was glad of the opportunity to tell him how happy I am that he has found both critical success and the peace of mind he was searching for so many years ago. After taking part in an *X-Men '97* panel at the 2024 San Diego Comic Con, we saw each other again at a private Marvel Studios party. It had also just been announced that Giancarlo would be playing Sidewinder in Marvel's new movie, *Captain America: Brave New World*. At the party we shared a laugh and a high-five as we shook our heads in amazement. After all, there we were in the thick of it, with Harrison Ford and Marvel boss Kevin Feige, who I also congratulated on the humongous success of our series and his recently rereleased film, *Deadpool & Wolverine*.

I mean, what are the odds that two theatre kids who had spent a lifetime overcoming trauma, honing our craft as actors, and aiming our bows at the stars, while just wanting to feel that we are "enough" just as we are, had somehow managed to become pop culture icons since those days lying in the grass in Central Park sharing our fears, hopes, and dreams?

It's something I'm sure many would love to experience. And all I can say is thank you to all who have helped me along the way. My cup is overflowing. And I just hope I can inspire others to follow their dreams and also do the hard emotional work that is necessary to overcome the many traumas and challenges along the way.

Once the play ended our run in New York it was time to go home to Toronto, where Jim Milan invited me to play Candy once again in a touring production of the play with a few of our original Poor Alex cast members. We travelled first to the Manitoba Theatre Centre, followed by a theatre festival in Mexico City (El Grand Ciudad de Mexico), where we were feted by feminist Bernie in our *Human Remains* tour. I also landed numerous guest roles in TV series like *Robo Cop* (with my first boyfriend, Charles Page Fletcher, starring in the title role), films such as *Cold Sweat,* and radio and TV voice-overs.

Upon returning to Toronto after all these adventures abroad I have to say, looking back, that it was really hard to return to a "regular" life back home living with a husband. It eventually became obvious that Ralph and I were no longer compatible and our relationship had become toxic. While I blame myself for much of it – having become, like the song, a "Wild Thing," Ralph, meanwhile, had become a "cranky old man" as he tried desperately to control my drinking – and control me. As any twelve-step group member of AA or Al-Anon can tell you, judging, nagging, criticizing, and attacking an addict either verbally or physically will not stop their addictive behaviour. It only makes things worse.

Experts say, "Alcoholism is a family disease" and that co-dependence is an underlying factor of the problem, because family members of alcoholics can become "control freaks" and therefore as un-balanced as the person with the addiction since they focus so much of their time trying to control the addict's behaviour (and basically every-thing and everyone around them) instead of focusing on their own life. I've seen this scenario play out myself, numerous times. In the case of my marriage, we were very sick individuals and our marriage was similarly unhealthy. But like a card game, you can only play the hand you're dealt, with the knowledge, skill, and emotional maturity you happen to possess. My husband and I had enjoyed a great life together – until it wasn't.

Ralph Dillon passed away in November 2022 and I can say with conviction that if it wasn't for Ralph, Rita MacNeil would never have become famous, and the world would have missed hearing her incred-ible music. Many others helped Rita along the way, including brilliant musicians Scott Macmillan, Gordie Sampson, and her manager, Brookes Diamond. But it was Ralph who put her on the map.

Upon hearing that he was in hospital in Sydney, Cape Breton, with stage four cancer, I called Ralph from Los Angeles to share a powerful dream I had received about a week before I'd even heard of his illness. In the dream, we met up in a place full of golden light and he was bopping around, happy and busy performing. Then he turned and his face lit up when he saw me. We gave each other the warmest hug and I remember thinking that, outside of my family, I had not received a hug full of real love like that for years. As Ralph and I hugged in my dream, we told each other that we still loved each other and forgave one another for all of the hurt we had caused each other.

In real life, on the phone, Ralph sounded weak but very happy to hear from me. Then I asked him to forgive me for "any and all past hurts I ever caused in our marriage" and he responded, with a catch in his voice, that he did, and asked if I would also forgive "any and all past hurts" he had caused me. I forgave him as well. Then we both cried and agreed it was time to put the past behind us and to cherish the good times. I told him I'd recorded some of the songs we had written together and would be including them on a new album, to be called *Strong Enough*.

At one point Ralph heard water in the background and said, "Hey, Kookaburra, are you in the bathtub, or somethin'?"

"Uhh, no ... Actually, I'm in a jacuzzi on my friend's rooftop in Hollywood watching the sun go down."

He chuckled at that and said, "Well, I guess some things never change," and we had a good laugh together. Then I sent him "a hug and unconditional love across the miles" from that rooftop in Hollywood, and he sent me the same from a hospital bed in the Palliative Care unit in Cape Breton, Nova Scotia. A couple of weeks later I received word that Ralph had "slipped the surly bonds of Earth." I was grateful I'd had the dream, grateful to old friends Kathy MacGuire and Max MacDonald (Best Man at our rock 'n' roll wedding) for contacting me about Ralph's illness, and so glad I had called to put things right between us. It's called radical forgiveness. It doesn't cost much but it sets your soul free.

Rest in peace, Ralph, old friend and lover. Your memory and your music, like Rita MacNeil's, live on.

CHAPTER 23

THE UNCANNY X-MEN

In 1992 I was cast in the role of Rogue for a new American animated show, *X-Men: The Animated Series*. I auditioned for the role in Toronto and, while I skipped the first auditions (because I considered myself a "serious actor," don't you know!), I was eventually convinced by my agent to show up for the call-backs. There was a lot of secrecy surrounding the show; we were told we were auditioning for "Project X" as far as I can remember.

As Elaine, my voice agent at the time, said, "Lenore, they have not been able to find the right actress to play this role yet – because it's *you*. Just get yourself down to the studio and audition!"

Elaine was right. She had also explained that the producers in L.A. were looking for "an actress with a low, husky, sexy voice who can do a Southern accent." I had just completed my first animated series ever called *Stunt Dawgs*, playing Sizzle, another character with a Southern accent, so I wasn't worried about the accent. And when I got to the studio, I took one look at the drawing of Rogue they showed us, in her classic Rogue stance with one hand on her hip and a sassy attitude, red hair flowing with that white stripe up the middle, and I thought, "Hell, yeah – I can do that!"

When I went into the studio I could hear the folks in L.A. in my headphones. I stated my name and the talent agency who repped me, and simply launched into the short monologue that had been provided, as written. I still remember it verbatim to this day.

"My daddy like to kill himself when he found out I was a *mutant*! I 'member, I had me a boyfriend when I was thirteen. Had me a boyfriend 'til I kissed 'im. Poor boy went into a coma for three days! Got so if I touched anybody, it just drove the life right outta them ... You know everythin', Beast. What makes us like the way we are, anyway?"

There was silence when I finished. Then suddenly I heard screams and shrieks coming through my headphones from the grown men in L.A. I didn't know what to do. Then came a voice saying, "That's her! That's Rogue! Don't let her leave the building!"

It took thirty years before I found out that was the voice of Larry Houston, the original director of our '90s series. But I'm proud to say this amazingly gifted artist, director, Emmy Award nominee, Inkpot Award winner, and Hollywood's first African American Saturday morning storyboard artist has since become one of my best friends.

X-Men: The Animated Series debuted on October 31, 1992, on the Fox Network as part of the Fox Kids Saturday morning lineup. Loosely adapted from famous storylines and events in the X-Men comics by Stan Lee and Jack Kirby, such as the Dark Phoenix Saga, and Days of Future Past, the series is about "The X-Men, a band of mutants who use their uncanny gifts to protect a world that hates and fears them." It features a team akin to that of the early 1990s X-Men comic books: Wolverine (voiced by Cal Dodd), Cyclops (Norm Spencer), Rogue (Lenore Zann), Storm (Alison Sealy-Smith), Gambit (Chris Potter), Jean Grey (Catherine Disher), Beast (George Buza), Jubilee (Alyson Court), Morph (Ron Rubin), Nightcrawler (Adrian Hough), and Professor Xavier (Cedric Smith).

The first season of thirteen episodes was unique for an animated series because it was the first time a studio had allowed a continuing narrative that flowed from one episode to the next, a coup for Larry Houston and his producers. However, once season three began airing, most episodes (except for multipart stories) were shown in random order. Over the course of our five seasons, we also did couple of cross-over appearances with *Spider-Man* in episodes "The Mutant Agenda" and "The Mutants' Revenge."

X-Men: The Animated Series ended with the episode "Graduation Day," which aired on September 20, 1997. By that time, our show was the longest-running Marvel animated series, lasting for six years, with five seasons and a total of seventy-six episodes until the record was beaten by the airing of one (seventy-seventh) episode of *Ultimate Spider-Man* in 2015.

Over the past thirty years *X-Men: The Animated Series* has become one of the top two animated series of all time and laid the foundation for Marvel's multibillion dollar "mutant" franchise globally. It's hard to believe now, but in the beginning when Larry Houston first shopped around his idea for the show, none of the studios in Hollywood wanted to make it. Larry says now, they just "didn't think a show about superheroes could be successful." Boy, were they wrong. It took a woman to make it happen: Margaret Loesch, who had just become president of Fox Kids Network. And the rest is history.

I believe the series endures because of its universal themes and storylines, and the fact that we never talked down to kids. Instead, our show is thought-provoking, reflecting social justice issues including civil rights, bigotry, tolerance, and equality – issues which, sadly, are still relevant today.

I'm often asked why Rogue is such a unique and popular character. The answer is complicated – just like the character – but from the very beginning, I have related to Rogue as if she was written for me. I have heard from many fans from around the world who say they love Rogue because although she is a kick-ass superhero (after all, she *is* the strongest woman in the Universe), they deeply relate to her vulnerability. I do too.

Rogue is universal in that way. Like many legendary, mythological heroes of old, Rogue is a hero with an Achilles heel, a unique vulnerability that could prove deadly. However, in Rogue's case, her greatest strength is also her Achilles heel. That's because Rogue, who exudes confidence, ease, sexuality, and a great sense of humour, is, at the same time, afraid to get too close to anyone because her unique ability to absorb their superpowers – thus becoming even stronger than ever – can also drain them of their life force as well. So Rogue can never touch anyone physically, skin to skin, which means she can never be intimate with someone. She can never allow herself to fall in love because, from past experience, if she was to let her emotions get the best of her, she can cause them serious injury – even death. Rogue can never let her guard down but must always remain vigilant, never able to give all of herself to anybody, which makes her a bit of a loner. And also very lonely.

Although it's clear she has deep feelings for her fellow X-Men colleague, that dashing Cajun, Remy LeBeau (Gambit), she knows better than anyone that she can never get too close (literally and figuratively) because she's afraid that loving Remy would kill him. There are other layers to Rogue as well, since deep down she doubts her own self-worth, and at times even hates herself. I'd say that's because she was given the message at an early age that if people knew her for who she *really* was, she would be rejected. She believed she was not worthy of love, and that no matter what she did or how hard she tried, she would never be "good enough." Again, I can relate.

In fact, I think this is a quality of Rogue's to which many people can relate. The pain of not being "good enough," of not being accepted as we are by our families, peers, or society, while desiring simply to *belong* is universal. That's why people join clubs, churches, and sports teams, and why lonely youth can fall prey to becoming gang members or joining cults. In all these cases, the human need to belong to a "tribe" or community is very strong. Rogue also feels a deep sense of guilt and shame for past actions, for the harm she has done to others – like Ms. Marvel – before joining the X-Men. It's something else that Rogue and I have in common. And guilt and shame, left untreated, can become toxic, turning into self-loathing, which can in turn be extremely destructive if we are unable or unwilling to face our own demons. Some people will act out and project their toxic shame and fear on others, while some turn it inwards, choosing the path of self-destruction, which can manifest as unhealthy compulsive behaviour or addiction, including extreme risk-taking.

Until we do the hard work of peeling back the multiple skins of our own onion to learn what makes us angry, afraid, and ultimately deeply sad, we cannot reach a place where we can even attempt to forgive those who have hurt us. But once we reach that place of forgiveness, we must next be willing to forgive ourselves. And that, my friends, can be the hardest part of all. Yet this is the path we must take if we are to finally love and accept ourselves as we are. Both Rogue and I ultimately managed to face our own demons to find healing, although, let's be clear, the pilot light is always on, so it's an ongoing process.

You know, when X-Men fans from around the world tell me that they hear my voice in their heads as Rogue when they read the comics, and that my portrayal of this character and our show changed their lives, helping them through tough times as kids, by giving them *hope*, I am overwhelmed. It brings tears to my eyes that something I am part of could have such a profound effect on so many. If only I had known back in the '90s just what a tremendous impact we were having on kids around the world, I wonder if I would have made different choices. I wonder too if our colleague Norm Spencer, the original voice of Cyclops, would be alive today had he known of the outpouring of love for our series. However, life is what happens while we are busy making other plans. And the trick to finding and holding onto joy and serenity is to accept what *is*, not what might have or could have been.

CHAPTER 24

LOSING THE PLOT
AND GOING ROGUE

Because there was no social media, Wikipedia, or even an internet in the 1990s, after several seasons of *X-Men*, our cast still had absolutely no idea of how successful our show had become. It was as if we were performing in a vacuum. Although fan mail addressed to us from around the world was piling up at Fox Studios in Los Angeles, nobody bothered to tell us, let alone forward it to our agents in Canada. Each year after we finished a season, we were told that was it; even the writers in L.A. were laid off after every season, so nobody ever knew if we'd be back for another season or not.

While I was still working pretty steadily as an actor, I was experiencing a greater and greater degree of frustration at playing similar roles, and a free-floating anxiety interspersed with panic attacks. I woke up every morning with a feeling of impending doom, like I was in a dark tunnel that was getting smaller and smaller, with no light at the end. My drinking increased exponentially, and I see now this was a way of self-medicating. It became a vicious cycle: I drank to deal with my anxiety, and my anxiety increased due to my drinking. It was on a trip to Cuba in the mid '90s with my husband Ralph, sister Tamara, and Brad, her then-boyfriend, that I really lost the plot.

I can remember now that I became particularly agitated after the Balkan war had broken out in Yugoslavia and news reports began coming out about the horrendous sectarian violence and a violent campaign of ethnic cleansing that was taking place in the country of my ancestors, including in Croatia, where the war raged on from 1991 to 1995. My drinking escalated in tandem.

I would often just stop in my tracks as I was walking down the street when I'd see a story splashed across the front page of the *Toronto Star*, *The Globe and Mail,* or *The New York Times* in a newspaper stand. I'd catch myself standing still as if in a trance, reading the front pages over and over. I couldn't get the images out of my mind. It was so horrendous, in particular the stories of women being kept in sex camps or raped in front of their families, and their husbands being murdered right in front of them.

It was then that I began having a recurring nightmare of being in a war zone with the young guy who raped me in Split ten years before. In my dream he was wearing a soldier's uniform, brandishing a sword in one hand while holding up a papaya in the other. Next he would place the fruit on the stump of a tree in front of me and split it open with his sword, then empty his semen into it. The papaya, split open, was shaped like a woman's ovaries.

I'd wake up in a sweat, shaking.

Looking back now, I find myself wondering once again why I never thought of getting psychological counselling for something that was clearly PTSD. All I can say is that I was so full of toxic shame and self-disgust that I did not, could not, would not bring myself to share the story of what had happened in Croatia with anyone. If I never talked about it, then it never happened, right? Wrong.

What brought me to my knees was that trip to Cuba with Ralph, Tamara, and Brad when I tried unsuccessfully to commit suicide. To this day I'm deeply sorry for the pain I put them through on that terrible trip. What should have been a fun vacation was a total nightmare – more for them than for me because I was already living in a nightmare. I was a runaway train with no brakes.

On this particular trip to Cuba, a place that had formerly always brought me joy, I was drunk every day to the point that my family did not want to be around me because my behaviour embarrassed them. And each night they'd wonder where I was as I'd go drinking by myself in bars and clubs all over the place. One night, very late, they found me at a bar once owned by Al Capone, doing a striptease to the Joe Cocker song "You Can Leave Your Hat On." I'm told that when Ralph tried to drag me out of the bar, a fight broke out because the male patrons didn't want me to leave.

I don't remember any of it.

I also don't remember walking down the middle of the street after that into oncoming traffic – although I fuzzily remember hoping to get hit by a car – but I'm told I hauled off and punched my sister in the face when she tried to pull me out of the way. Me, who had never hit anyone in my life. (Although in Grade Two I did shove a kid and kick him because he made fun of my best friend Vivian, who had a deformed finger, and he made her cry).

But who was this madwoman in Cuba? Even I didn't recognize myself anymore.

Finally, one night near the end of our stay, on a night when the moon was full, I decided to put an end to the madness. I just couldn't stand the pain anymore and I saw no way out. So I went to the beach by myself and drank a bottle of Havana Club and swallowed a bottle of sleeping pills. Then I took all my clothes off and swam out to sea, hoping to drown.

Needless to say, it didn't work. As I swam and swam around, I seemed to become more and more energized. It seemed like the moon was filling me with energy and vitality, and it was really starting to piss me off that my constitution appeared to be just too strong to kill. After what seemed like hours, I finally got bored with swimming around waiting to die, so I swam back to shore. And promptly passed out.

I woke up in my hotel room the next day covered in puke. It was all over the bed, and even on the walls. I had no idea how I got there. But apparently hotel staff had found me and brought me to my room. Ralph was gone; he told me later he'd become disgusted when I started vomiting and had moved to another room. My sister was also disgusted with me.

I don't blame them. Most people would have no idea how to handle an alcoholic who is out of control and hitting bottom. That's why it usually takes a sober alcoholic to help one who is still active. We don't judge; we empathize. Because we've been there. That is why I often say, "There but for the grace of God go I."

But not to put too fine a point on it, I was one hot mess. I was ashamed and broken and disappointed to find myself still alive when all I really wanted was to die. I never did tell Ralph or my family that I had attempted suicide that night. They just assumed it was yet another "wasted day and wasted night" of drinking. And maybe the puking saved my life. While I hadn't drowned I also didn't end up overdosing on sleeping pills and booze – my body had expelled them naturally. I was lucky too that when I passed out, I hadn't drowned in my own vomit. Otherwise, my family would have had to take me back home in a body bag.

Needless to say, I am not proud of these actions, and, for many years, I was full of shame. But as I've said before, shame is not a healthy state of mind, and can become toxic if left untreated. As we say in twelve-step recovery programs, "You're as sick as your secrets."

Even after sobriety is gained, forgiveness by an addict's family can take time. And we are powerless over the thoughts, feelings, and behaviour of others. So as long as we clean up our side of the street by taking responsibility for our own actions and making amends for past behaviour, we have done our part and are on the road to recovery and the serenity that brings. It is up to the families of addicts to realize this as well and get help to stop their own controlling behaviour – which is also compulsive in nature – so they too can find peace of mind.

Old wounds are hard to heal, and scars in families can run deep. I've made amends to mine, but even yet I feel a profound sense of sadness and loss. However, in recent years, as I've done ancestral research into our family history, unearthing medical and death certificates, I've been shocked to discover just how rampant alcoholism has been in past generations on both sides of the family tree, leading to many early deaths. And while this must have been very hard on the families, this knowledge has helped me come to terms with my own disease, as it is clearly inherited. It's not a choice. In the words of Lady Gaga, I was born this way.

However, upon returning to Toronto after that fateful trip to Cuba, while I was reaching the bottom in my drinking journey, I was not yet ready, willing, or able to quit. I just couldn't hide my disease anymore, and my agent and friends were worried. I'll always be grateful to close friends like Ferne Downey, playwrights David French (*Salt Water Moon, Leaving Home*), Paul LeDoux (*Fire, Dream a Little Dream*), and filmmaker

Don Shebib (*Goin' Down the Road*, *Change of Heart*), who did their best to help when I needed it most.

Finally, I realized I was at a turning point. If I was even to attempt to get sober, I didn't think I could do it in Toronto where I had so many drinking buddies and favourite watering holes to avoid. I also knew I couldn't do it in Nova Scotia because I couldn't bear the thought of bringing them any more grief. So I bought a one-way airline ticket to Los Angeles and got a hotel room at the Bayside Motel by the beach in Santa Monica, determined to either end my life for good or get sober and, at the time, I really didn't care which. I just knew it had to be one or the other – no in-betweens.

For the first couple of weeks in L.A., I did nothing but walk along the beach by myself, drinking every day, and eating nothing but vanilla ice cream with chocolate chips. That was the only kind of "food" I was able to keep down. And my drink of choice was champagne and vodka. I lost a lot of weight. I didn't see it then, but at the time I was the same age as Marilyn Monroe when she died at thirty-six (also in Santa Monica) back in 1962. Naked, alone, and lonely, Marilyn had died from what was very likely the same disease, culminating in an overdose of booze and pills. Ironically, I had already acted out her death scene at the ripe age of twenty. Now here I was about to re-enact it in real life.

At night when I'd tumble into bed, I dreamt that a monster was chasing me. I was terrified it was going to catch up with me. For many nights in a row this nightmare haunted me. Until one day when I woke up, sweating profusely, I realized the monster was *me*. And that really gave me something to think about on my daily sojourn to the sea.

After a couple of weeks, I had a dream that I was standing in the bottom of a very deep pit, unable to climb out. But suddenly my great-uncle Ambrose appeared, peering over at the top of the pit, his hand outstretched. I tried to climb up the wall to his outstretched hand when I realized I had on a huge backpack that was holding me back. "Come on! You can do it! I'll help you!" Uncle Ambie called out.

"But," I said, forlornly, "I can't. I've got too much baggage. It's too heavy!" Then Uncle Ambie said the magic words that I needed to hear.

"Just let it go. Drop it. You don't need that baggage anymore."

And I awoke to another sunny day in Santa Monica, still feeling like ten pounds of shit in a five-pound bag, but knowing I'd had a real "Aha!" moment. I knew what must be done.

CHAPTER 25

THE CURE

Beachwood Canyon, Los Angeles, April 2024.

> "All life is interrelated – all men connected by an inescapable network of mutuality tied in a single garment of destiny. Whatever affects one directly affects all indirectly. I can never be what I am meant to be until you are what you are meant to be. And you can never be what you are meant to be until I am what I am meant to be. This is the interrelated structure of reality."
>
> – Dr. Martin Luther King, Jr.

As I write this, I'm back in one of my old haunts: in Beachwood Canyon, in a little apartment nestled high in the trees, not far from the Beachwood Café where my friend Dawna and I used to go for brunch when we lived down the street, on Cheremoya Avenue. With the Hollywood sign above, the Beachwood has always been a great spot to hang out, eat, and people watch. While it's had its highs and lows over the years like most long-running establishments (and most of us who are also long-running), it's currently trendy once more, thanks to Harry Styles, who wrote a song about it.

As I look around at the other patrons, some of them clearly young actors, excited and full of hope, I find myself thinking back to when I was here in my twenties, excited, naive, and ready for action. Had I known the difficult road ahead, would I have continued?

Hell, yeah!

Nothing worthwhile is a walk in the park. And while my life has certainly had its challenges, the things I craved most were never monetary, not fame and fortune. They were ephemeral things like experience, knowledge, wisdom, a desire to belong, to be respected, and to love and be loved enduringly.

At one point when I was in my early twenties, I remember waking up out of a blackout drunk and telling my young sister, Tamara, when she was still a teenager, "Life is a roller coaster. You've just got to hang on!" I scared the shit out of her that morning, rising up in my bed out of a dead sleep like that (a bit like *The Exorcist* but without the pea soup). Terrified, the poor kid ran downstairs to tell our parents, so Dad had to come up and give me a talking to. From this and other experiences, I decided early on that it was best for me not to have children of my own because, A) I suspected I was an alcoholic and didn't want to burden my children with it, and B) because I was afraid that if anything bad ever happened to a child of mine, I would be so destroyed, I wouldn't be able to handle it.

And while I was always searching for my self, and the meaning of existence, I was also searching for a true soulmate who was compassionate and kind, but also strong enough to provide a sense of calm, safety, and protection that I had never known with any man other than my father.

But after all my searching, by April of 1996, I found myself at a crossroads. And, like a moth to a flame, I was drawn to L.A., as if this City of Angels was a crucible calling me to come and, like a proverbial sorcerer, pour in all of my elements, heating them up to such a fever pitch that the gold inside me would separate, like magic, from the other base metals obscuring its gleam.

Now keep in mind, Los Angeles is a city that can make or break people. Success and money are on display everywhere. But so is poverty, desperation, and despair. So it's not the kind of place you'd really choose to hit bottom. Well, I've always played the odds and, like Rogue and Gambit in *X-Men*, the odds have usually been in my favour. Not always, mind you, but often enough to continue rolling the dice.

And so it was that on April 11, 1996, I awoke at the Bayside Hotel in Santa Monica, not sure if I would live or die – and not caring which – but for some reason I knew that particular morning deep in my soul that a paradigm shift was about to occur. I had no idea whether it was for good or bad, but I just knew I was on the threshold of change.

I crawled out of bed, squinting at the bright sunlight outside my window, and lurched into the bathroom to perform what had become a morning ritual. There were only two choices to be made each time I opened my eyes. Similar to Hamlet's pithy question, mine went something like this: "To drink? Or to puke? That is the question." That's what my life had become. Every. Single. Morning. Don't think it was a choice. It wasn't. Not by a long shot. It was simply what I *had* to do. A compulsion. And it didn't matter which action came first, the other would immediately follow.

That morning the action I chose was "Puke."

I was on my knees at the white porcelain throne, puking my guts out (what little I had in my stomach), when I suddenly noticed the white toilet was filling with ruby red blood. My blood. That's the first time that had happened in all my years of drinking. And my immediate reaction was a dark, masochistic smile because it meant I was closer to my goal of destroying myself than I'd ever been. I wasn't afraid of death. I was afraid of life!

But after that initial reaction, a new thought floated into my consciousness, unbidden: that at this rate, it would be relatively easy to continue on this path barrelling towards death, but wouldn't the braver choice be to *live*, and face my fears? And I asked myself, "How do you cure a sickness of the soul?"

Then suddenly I remembered an episode from *X-Men: The Animated Series* called "The Cure," which I had recorded in our very first season. It's one where Rogue almost gives up everything in the reckless hope of being "cured" of her mutant powers so that she can be "normal" and able to love and be loved, like everyone else. But by the end of the episode Rogue has an epiphany, like a lightning bolt from the Universe, or St. Paul on his horse. She realizes that it is her unique superpowers that actually make her who she is, and that in order to cure her own soul sickness, she must embrace her powers and accept herself for who she is, just as she is. And use her powers for good. In this way, Rogue has what I would call a spiritual awakening, a deep inner shift in consciousness and the innate knowledge that comes with it: that she has a greater purpose in the Universe than just herself.

That's what happened to me in that hotel bathroom in Santa Monica.

I was already naked and on my knees anyway, so I cried out a prayer from the depth of my being, "Universe, oh Universe, I can't do this anymore. I'm in pain. I'm in fear. I need help and I can't do it by myself. Just take me away, I'm yours! But please take away my desire for alcohol." And it did. I felt like a window had opened somewhere above me, and golden light was flowing down upon, and over, and all around me. I suddenly "knew" with a deep sense of wisdom (as if somewhere inside me was an ancient being, a Higher Power as I soon came to discover) that I was a very sick woman – and that it was not my fault. I got up from the toilet, had a shower, and looked up the phone number for AA in the hotel phone book, then called them immediately, saying I was ready to get sober and needed help. But I had also been invited to dinner that night by my Aussie uncle Jim, who was in town for business with his daughter, Christine, and I didn't want to let them down.

The folks on the twenty-four-hour AA telephone help line told me, "Well, if you have to go to this dinner, then go, and we'll send someone to come get you in the morning to take you to a meeting. But just don't drink. Do you think you can do that?" I said I thought I could.

On a visit to Australia for Christmas 2023, cousin Christine and I, having both recently lost our beloved fathers, reminisced about that dinner, and she told me she remembered very clearly that while neither she nor Uncle Jim suspected I had a drinking problem, they were both concerned about how terribly thin I'd become. I was finally able to tell her why.

I kept my word to the AA help line people that night. But I will not lie – that first night was pure *hell*. I didn't drink at dinner and went straight to the motel room afterwards and tried to sleep without my usual nightcap (or ten). I tossed and turned and kept throwing up; my stomach was aching, and I had the heebie-jeebies, shaking and sweating all night. But I didn't drink. In the morning there was a knock on the door and when I opened it, there stood an *angel*. She was glowing, radiating with warmth, kindness, serenity – and hope. And there I stood, a tiny, wet, little white mouse full of fear and despair. I desperately wanted what she had.

She said her name was Amanda. And she saved my life.

As it was a Saturday morning, Amanda took me to an early meeting on Martin Luther King Boulevard. The meeting had just started and an older African American gentleman was speaking at the podium. He called himself Leon, and when our eyes met it was as if we had known each other for eons. He knew me, and I knew him. And he began telling his story, one that reminded me of me. Although we were from different countries and had different life experiences, we had one thing in common. We both had the same disease, and it was called alcoholism. Our emotions too were very similar. And old Leon made a point of that for everyone in the room.

As it turned out, serendipitously, Leon was celebrating his thirtieth sobriety birthday that day. He had gotten sober exactly thirty years before, in the middle of the Watts race riots in Los Angeles, when a white woman stopped and asked him how he was doing. And she said, "You're in pain, aren't you? I was once like you are now, but now I know I don't have to live like that anymore. Are you ready to do try something new?" And Leon said he was so sick and so tired of being sick and tired that he agreed, and the woman took him to her car. As Leon said, "She took me by the hand at a time when whites and Blacks would never be seen walking down the street together, let alone holding hands, and she got me in her car and took me to my first AA meeting in Pacific Palisades. And I was the only Black person at that meeting."

Leon went on to say that the woman and her AA friends told him that he was not a bad person, that he was just very sick, suffering from a malady of the body, mind, and spirit. And here he looked straight at me and said, "Those wonderful AA people looked beyond the colour of my skin and saw the soul inside – and up 'til then I didn't really like white folks 'cause they was always causin' me grief. Ya know? But these folks was different. They said we was all the same and that I just didn't know how to love myself. But that they would love me 'til I was able to love myself. And that's what we are gonna do for *you*. And for *anyone* who walks through these doors of Alcoholics Anonymous who needs our help." Old Leon and Amanda taught me many things that day and afterwards about the disease of alcoholism and how to break free from its clutches.

After the meeting Leon told me, "There is a beautiful, powerful woman inside of you. I can see her in your eyes. But the alcohol and the addict inside, they's always tryin' to destroy her. Don't let them. Just don't you pick up a drink – one day at a time – and you'll get to celebrate thirty years too. But once you've got it, you can't just keep it to yourself. No … You gots to give it away. That's what we do here in Alcoholics Anonymous: our purpose is to save the folks who is still out there sufferin.' It's a physical and mental disease with a spiritual remedy. And that remedy is *love*. Pure, unconditional love.. That's what it is. And that's what we do. We got to spread that love around." That was twenty-eight years ago: April 12, 1996. And the experience was so powerful, so imprinted on my mind that I've never had a drink since.

I believe it was no coincidence that I was drawn back to L.A. at that time. There was a method to my madness. Something or someone (my Higher Power) was telling me where I needed to go to hear the message of AA from the specific people who shared the message with me. I felt so comfortable with Leon, Amanda, and their AA community that it felt like coming home.

That night Leon had a huge sobriety birthday party at a swanky hotel, and invited me. I didn't want to go because I was feeling so sick, and my nerves were shot. But Leon insisted. And Amanda said they'd worry about me if I was by myself, so she and her friends took me with them. They even took me to a nail salon beforehand to get my nails done because they said they wanted me to start feeling good about myself. Can you imagine? I was a stranger, from another country even, yet they did not judge me. Instead, they gave me love and compassion, the two things I needed most to begin to heal.

There were several hundred people at the party, all dressed to the nines. I felt like Cinderella at the ball but covered in cinders. I had to keep going to the bathroom to throw up, and Amanda and her friends would take turns looking after me. At one point I was shaking so hard I could barely stand upright, and I said, "Can somebody just get me a gun so I can put myself out of this misery?" And they just laughed at me and said, "Hell, no, child! You just shaaake and quaaake and shake this one off – and don't pick up another drink – and you'll never have to go through this again!"

At one point I overheard two older gentlemen greet each other. One of them was Amanda's husband. "How are you doing, Henry?"

I'll never forget Henry's response: "It's a beautiful day."

It's a beautiful day. Wow! I thought. I can't remember when the last time was that I could say, "It's a beautiful day" and mean it. I certainly had a lot to learn. And whatever those folks had that made them happy and at peace with themselves – without any liquor – that was the remedy I wanted. The fog in my brain was just beginning to thin out a little. I had a long way to go but I knew I was where I needed to be.

At one point in the evening, Leon got up to the mic and thanked everyone for coming. Then he announced that they were going to have a countdown of how many years, months, and days of sobriety everyone had. At the very end of the countdown Leon made another announcement. "Now I want to introduce y'all to my new friend, a very special young lady. She's here all the way from up north – Canada. Lenore, can you please stand up and tell all these fine folks how long you've been sober?"

I was terrified and also confused. Why would anyone want to make a fuss about *me* being here, when I was brand new to this sobriety thing? Surely the people who had years under their belts should be congratulated. I just wanted to disappear under the table. But with Amanda and her ladies all urging me on, I reluctantly stood up and said, "Happy Birthday, Leon, and thanks for inviting me to your party. My name is Lenore. I'm an alcoholic. And I've gone twenty-four hours now without a drink."

Well, from the roar of approval and cheers that went up from the crowd you'd have thought I'd won an Academy Award. And now I was completely perplexed. It was then that Amanda explained that a person who is freshly sober is like a gift to the "old-timers" of AA (people who have years of sobriety) because the "newcomers" usually arrive so messed up it reminds everyone why they got sober in the first place. After the countdown, for the rest of the evening people were introducing themselves and congratulating me right, left, and centre. What an interesting program, I thought, one where "The first shall come last and the last shall come first."

Over the next days and weeks, I learned many more "sobering" facts about the disease we all shared. For instance: there is no "cure" for alcoholism. One can only keep it at bay by remaining abstinent. And the reason why we say "one day at a time" is because it's easier to stay sober when we think in short time allotments of twenty-four hours, rather than an entire lifetime. I also learned that people who try to quit drinking but don't go to AA meetings are more likely to start drinking again. The meetings are like medicine for the soul. Years of research shows that alcoholism will kill them, one way or another. AA members, on the other hand, have the best rate of staying sober, with 22 percent of members able to stay sober for twenty or more years. The more AA meetings a member attends, the higher the chance of remaining abstinent. Statistics show that this is true for all twelve-step groups, which is why I chose to attend "90 meetings in 90 days" in the beginning of my recovery. I made a point of getting to each meeting no matter what, as if my life depended on it. Because it did.

Fortunately, more North Americans appear to be cutting back on drinking. Studies show that over 41 percent are trying to drink less in 2024, an increase of 7 percent from 2023. And younger generations, especially Gen Z, are adopting this approach with 61 percent of Gen Z planning to drink less in 2024, up 53 percent from 2023.

While it doesn't bother me to be around others who drink, I can say with certainty that if I had not quit drinking when I did, I would not be here today to tell my tale. And when I think back to old Leon's sobriety story and my own, I see the link between us so clearly. We were like the yin and yang symbol: opposites but reflecting each other.

Old Leon has sadly passed away, but I'll always be grateful to him, to my Angel of Mercy, Amanda, and to the good members of Back to Basics on Martin Luther King Boulevard. They opened my eyes to the fact that, like Rogue, we all need to accept ourselves, to embrace our own unique powers and use them to help others who are struggling. You could say that they helped me awaken my inner superhero.

In the ensuing years, Sparrow Hawk has been shifting and growing into Golden Eagle. It's an ongoing, ever-evolving process. And as Rogue says at the end of "The Cure," "There ain't no cure for who you are. I am my powers. And the good they can do. And I reckon I can live with that."

CHAPTER 26

WAITING FOR TAKEOFF:
PABLO THE INTREPID

San Francisco, March 11, 2024

I'm sitting in a plane on the tarmac of San Francisco waiting for take-off (both literally and figuratively) and images from the summer of 1968 roll across my mind like the flickering frames captured on my dad's first video camera – which he bought in preparation for our big ocean voyage to a new home on the SS *Canberra*. It's been many years since I was here as a little girl of eight, yet when I close my eyes, once again I see Flower Power: Love and Peace signs everywhere, vibrant flowers on every street corner, young men with long hair and beads, women wearing halter tops with flowers in their hair, the enticing scent of burning incense wafting on a warm breeze, and the pungent flavour of the succulent peach I've just tasted, the largest and sweetest peach I had ever seen.

Now, swoosh! I am onboard our ship, the *Canberra*, watching from the deck as we dock in the port of L.A., Dad with his ever-present video camera documenting our arrival, then another swoosh! Now I'm outside our hotel which is located right beside The Pink Pussycat Club, and I find my adult self wondering if Dad had known about that in advance, or was it just a coincidence? Sadly, I'll never know as my beloved father passed away five months ago, just a few months after his ninety-first birthday. And while he'd had a long, happy, and truly amazing life,

I still feel robbed of a dear friend, confidant, co-conspirator, kindred spirit, and one true champion.

I've heard it said that when a storyteller dies, it's like a thousand libraries have burned. And so it is with my dad, Paul, or Pablo, as he liked to call himself when, after retirement from teaching, he and Mum would get a reprieve from the harsh Canadian winters for a few months by escaping to the small coastal village of Nerja, on the Costa del Sol of Spain.

I began calling Dad Pablo the Intrepid due to his sheer unflappability in the face of the unexpected, including misadventures like heading off to Spain despite the Covid-19 pandemic, which meant that, at one point when I switched gears to become an elected Member of Parliament, one of my first responsibilities was to try to repatriate all Canadian citizens abroad, including my octogenarian parents, along with all my other constituents who found themselves stuck somewhere outside of Canada with no way of getting home due to the grounding of airlines worldwide in those first few months of Covid-19.

I can't tell you how much added stress that caused. However, that and other stunts were Dad's modus operandi, as he refused to let age, Mum, my sister Tamara, the doctor – anybody or anything – stop him from doing what he truly wanted to do. Some may call it stubbornness, a streak which likely also runs in the Zann family and one which I'd have to admit I have also inherited. However, it certainly gave Dad great courage and chutzpah to take on many challenges, which took him on adventures to places where no other would dare to tread. Hence Intrepid is a moniker that befits the man I am blessed to call my father.

Dad himself was blessed with great health and stamina throughout his long life, rarely catching a cold or the annual bout of bronchitis that has often plagued the rest of us. But the last eight months of his life found him in consecutive long hospital stays, first in St. Elena's Hospital in Torremolinos, Spain, then back to Nova Scotia in a rehab facility in Pictou, and finally the Colchester East Hants Hospital in Truro, where he was placed in the Palliative Care unit not once but three or four times as his constitution was so great the man just refused to die.

Until he decided he'd had enough. And after coming to the realization that he would never be able to go home again, he opted for medically assisted death, which is legal in Canada. And once again Pablo the Intrepid chose to leave this world on his own terms, in his own way, in an act of courage that many of us are afraid to contemplate.

In the eight months leading up to his death, I decided that the best thing I could do for my father was to "sow the seeds of joy" in the final chapter of Dad's journey in this lifetime, and send him off "into the mystic" feeling as calm as possible, knowing without a doubt that he was loved and appreciated. I did this by remaining as cheerful, positive, and optimistic as I could, despite my own fears and grief, knowing I was losing my best friend, while also dealing with the fear and grief of my mother and sister, who were doing their best to look after Dad in their own ways as well. And we were all dealing with the compounded grief and trauma from losing Maia, Tamara's seventeen-year-old daughter, to cancer just two years before. However, as I told Dad at one point, even if one receives a diagnosis of cancer, surely it's better not to behave as if we are "dying from cancer" but, instead, that we are "living with cancer." After all, why bring the curtain down before the play is actually finished? It ain't over 'til it's over.

To keep Dad's spirits up I began reading to him each day, or sometimes twice a day, including at night, to keep him company and help him drift off to sleep with a familiar, reassuring voice in his ears – although Dad's favourite books happened to be murder mysteries. Hardly the kind of stories that would make me sleep, but Dad found them enjoyable, so that's what he got. And in the end we read seven books before Dad passed, our favourites being The Thursday Murder Club series by Richard Osman. We loved the main characters because they were in their seventies and eighties, but still solving murder cases. And the most recent release in the series, for which Dad and I had been waiting impatiently, was aptly named *The Last Devil to Die*, which we both had to admit was quite fitting given our own circumstances.

To be honest, I think I had been hoping that we were like Scheherazade in the famed Persian story of the princess who managed to stay alive by spinning nightly stories to a murderous king, captivating him so much with her tales that he wanted to hear how the story ended. It never did. And so her life was spared. I too was using this storytelling device, but in a bid to keep my dad alive. We both looked forward to the next night of reading, to our time spent together, and we didn't want it to ever end.

And so we passed the time, reading all the way through a Spanish spring, followed by a spectacular Nova Scotia summer, which faded into fall. Deep down, of course, I knew a fairy tale ending was impossible, but my deep love for Dad kept me spinning the tales as long as he was willing to listen. It was my final gift to my father. Many nights as I neared the end of a chapter, if I thought Dad was falling asleep, I'd say softly, "Dad, are you still with me?" If he didn't respond I'd close the book, get up and stretch, pull the super-soft checkered blanket I'd given him up around his neck, kiss his forehead, and whisper "Goodnight, Dad. I love you ..." Often, he'd murmur a response: "And *I* love *you* ..." Then I'd tiptoe out of the room, say goodnight to the nurses on duty, head down the now-empty hospital halls, get in my car, and go home alone – with tears streaming down my face.

But, more often than not, even if Dad had started snoring, when I'd say, "Dad, are you still with me?" he would open his eyes with a start and pretend he was right up to speed with the story.

"Oh yes," he'd exclaim. "Keep reading. Don't stop." And I would dutifully obey. But I'd take it back to a place in the chapter where I'd first caught him drifting off.

Sometimes when I'd get to the end of a chapter and thought he was tired, I'd say, "Okay, Dad. Maybe we should just leave it there for tonight, shall we, and I'll pick it up again tomorrow?"

Without fail, Dad's response was that of a little boy, as he'd say "No! Another one! Another one! Please! Keep reading!" And I would happily comply.

It was then that I saw how things had come full circle, that my dad and I had switched places because, as a child, I used to say the same thing to him. Dad would often read to me at night to help me get to sleep. Like Dad, I never wanted the reading to stop or for our time together to ever end.

But nothing lasts forever. And the only thing constant in the Universe is change. Or, as my Buddhist teacher Gen Lekma, says, "Everything is impermanent."

I was glad to have several opportunities to talk to Dad about spiritual matters, including Indigenous spirituality and Buddhism, both of which interested him greatly. And as usual Dad's thoughts on that were, "Anything is possible."

Now as I left the hospital each night, I found myself singing an old Joni Mitchell song, "We go round and round in the circle game." And with the last gasps of summer, I knew my time with my father was coming to an end. The spectacular Nova Scotian summer turned to fall with hues so bold it seemed the glory of the world was reflected in the leaves of gold. The maples too seemed especially rosy – or is it just that when we are aware our time is short, we see and appreciate things more acutely?

About a week before Dad died, I had a dream that he was lying on his deathbed, and half of his face was a skeleton, but the other half was still the Dad I knew and loved. He called me over to his side and said, "Don't stop what you're doing on my account. Keep going! Keep travelling! Keep touching people with your gifts. Go out and set the world on fire!"

There it was, again.

Finally came the time to say goodbye, the time I'd been dreading. It was now October 2023.

The night before Dad died, I read him the last chapter of our book, which, in yet another instance of head-scratching serendipity, touched on the issue of assisted suicide. This in turn gave us the opportunity to talk about Dad's own decision to have the same procedure at noon the following day, and once more I was reminded of the power of books, and how they can open up channels of communication and discussion of topics that might otherwise be too difficult to discuss without the protective layer or cloak of characters and plot points.

After I'd said goodnight and kissed his forehead for the last time, Dad told me that he was proud of me. "And I'm not just proud of your *accomplishments*, which are many. I'm proud of who you are as a *person*, the woman you've become." I will forever be grateful for those words from the one person in this world who knew me better than anyone, and whose opinion counted most. Who could ask for anything more from a father?

That night as I drove home, an autumn mist rose up and once again I was reminded of Mother Earth, breathing. As I rounded the final bend in the Marsh Road which takes me home, I saw a form standing in the middle of the road. So I slowed my Miata down and came to a stop.

It was a large stag with a beautiful set of antlers reaching up to the skies like a huge crown. We observed each other calmly. And, still calmly, but aware of my every heartbeat, I got out of the car and walked slowly towards him. Unafraid, the stag let me approach until we were an arm's length from each other.

"You're so beautiful. Thank you," I whispered. "Look after yourself."

Then with a curt nod, and a soft snort, he turned and disappeared into the mist as tears sprang to my eyes, unbidden: tears of wonder, joy, and grief intermingled. And I felt – no, I *knew* – that the stag had come to me with a message – some medicine or totem – from the Universe, and my instincts told me it was about my father.

In many cultures around the world, including First Nations people, the stag has symbolized regeneration, wisdom, maturity, vitality, stamina, virility, instinctual nature, protection, and spiritual enlightenment. Mature and wise, non-aggressive unless provoked, the stag has endured life's many challenges, which means his antlers are like a crown that he has earned. And because he sheds his antlers and grows new ones each year that are even stronger and larger, he symbolizes the life force and regeneration, life after life, which is also why the Celtic people worshipped the stag god Cernunnos, and the Greek goddess Artemis, who never married, is often pictured running wild through the woods with a stag.

I remembered what my dad told me after he'd had his first stroke, a number of years before: "You are blessed with a great deal of vitality. Protect it." While Dad's own vitality waned over the next few years, his sense of humour and thirst for adventure remained, and he and Mum continued to travel to Spain each winter, though now with the help of wheelchair assistance at the airports and sporty Spanish walking canes.

Now, this stag reminded me of Dad – of a strong, secure male who stands his ground, unintimidated, yet with no hint of toxic masculinity either, because he is entirely comfortable in his own skin, and therefore has nothing to prove. Yes, a fitting symbol indeed of the man who had seen and done so much and was now ready to shed his earthly antlers and sojourn off to another plane of existence, on his own recognizance. Pablo the Intrepid. A man among men. Society would be so much healthier and happier, and the world would be a much better place, if everyone was blessed with such a father, who shows by example what healthy masculinity is truly like. All I can do is to act in line with the principles my dad taught me and try to embody that same compassion, curiosity, and kindness he showed for all people. And maybe, just maybe, I can inspire others to do the same. We are all "waiting for takeoff" in one way or another.

So thank you, Dad. As my career once again takes flight, I will carry you in my heart, always.

CHAPTER 27

ROGUE GOES TO PARLIAMENT AND THE X-MEN TAKE HOLLYWOOD BY STORM

The Roosevelt Hotel,
Hollywood,
March 14, 2024

Last night I attended the Hollywood premiere of our new Disney/ Marvel series, *X-Men '97* at the El Capitan Cinema before its official release next week. And Disney kindly put us up for the night at this famed hotel – The Roosevelt – where, serendipitously, Marilyn Monroe used to stay. Judging from the fans' reaction at the premiere, I have a feeling the series should be a huge hit. One can only hope!

What would the little Aussie girl say about this incredible turn of events? The eight-year-old who sailed around the world but was most excited about going to Disneyland. What would she say if told that one day she'd be working for the Mighty Mouse herself, playing an iconic superhero touted as "the strongest woman in the Universe" in one of the most popular animated series of all time?

And what would the lonely nineteen-year-old star of *Hey Marilyn!* say? The one who had to summon up her own inner superhero to fend off the constant, unwanted sexual advances of her director? What would she say if told that Disney would one day be footing the bill for her stay at The Roosevelt Hotel where Marilyn herself spent so much time?

I think of Tiny Tim and his mantra: "You've gotta get a gimmick if you wanna be a star!" And I look at my choices throughout my career to resist being typecast in any particular role. Like Madonna, that '80s and '90s icon, I chose instead to "morph" into different versions of myself, constantly recreating myself so that nobody could pin me down, no matter how hard they tried. Instead, I focused on manifesting the types of roles and projects that continued to interest me and which I hoped could influence others to become better versions of themselves as well.

From watching *The Wonderful World of Disney* every weekend on our little black and white TV in Sydney, Australia, to being magically transported to Hollywood on the enchanted wings of Disney, I hope that *A Rogue's Tale* might inspire a whole new generation of young people to take that leap of faith needed to follow their dreams, and to stand up for their fellows.

Reach for the stars, my friends, as you may just make it to the moon! If you don't at least try, you will never know what could have been, but you can be damn sure that nothing will happen.

I'm honoured and grateful to be able to continue doing what I love, both onscreen and off. And I appreciate the commitment of Disney and Marvel to our original cast of *X-Men: The Animated Series* as it's a testament of their dedication to our show that most of the original cast was invited to reprise our roles or play new ones, enabling some of our "Legacy" cast to record from Toronto and Vancouver, while allowing me to record most of my episodes in Halifax, Nova Scotia.

X-Men '97 is an ode to our OG (original) show and we are blessed to have a multitalented, passionate, vibrant creative team making magic once more: the producers, directors, writers, artists, cast, and crew. We were so lucky to be able to reprise the creative energy of *X-Men: The Animated Series*.

Without the fans, however, *X-Men '97* would not be happening. So thank you to each and every one of you from all of us. It's great to be back in the saddle again in my green and gold colours (like Aussie sports teams). And with all of the horrendous events that are happening around the world, I'd say it truly is time for the X-Men to return.

Some of you may also be wondering what I've been up to since "Graduation Day." So here's a quick rundown:

After recording that last season of *X-Men,* newly sober, I continued performing in film and TV, including playing the lead role in a feature film, *Babyface,* by Jack Blum and Sharon Corder, with Atom Egoyan as executive producer, which premiered at the Cannes Festival in 1998.

In 2000 I began writing my first play, *The Marilyn Tapes* (a one-woman musical about Marilyn Monroe), which I performed at the Marigold Cultural Centre and Neptune Theatre in Nova Scotia to hometown audiences, before taking the show to New York, where I performed it first at Don't Tell Mama (an iconic cabaret theatre near Times Square), followed by an off-Broadway run at The Blue Heron Theatre.

When I had gone to New York at that time, I had only three intentions in mind:

1. To get *The Marilyn Tapes* produced off Broadway,
2. To get a review in *The New York Times* (preferably a good one), and
3. To book a guest role on *Law and Order* and perform in *both* the law and the order sections of the show.

Remember when I said the odds are often in my favour? Well, Lady Luck was clearly blowing on my dice, as I managed to fulfil all three goals, and this second New York era was another highlight of my career so far.

I loved performing live every night while sharing a brownstone apartment on St. Mark's Place in the East Village in a building known as in the Physical Graffiti with a couple of Canadian pals. (So named because it appeared on the cover of an old Led Zeppelin album called *Physical Graffiti.* My roommates were actor Ben Bass, who had played Elvis when I portrayed Priscilla in *Are You Lonesome Tonight?* back in 1987 but is best known for his role as officer/detective Sam Swarek on the Global/ABC series *Rookie Blue,* and singer Doris Mason, who was in New York from Nova Scotia playing Mama Cass on Broadway in the musical *Dream a Little Dream,* co-written by our treasured friend playwright Paul LeDoux and singer Denny Dougherty of The Mamas and Papas fame. Other than Ben (who hailed from Vancouver), we were all from Nova Scotia and while this was long before *Come from Away* gave New Yorkers a taste of Maritime kitchen parties, let's just say that wherever we went in the

Big Apple a good time was had by all. And with Marilyn Monroe, Mama Cass, and Elvis all living together, our little Physical Graffiti apartment was the mecca for a rockin' good time.

While my play received a number of good reviews (including from *The New York Times*), I also booked a number of TV shows: a TV pilot with John Waters; a film, *Favourite Son*; and voice work, including the children's series *Word World* for PBS Kids and *Teenage Mutant Ninja Turtles*. However, when my third wish was fulfilled by landing a guest starring role on *Law and Order* where I got to perform in scenes with Sam Waterston (whom I had loved since the *The Great Gatsby* and *The Killing Fields*), Jerry Orbach, and Jesse L. Martin, my dreams had come true.

I'll never forget singing love duets from Broadway shows in the back of Jerry's limo with him in between takes on those cold February New York streets, and Jesse L. Martin asking me for my autograph as Rogue because he said he loved watching the show with his nephew and Rogue was one of his favourite characters.

After this second New York stint, I felt it was time to go home to spend time with my family since my parents were getting older and my sister's three kids were still toddlers. I didn't want to be just a photograph on a refrigerator. I wanted to be a full-on, hands-on fun auntie.

But before I made the move back to Nova Scotia I did more TV guest star appearances in Vancouver, where I had a condo, including *The L Word* in 2007. I ended up playing a rather interesting "role" in the next chapter of my life, when I moved home to Nova Scotia and was asked to run as a candidate for a political party my parents and I had supported for many years: the New Democratic Party (NDP). You may wonder at the connection between this TV series and my NDP candidacy. Read on.

I was in New York doing an audition the day the party announced I'd be running for them in the upcoming provincial election. But no sooner had it been announced than the party called me to say that one of the opposition parties had sent a picture of me from some show I'd done to CBC TV's *Evening News*. The problem was, they said, it was a topless photo.

"Which one?" was my response.

"You mean there's more than one?"

"Well, yes, of course. I'm an actor. I've done a number of nude scenes in the course of my career. I told you that when you signed me up. So they likely had a field day trying to decide which one to use."

It turned out they'd used a screenshot from a shower scene I appeared in for *The L Word*. And why would they use that shot? I wondered. Could it be because that particular series was about lesbians – hence the title – so were they counting on stirring up some homophobia in the constituency called Truro-Bible Hill?

In any case, the attempt to cut me down before I'd even had a chance to get my campaign going backfired completely. The day after the news story broke (on CBC no less, the network for whom I'd done so many productions over the years), more news outlets descended upon Truro and Bible Hill with cameramen chasing down every little old lady they could find and asking them, "What do you think about this woman running for office in your community?" And I've never been so proud of my home-town as each and every person asked said the same thing: "What are you talking about? This is the twenty-first century. She's an actress. That's her job. Get over it!" God bless every one of them. That was my introduction to politics in 2009, a baptism by fire. But when, against all the odds, I won the election with a huge majority of votes, the media dubbed it a "Zannslide!" The win was extra sweet.

I ended up winning four consecutive terms in office as an elected representative, for two different levels of government: first as a provincial Member of the Legislative Assembly of Nova Scotia (MLA) from 2009 to 2019, then federally as the Member of Parliament (MP) for Cumberland Colchester from 2019 to 2021.

Anyone who thinks being a politician is easy has absolutely no idea of the work it entails. And you would imagine that in this day and age, being a female politician should be accepted without question, wouldn't you? I can assure you from personal experience that when a woman attains any kind of political power, the misogynists and bigots come out of the woodwork, attacking and criticizing everything from our hair to our weight, to whether we have a right to make our opinions known. I kid you not. Female politicians also receive more hate mail and threats – including death threats – than our male counterparts. It's truly shocking.

Luckily, Alexa McDonough, the first female leader of a political party in Canada, was instrumental in giving me guidance and political mentorship during my time in office. I'll always be grateful to Alexa, and to the many wonderful volunteers who contributed time and money to my political campaigns. My parents were also incredibly helpful during election campaigns, and Dad in particular loved driving his van around, which we dubbed The Zann Van because he had logos with my name emblazoned in large lettering on both sides. Before I ran for the NDP, they had never once won an election in our region. So that first victory was particularly satisfactory.

Once in office, my staff were extremely important as well in the day-to-day running of constituency offices, casework, and committee meetings. I'm indebted to Stephanie MacNeil, Darlene Blair, Deb White, Sharron Timmons, Jane Bolivar, and Matthew Guy.

In one of my final private heart-to-hearts with Dad before he passed away, I asked him to name something during his long life that made him really happy. "Well, now, let me think ...," he said, closing his eyes. He thought for so long that I assumed he must have drifted off to sleep. But suddenly he sat up, eyes blazing, and exclaimed, "When *we* went into politics! Now *that* was exciting!" I had to laugh.

Two years before, while I was a Liberal Party Member of Parliament, shortly after losing Maia to cancer, I had received word from the Prime Minister's Office that the PM wanted to call Dad to give him his condolences and wish him a happy birthday as Dad was turning eighty-nine. Although Dad had announced to the family he would not be celebrating that year, I figured that a call from the Prime Minister might help cheer him up.

When the time drew near for the PM's call, I drove over to the family homestead on Willow Street to find Dad lying on top of their bed, fully clothed, reading, the little glasses perched on his nose that always made him look like Bilbo Baggins in *The Hobbit*. When my cell phone began to buzz and I saw the 613 area code, I knew it was from Ottawa, so I said, "Dad, I believe this call is for you."

"Who would that be?" Dad asked, puzzled.

"I think you'll recognize the voice," I responded, and answered the phone.

"Hi, Lenore. Is your dad handy?" It was Prime Minister Trudeau.

"Yes! I've been expecting your call. Thank you. He's right here," I said and turned my cell on speakerphone so I could hear every word as I handed the phone to Dad.

"He-llo!" Dad said in that cheerful way he had of answering the phone, no matter the circumstances. (God, I miss that so much!)

"Yes … Mr. Zann. Hello. It's Justin Trudeau …"

"Well, hello, Justin. To what do I owe this pleasure?"

"Paul, I just wanted to tell you, personally, how very sorry I am for your recent loss of your granddaughter. I was so hoping that Maia would have a full recovery. So please give my sincere condolences to her mum and dad, Tamara and Tim … I also know it's your birthday today, and I know you don't feel like celebrating this year, which I completely understand. But I just feel that you have contributed so much to your community and to Canada over these many years – including lending us your daughter Lenore, who is such a great member of our team – that it's important to acknowledge your incredible eighty-nine years on the planet."

I could tell Dad was thrilled. But he took it all in stride as if a call from the Prime Minister of Canada was a regular, daily occurrence. After that, Dad and Prime Minister Trudeau proceeded to have a long, very comfortable conversation, during which the PM told him that he too had suffered the loss of a younger family member much too soon – his younger brother, twenty-three-year-old Michel. And he told Dad, "The public knows that we lost him in a tragic skiing accident, but what they don't know is that we *almost* lost him not long before that, when he was involved in a terrible car accident."

The Prime Minister went on to describe how scared he was when he thought he would lose his younger brother, and that they were given several months of reprieve while Michel slowly regained his health, during which time he visited him every day. After his recovery, Michel decided to go on a ski trip with friends to British Columbia, where he got caught in the freak avalanche that killed him.

The PM said he and his family were gutted but that he came to realize he had been granted an extension of several precious months with his brother which he cherished to this very day, and that he carries his brother with him in his heart wherever he goes. He concluded by saying that he imagined Dad might feel the same way, since we too ended up having about six months longer with our Maia than the doctors had predicted with her terminal cancer diagnosis.

Dad listened carefully to the Prime Minister's story and thanked him for sharing, admitting that he too felt as if we were blessed with some extra time with our sweet girl. Then he said, "Now I know you have many important things to do so I'll let you go. Thank you for taking the time to cheer up an old man."

"Not just *any* old man," replied the PM.

"Now before I go," said my dad, "there's one more thing I'd like you to know. You are doing an *excellent* job of running the country. Keep up the good work. I'm very proud of you, my boy."

There was a slight pause on the other end of the phone. But I could tell the PM was genuinely moved when he said, "Well, thank you so much, Mr. Zann."

"It's Paul, Justin."

"Uhh ... thank you so much, Paul ... That's very kind of you to say. I really appreciate your support. And that of Lenore. She's a breath of fresh air in Parliament. And I can certainly see where she gets it from. Happy Birthday, Paul. I know it's not an easy one. But don't forget to take the time to celebrate."

I took a deep breath at the end of that call, feeling like I'd just witnessed an incredible scene from a movie. After all, the PM's father, Prime Minister Pierre Elliott Trudeau, was the reason Mum and Dad had decided to move to Canada in the first place. Trudeau Sr. had been dead for more than two decades, but even so, who would ever have the audacity of calling the Prime Minister of Canada "my boy"? Only my dad – Paul the Intrepid – that's who.

There is so much more to tell about the time when "Rogue Goes to Parliament," but that, my friends, is a tale to be told another day. Suffice to say that, in spite of the many challenges that came my way, I'm truly grateful to the good people of Nova Scotia who believed in and trusted me to represent their best interests for twelve years – and four consecutive terms. They had good reason to do so, since both of my parents gave me the gift of a strong moral compass. And my motto as a politician is simple, for as Joseph Howe, the famed Nova Scotian parliamentarian (and father of responsible government), once said, "What is right? What is just? What is for the public good?"

These days, however, it seems like the whole world has gone crazy. Wars are raging around the world, leaving thousands dead and millions suffering and displaced, famine and pestilence taking even more inno-cent lives, and the worst global pandemic in hundreds of years has al-ready killed millions. Book-banning has once again become a common occurrence. (*The Uncanny X-Men: The Trial of Magneto* comic book by Chris Claremont was recently removed from public libraries in Edin-burgh of all places. That beautiful cultural city that hosts the Edinburgh Fringe Theatre Festival!)

Laws are also being enacted daily in a twisted attempt by right-wing lawmakers to prevent the teaching, or even *discussion*, of sex education and the history of racism in classrooms, libraries, and school counsellors' offices, with a rolling back of human rights, including LGBTQ2SIA+ and women's reproductive rights. Bigoted attacks on LGBTQ2SIA+ individ-uals and people of Jewish and Muslim faiths have been climbing around the world. George Orwell was clearly prescient when he wrote his famous books *1984* and *Animal Farm,* each of which could describe some of the ridiculous political maneuverings evident today.

If you are anxious about the future my advice is to *get involved.* Join grassroots environmental organizations as well as political cam-paigns in your community, volunteer to canvass door-to-door, host neigh-bourhood events, and donate your time and/or money to help support the progressive candidates in other regions where the fight to get them elected will be tighter. If not running as a candidate yourself (but why not?), get involved in school board elections and other campaigns for seats in other levels of government by volunteering for your candidate who has the same compassionate, inclusive values as your own. Because, believe me, the right-wing crusaders are doing that. It's why these horrendous backward laws are being enacted. And for God's sake, get out and *vote.* Don't believe the folks who say your vote doesn't count. It does. Take it from me. Progressive politicians need every vote they can get in order to defeat those who would take our civil rights away. Don't let them.

EPILOGUE
TO ME, MY X-MEN!

It's been thirty years since *X-Men: The Animated Series* first aired on Fox Kids TV. Decades later, on March 20, 2024, our loyal fans finally found out what happened after the final episode, "Graduation Day," aired back in 1997 – and the response has been astounding. Fans and critics alike have been raving online and off, giving each episode stellar reviews, with a 100 percent approval rating on Rotten Tomatoes and 99 percent on IMDB. We even managed to break the internet several times as a "trending" topic of conversation. Simply beyond our wildest dreams!

And season one is a long and rocky road for Rogue, reflective of the trauma of so many who have lost beloved family members in recent years, due to the Covid-19 pandemic as well as natural disasters, hate crimes, gun violence, and wars. With so much suffering both near and far, it sometimes seems too much to bear. But we must not lose hope.

The beauty of art is that it helps to reflect our inner world and the outer events that affect us. *X-Men '97* is a perfect example of the heights and depths to which art can take us.

It's not "just a cartoon." It's an allegory for what humankind is currently experiencing – and has for many years. Love, desire, temptation, confusion, hatred and bigotry, grief, rage, revenge, bravery, and celebration – all these are touched upon in our series. And Rogue is often at the epicentre of these moments. As a professional actor this role has been a real gift for me. First, I have been given the opportunity to portray such a charismatic character on a powerful roller coaster of joy and despair, but the role also gave me the opportunity to draw from the deep well of my own emotions at a time when I too was traumatized by recent personal loss. Not only did *X-Men '97* provide an outlet to channel my own trauma, but it also gave me the opportunity to authentically convey Rogue's grief, pain, fear, rage, loneliness, and loss of identity. So I made the conscious decision to channel all of this energy into my performance in the hope that by doing so, my voice might resonate and touch the audience's own deep-seated emotions, providing a cathartic experience by way of an emotional release that would be therapeutic – even for those who were unaware that they needed healing.

Now that the first season of the series has proven to be such a massive hit, experiencing the public's response to our show via social media and in person at Comic Cons has been so fulfilling. As of this writing our series has received a Primetime Emmy nomination for Best Animated Production specifically for Episode Five, "Remember It," which is my big episode of the season (followed closely by Episode Seven, "Bright Eyes," in which, famously, "Rogue goes rogue"). I've also just received an ASTRA Award nomination for my performance. Who knows what may happen. After years in showbiz and Buddhist studies, I've learned not to get too attached to the outcome. However, it's incredibly heartwarming to see *X-Men: The Animated Series* finally being recognized as powerful drama and storytelling – something our loyal X-Men fans have known all along.

It takes outstanding team effort to create a show of this calibre. I'm proud of our entire cast and creative team. And extremely grateful to be an integral part of it – not once, but twice. When all of the various elements of *X-Men: The Animated Series* came together in the '90s, as our original director, Larry Houston, likes to say, it was like "lightning in a bottle." I would add that the runaway success of *X-Men '97* proves that, with the right people involved, lightning really can strike twice.

At the end of the day, my message is simple: The Phoenix always rises, reborn, from its own ashes. So never give up, even when the task ahead seems impossible, or life has just thrown you a curveball that has brought you to your knees. When you feel like you've hit the wall, or you're free-falling, or have reached an impasse, or the end of the road and you don't know where to go, try to cultivate a feeling of "faith versus fear." And wait … There is always something beyond that bend, around this corner, or over the next hill that you can't yet see.

So hit the pause button. Take time to meditate. Have a moon bath. Or a sun shower. Take a walk on the "wild side": in a forest, or through a park, or by the sea. Waltz with the waves. Run with the wind. Taste your tears. Smell a coming storm. Listen to birdsong and the music of the spheres. Talk to the trees. Plant a garden. Sing to flowers. Lie wrapped in a blanket and stare at the stars … Feel the energy that connects us all.

And when your heartbeat is steady, your mind clear and calm, ask, "What is the lesson I am meant to learn?" Give it time, but have faith. For the answer will come. In the words of John Burroughs, "Leap – and the net will appear." Find your own "superhero" within. Get in tune with the Universe – and with your self. And above all … believe.

As I write this, I am also honoured by the fact that the federal bill I crafted so painstakingly and introduced in February 2020 as a Member of Parliament (now labelled Bill C-226, the National Strategy Respecting Environmental Racism and Environmental Justice Act) has finally passed in the Senate, and I am now in Ottawa to witness this and finally Royal Assent by Canada's Governor General. It took a decade to accomplish, but I hope this can prove to other like-minded individuals that persistence pays off, and that working together, across party lines, is the way to get things accomplished in government.

But one can't do it alone, so I'm incredibly grateful first to Dr. Ingrid Waldron for bringing this important issue to my attention, and for all the support I've received from the bill's 2015 infancy in Nova Scotia as Bill 111, An Act to Address Environmental Racism. The grassroots support for this bill was crucial and includes Grassroots Grandmothers from coast to coast, as well as Nova Scotians Dr. Lynn Jones, Doreen Bernard, Chief Andrea Paul, and Louise Delisle, and hundreds of youth and civil rights, environmental, and social justice organizations from across Canada. In particular I appreciate the strong public endorsement of Canada's top environmentalist, Dr. David Suzuki, and Lisa Gue from the Suzuki Foundation. Dr. Waldron and I celebrated our victory in Ottawa with MP Elizabeth May, Nova Scotian senators, and environmental and social justice organizers from across the country. We drank a toast to Mrs. Ping, and to all the Grassroots Grandmothers around the world who are still fighting to protect and preserve both their human rights and the rights and well-being of Mother Earth.

Finally, many thanks and deep gratitude to MP Elizabeth May and Senator Mary Jane McCallum for reintroducing and carrying the bill across the finish line in the House of Commons and Senate; to Liberal Environment Minister Steven Guilbeault; and last but certainly not least, to Prime Minister Justin Trudeau, whose unwavering support made this victory possible. While governing is in many ways a thankless job (as it's impossible to please everyone), his leadership has been imperative to keep Canada moving forward with progressive, inclusive, and compassionate values, while creating laws that turn ideas – and ideals – into action. I was pleased to be able to remind the PM of the words of my late father: "You're doing an excellent job of running the country. I'm very proud of you, my boy."

As my Rogue's Tale comes to a close, I am incredibly grateful for every good thing that is currently happening, and I hope to continue doing the work I love – performing, writing, and politicking – to help improve the well-being of my fellow citizens for many years to come. After all, the fight for social justice never sleeps. And in the words of that great Canadian statesman and politician Tommy Douglas (the Father of Medicare in Canada and grandfather to actor Kiefer Sutherland), "Watch out for the little fellow with an idea ... Courage, my friends, 'tis not too late to build a better world."

This book, my first, is meant to inspire you to keep going when the going gets tough. If people like it, I have many more tales to tell, and learned lessons to share. At the end of *X-Men: The Animated Series*, Professor Xavier sums up my character: "Rogue: unable to touch, yet look around you – you will find that you've touched us all." One can only hope.

Excelsior!

ACKNOWLEDGEMENTS

Wth heartfelt thanks to:

~ My dear mum, Janice Rose Zann, and grandmother, Elizabeth Marshall, for instilling in me the courage to stand up for my convictions, and to our Aussie and Canadian Zann Clan for their continued love and support.

~ My publisher Lesley Choyce, for believing I had a story worth telling, and to both Julia Swan and Debra Englander for their keen eyes, astute observations, and great editing.

~ The Honourable Alexa McDonough (MP for Halifax, and first female leader of a recognized political party in Canada) and Dr. Burnley ("Rocky") Jones for their political mentorship, and my fellow Nova Scotians, who put their faith in me as their elected representative for four terms.

~ Marvel Studios and Disney, Stan Lee, Chris Claremont, Michael Golden, Larry Houston, Margaret Loesch, and Eric and Julia Lewald for the gift of Rogue, and X-Men Fans around the world whose loyal support helped bring us back a second time – and create a hit show.

~ My niece Maia Li Hazel Zann-Roland, who, at just seventeen, shone her light so brightly in spite of her terminal illness with the dignity and grace of a true Jedi warrior. Maia is the inspiration for my performance as Rogue in *X-Men '97*, Season One, Episode 5, "Remember It."

~ My dear father, Paul Zann, who staunchly encouraged me and many others to follow our dreams. I encourage you to do the same. And don't let anyone tell you it can't be done!

ABOUT THE AUTHOR

Award-winning actor-politician Lenore Zann was born for the world. A ground-breaking artist and political trailblazer, her explosive career has spanned North America and the globe. Her unique, powerful voice has inspired the public from stages and screens to the heights of political power. Thanks to her strong political stances as well as her iconic performance as Rogue (the superhero fittingly recognized as "the strongest woman in the Universe") in *X-Men: The Animated Series* and Marvel Studio's *X-Men '97*, Lenore Zann has become the voice of an entire generation.

Born in Sydney, Australia, she moved to Canada with her teacher parents at the age of eight. With a natural talent for performance, Zann burst onto the entertainment scene at just nineteen with her haunting portrayal of Marilyn Monroe in the rock opera *Hey Marilyn!* At twenty-six she won Canada's national ACTRA Award for Best Actor in a Radio Drama for her performance as Mary Snow in CBC Radio's *Salt Water Moon* by David French. At thirty she was sponsored by producers in New York to play Candy in *Unidentified Human Remains and the True Nature of Love* by Brad Fraser, first at the Hampstead Theatre in Chicago, followed by an off-Broadway run at the Orpheum Theatre. She followed this up by writing and performing her first play, *The Marilyn Tapes*, first at Don't Tell Mama's Cabaret and another off-Broadway run at The Blue Heron Theatre. With hundreds of credits in TV, film, theatre, radio, animation, and interactive games, she has electrified audiences with her performances. Fans tell her she has empowered them in their own lives.

A tireless champion for environmental and social justice, Lenore put aside her acting career for a dozen years to serve as an elected representative on both provincial and federal levels of government in Canada from 2009 to 2021. She introduced many progressive legislative bills, including two historic Private Member's bills which are considered to be the first of their kind in North America: Bill 111, Act to Address Environmental Racism (introduced while she was a Member of the Legislative Assembly in Halifax, Nova Scotia, in 2015) and Bill C-230, National Strategy Respecting Environmental Racism and Environmental Justice Act. Introduced while Lenore was a Member of Parliament in Ottawa in 2020, Bill C-230 received Royal Assent as Bill C-226 on June 20, 2024.

Now, the magical wings of Disney have helped Lenore soar to new heights of fame. Fans and critics alike have hailed her stunning performance in *X-Men '97* as Emmy-worthy with both the show and Lenore garnering numerous award nominations, including a Primetime Emmy nomination for Best Animated Production. An album of songs is currently in the works, as well as several feature film and TV roles. *A Rogue's Tale* is her first book.

Lenore is the recipient of the Duke of Edinburgh Gold Award for Service to Community & Country and a Lifetime Achievement Award for Contribution to Arts and Culture.